Philip Allan
Publishers

A-Level

Exam
Success
Guide

E
H
1

Joh

Titles available

A-Level

British History, 1815–1951

European History, 1789–1945

History: Europe of the Dictators, 1914–1945

Biology: Essays

Business Studies: Essays

Chemistry: Multiple Choice

Chemistry: Structured Questions & Essays

Computing

Economics: Data Response

Economics: Essays

Economics: Multiple Choice

English: Practical Criticism

French

Geography: Essays

Law: General Principles

Media Studies: Essays

Physics: Structured Questions & Multiple Choice

Politics: Essays

Pure Mathematics

Religious Studies: The New Testament — The Gospels

Religious Studies: The Philosophy of Religion

Sociology: Essays

Philip Allan Publishers Limited
Market Place
Deddington
Oxfordshire OX15 0SE

Telephone: 01869 338652

Formerly published by Richard Ball Publishing
Revised 1998

ISBN 0 86003 307 4

This is a revised (and combined) edition of *A-Level European History, 1789–1870* and *A-Level European History, 1870–1945*, both published by Richard Ball Publishing in 1996.

Typeset by Alden Bookset, Oxford and printed by Information Press, Eynsham, Oxford

Contents

Contents

Introduction

This book is concerned exclusively with essay technique. It is not a comprehensive study guide. It contains no advice on reading or the most effective way of making notes. It is devoted to the ultimate product of much of your preparation – the writing of an essay within the 45 minutes allowed in most examinations. For you, undertaking a two-year course in Advanced level History, essay skills are progressively developed and refined, assisted by a growing command of language and syntax. Your relish for this mode of expression should increase with your confidence. Take pride in your fluency on paper and your ability to marshal arguments persuasively and cogently. Whichever professional path you tread in future, clarity of expression will serve you well.

You may be learning to drive. At first the manipulation of the gears may cause you difficulty, but a combination of your own resolve and your instructor's patient encouragement will enable you to overcome this problem. Even at an early stage, after awkward gear changing, you will discover that propelling your car at 30 miles per hour along an uncluttered, straight road is a fairly easy task. Eventually, however, you will need to stop. Your instructor will expect you to manoeuvre the gears so that your car gradually loses speed and gently halts. Thus, the actions needed to gain speed from a static position and the steps taken to return to immobility are complex, whilst the intervening activity of driving at some speed usually presents few problems. Similarly, composing a first paragraph and a final paragraph may present you with greater challenges than fashioning the intervening paragraphs.

Why should this be? The first paragraph demands that you should explore the implications of the question set. It may be presented in the form of a quotation, the justification of which you are invited to assess. 'To what extent', or 'how far' may the quotation be considered justified? It may take other forms: 'Discuss the view that...'; 'How important was...?'; 'How successful in...?'; 'Account for the success...'; 'For what reasons...?'; 'To what extent, and why, did...?'; 'Compare and contrast...'. You will become accustomed to the varying characters of the questions. A question may include a technical term – like 'liberalism', 'welfare state', or 'despot' – which you cannot afford to delay in defining before you can continue. Suffice to say, by the end of your introductory paragraph, whatever the question, you should have indicated to the reader the lines on which you intend to develop the essay. It may be considered as a microcosm of the whole essay. That is why it demands, from the moment you decide to respond to the question posed, the most concentrated thought. From that first paragraph, subsequent paragraphs will be derived. Your introduction may be largely shorn of detail, but it should contain crucial arguments which, perceptively expressed and given an order of priority, will be amplified later. Once composed, the first paragraph is the indispensable springboard for the analysis and supporting illustration which should follow.

As you begin the second paragraph the essay should be moving into top gear, the content of the first paragraph representing the gear manipulation needed to increase speed from 0 miles per hour to 30 miles per hour, without which smooth progress cannot be assured. The whole essay may be seen as a journey to a destination. The stages of that journey should witness a close examination of the principal arguments mooted at the outset.

Eventually, the final paragraph, terminating the journey, has to be written. Again, the gears have to be manipulated so that your essay is brought to a persuasive conclusion. As a literary device it confirms the unity of the essay. If it is an opportunity to consolidate points already made, try to make them from a fresh angle. Avoid a mechanical repetition of that which you have already expressed with clarity earlier in the essay. Keep an idea – or ideas – in reserve for your concluding statements. When the final full stop is placed, you should convey the impression that your analysis is complete, your literary and historical journey ended.

The framework for your essay may be as follows:

PARAGRAPH ONE: Points (a), (b), (c), (d) and (e) essentially raising the critical issues demanded by the question posed.

PARAGRAPH TWO: Detailed consideration of point (a).

PARAGRAPH THREE: Detailed consideration of point (b).

PARAGRAPH FOUR: Detailed consideration of point (c).

PARAGRAPH FIVE: Detailed consideration of point (d).

PARAGRAPH SIX: Detailed consideration of point (e).

PARAGRAPH SEVEN: Conclusion.

Of course, an essay may be written without the rigid application of this formula, but if you lack confidence in your ability to structure essays, this should enable you to organise your thoughts logically. Ultimately, you will so refine the formula that it accommodates your own ideas and planning. In any event, you will need to paragraph carefully so that the arguments raised at the outset can be developed fully and clearly subsequently. As a rough guide, a 45-minute essay will require six to nine substantial paragraphs. Each point raised in the introduction needs to be carefully weighed. You may need to modify its original tenor by presenting conflicting evidence. Your judgements should be carefully balanced. 'Moreover' and 'furthermore' are useful adverbs presaging the strengthening of an argument, whilst 'nevertheless', 'notwithstanding' and 'however' foreshadow the presentation of a contrary view. For the reader such words are invaluable in signalling the direction of your thinking. You should state the key sentence of each paragraph early – not necessarily in the first sentence, which may be no more than a link with the previous paragraph designed to ensure continuity. The thought contained in that key sentence should be sustained by carefully chosen evidence and qualified by the presentation of any contrary argument, again supported by appropriate detail.

From the second paragraph to the penultimate paragraph you should be accumulating arguments – supported by illustration – so that your overall analysis is validated. Each sentence in each paragraph should carry weight and usually contain argument and evidence, the latter meticulously and sparingly selected. This is your detailed analysis. The more skilled you become at composing complex sentences of this character, the more succinct, polished and persuasive will be the presentation of your thoughts. Should you find yourself writing narrative, unaccompanied by analysis, you can be sure that you will be failing to answer the question. A too generous allocation of illustration will soon weaken an essay's structure and arguments. You will not impress an examiner merely by displaying an encyclopedic, undiscriminating knowledge of the facts.

Avoid being dogmatic in your judgements, but do not abdicate responsibility for drawing conclusions. The language used by historians is well suited for conveying degrees of commitment to a viewpoint. There is a wide variety of phrases which suggest degrees of adherence to a particular analysis of the subject – 'it is possible that' and 'it is probable that' are two such. 'It may be inferred from the evidence' and 'The evidence would (seem to) suggest' are clearly fashioned to avoid an uncompromising expression of an opinion. The prose of the historian is formal. Colloquial expressions should be avoided. The studied detachment implied by the use of the third person reinforces the historian's quest for objectivity in his/her analysis.

You must practise essay writing in order to gain a self-assured facility in this mode of expression. Writing essays under timed conditions will be an invaluable help to you. In addition, you should organise your own practice. Scour past papers for questions for detailed consideration. In any case, you should be well informed about the structure of the papers with which you will be eventually confronted with in the examination room. Assemble a variety of questions on a similar theme. Each answer will require a distinctive approach, even though each may draw upon similar evidence for supporting arguments. Write introductory paragraphs for each, which emphasise the differences of emphases in the questions posed. Devise headings for succeeding paragraphs, each of which will be determined by the analytical content of the first paragraph. In this way, a session of study, involving hard work and thinking, should have an invaluably practical outcome. Such exercises will make the culmination of your study of a particular theme purposeful and dynamic. It is immeasurably better to approach your study of history in this way than to adopt the inefficient practice of dourly turning over the pages of often turgidly composed notes and making desperate, often unavailing, efforts to memorise detail and analysis. Such a limited approach will not be your salvation in the examination room.

You will be mistaken if you consider that the essays in this book should be memorised for detail and argument. This would prevent you from acquiring the flexible thinking demanded when, in the examination room, you are faced with a question on a familiar theme worded in an unfamiliar way. Rather, study the essays for the purpose of understanding the techniques employed. You may not necessarily agree with the analysis presented in any one essay. There can be no definitive essay. The relative importance of decisions, actions and events must remain a matter of individual judgement. The essays here presented are one person's view of what seemed to be lucid and persuasive interpretations of the demands posed by the questions set. It would be good practice for any one of the essays contained here to be dissected by you and your fellow students. You may well find yourself very critical of the conclusions I have drawn. Ask questions of the essays. Why has this been left out? Why has this been included? Has the approach been too narrow? Have the full implications of the question been considered? Who says it should be written this way anyway? In truth, there would be scope for considering any of the essays in this book in a quite different way from that explored here. Other interpretations may be equally – or even more – valid.

If there can be no definitive essay, look for the recurring features of good practice in essay writing. These are:

(a) the logical accumulation of arguments in the introductory paragraph;
(b) the nice balance between analysis and supporting illustration in subsequent paragraphs, where the arguments of the introductory paragraph are amplified;
(c) the drawing together of the arguments at the end of the essay.

Each paragraph may be compared to a movement of a symphony – there is a clearly defined structure, but the quality of expression, as in a musical composition, reflects the ingenuity, the capacity and the perceptions of the individual.

Each essay is written in fewer than 1,000 words so that it matches the length which many students are able to write in 45 minutes under examination conditions. You may write an excellent essay employing substantially fewer words than this, say 700 words or, indeed, rather more than 1,000 words – if you have the physical stamina – without sacrificing a clearly defined structure. Each paragraph needs to be substantial, but a simple calculation will reveal that if you write six to nine paragraphs in each essay, it is crucially important to be concise. Your time in the examination room will be short, but after much practice you should enter it with the acquired habit of disciplined, rapid thought necessary for teasing out the implications of questions to which you intend to respond, and with a capacity for concise, fluent expression.

At the end of your course may you not lament with Samuel Johnson that 'I find so much of my life has stolen unprofitably away, and that I can descry in retrospection scarcely a few single days properly and vigorously employed'.

Question 1

'The flight to Varennes in June 1791 sealed
the fate of Louis XVI.' Discuss the truth
of this statement.

 Tackling the question

Charles I, Tsar Nicholas II and Louis XVI, all ill-fated monarchs, exhibited certain damaging
characteristics in common. They each possessed a capacity for self-deception that
exceeded their ability to deceive others. Charles I never wearied of 'handsome denying'
answers when negotiating with his opponents, always hoping that he would be able to play
off one group against another and steal some kind of political advantage, which he could
use to restore to himself the authority that he believed unwaveringly was his. Tsar Nicholas
II, faced with the real danger of being violently overthrown, reluctantly agreed to political
concessions that appeared to turn him into a constitutional monarch. However, once the
crisis of 1905 was over he sought a reassertion of his autocratic powers, thus causing his
subjects to feel a sense of betrayal which, when war came in 1914 – and with it many military
reverses and much social and economic misery – was by 1917 translated into an emphatic
rejection of his rule. As the response to this question will show, Louis XVI, before and after
his unsuccessful attempt to flee from France in June 1791, demonstrated an
untrustworthiness that steadily removed any residual hope that he might just salvage from
the undermining of his autocratic powers the status of a constitutional monarch.

Answer

Guidance notes

It was more than a year after his abortive attempt to flee France
in June 1791 that Louis XVI was suspended from his royal duties,
a prelude to the abolition of the French monarchy. That he
remained King for a period suggests that, despite the humiliation
of being thwarted in his intended flight, there remained some
prospect of his retaining his throne permanently. Yet none of his
actions before his flight indicated a willingness to accept grace-
fully the irretrievable loss of his absolute powers and the establishment of constitutional monarchy. After June 1791, Louis was
discredited and his formal acceptance of the Constitution
(September 1791) did little to allay criticism of him. Moreover,
not only were the considerable residual powers vested in the King
contentious, there was also much resentment that the Assembly
had decided that the possession of property was the foundation

Explain, in general terms, why
Louis XVI's conduct before and
after his abortive attempt to
flee from France in June 1791 did
not augur well for his securing
his throne as a constitutional
monarch. Stress that the
Constitution of September
1791 was divisive in its effects
in any case.

Question 1

for electoral and suffrage qualifications, thus excluding most people from the political process. Political and social divisions deepened inevitably. These were exacerbated by the King's provocative use of his constitutional powers and the prevailing sentiment in an increasingly radically politicised Paris that the exercise of constitutional powers by an untrustworthy monarch was indissolubly linked to the defence of property.

How did Louis XVI react to events at the outset of the Revolution? Cite his responses to the August Decrees and the Declaration of the Rights of Man and the Citizen. Why was he obliged to reside in Paris and not in Versailles by October 1789? How did this development constrain the monarch?

From the outset of the Revolution, Louis had been loath to accept the powerful symbolism of the fall of the Bastille (14 July 1789) attesting to the demise of monarchical absolutism. He was reluctant to co-operate with the new order. He refused to accept the August Decrees, which abolished much of the established structure of French society, called by the Assembly the 'regime feodal'. Nor would he accept the principles embraced by the Declaration of the Rights of Man and the Citizen (26 August 1789). Such actions suggested that he would not entertain formal institutional restraints on his powers. His provocative action in the summoning of the Flanders Regiment to Versailles (October 1789) was interpreted as a sign that he might be ready to reimpose his traditional authority by force. This goaded Parisians to insist on his removal from Versailles and 'corrupt' court influence. Once the King was resident in Paris – together with the Assembly – he and the Assembly were thereafter prisoners, susceptible to the intimidations of the Parisians.

Now consider the immediate consequences of the King's attempted flight. What were the effects on the Assembly of their reluctance to remove the King when evidence suggested that he was thoroughly untrustworthy? Consider the significance of the demonstration on the Champs de Mar in July 1791.

Although the King's flight and enforced return (June 1791) increased anti-monarchical sentiment and the fear that France faced imminent invasion, the Assembly, about to complete a monarchical constitution, merely 'temporarily suspended' him. When it was discovered that the King had left behind him incriminating documents condemning the acts of the Assembly, which, disingenuously, he had accepted at the time, popular agitation for his removal was accompanied by fast diminishing respect for the Assembly. Its continued co-operation with a discredited monarch prompted a popular demonstration on the Champs de Mar (17 July 1791) demanding the King's dethronement. The demonstration was dispersed violently by the municipal authorities. This event defined with some clarity the line between those who would and those who would not compromise with the King. Many who had supported changes in 1789 now feared that the popular movement in Paris threatened their wealth and property as well as the King. Thus, the alliance of differing groups that had carried the Revolution so far was ended.

Indeed, after June 1791 there was no appeasing Parisians hostile to the monarch. The King's acceptance of the Constitution (14 September 1791) did not impress them. In any case, it sanctioned a restricted franchise of which they disapproved. Even so, many noble deputies disliked it and became *émigrés*. The delicate position of the King was rendered even more precarious when he exercised his suspensive veto provocatively: firstly, when he vetoed a decree declaring emigrants suspect of conspiracy against the state and ordered their return (12 November 1791); and secondly when he vetoed a decree against non-juring clergy (19 December 1792). In a tense atmosphere, the newly elected Legislative Assembly, containing no members of the earlier National Assembly, and much influenced by Girondins seeking war to expose counter-revolutionaries, was at one with the King in this matter, although Louis wanted war in order to reverse the Revolution. The Feuillants, seeking co-operation with the King as a constitutional monarch, and the Jacobins, implacably hostile to the King, sought the avoidance of war. When a Girondin ministry was appointed (March 1792) war was imminent and soon declared (April 1792). Thereafter, economic hardship and early military reverses made the King's position even more desperate.

> Show how the King continued to aggravate his personally precarious position after June 1791. Examine his provocative use of his suspensive veto, granted to him in the Constitution. How did war come about in 1792? Who supported the war and who did not? What were the effects of the outbreak of war on Louis' position?

When an insurrectionary force attacked the Tuileries (10 August 1792) and a massacre ensued, the consequences were momentous and historians speak of a 'second revolution', more radical than that of 1789, being initiated. The Legislative Assembly was forced to accept the demands of Robespierre and the *sans-culottes* for the election of a new Assembly, the Convention, by universal male suffrage. The King's reign was over – terminated formally on 21 September 1792 – and, with his enforced abdication, the Constitution of 1791 was dead.

> What were the dramatic consequences of the attack on the Tuileries on 10 August 1792?

The King's capacity to rule had been radically curtailed since 1789, and his possible survival depended partly on his ability to embrace constitutional changes willingly, and partly on economic and political factors beyond his control. At best, from the King's viewpoint, a constitutional arrangement was attainable – at worst, constitutional reforms would pave the way for a Republic. The flight to Varennes in 1791 not only virtually ensured that he would not survive as the French King, but undermined the hopes of traditional royalists, many of the bourgeoisie – including the majority in the National Assembly – and many people of all classes in the provinces, where traditional values and practices were cherished.

> Conclude by explaining how Louis XVI might have survived as King of France. Why did the failure of his attempted flight have such grave consequences for the course of the Revolution?

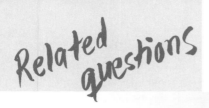

1 'It cannot be said that any one event in 1789 was the most revolutionary of all.' Discuss the truth of this statement.

Arthur Young mistakenly believed in June 1789 that 'the whole business now seems over, the revolution complete'. In fact it was merely beginning, its course thereafter complex and unpredictable. Outline at the start the succession of events in 1789, each replete with dramatic implications, which in aggregate represented a crumbling of the restraints that held in check the disparate forces active in pre-revolutionary France. Of all the events of 1789 that may be cited in this essay, the least specific must have been the rumours and violence that became endemic in many parts of France during that year. May one say that any single event or development was the most important of 1789? Having outlined these points in the introduction, each event should be considered in detail. How and with what results did the National Assembly come into being? What was the significance of the fall of the Bastille on 14 July 1789? What were the consequences in 1789 of Louis XVI giving the impression that he was loath to accept constraints on his authority? What was happening in the rest of France while dramatic events were occurring in Paris? Finally, how valid is the claim made in the question set? You may conclude that to isolate a single event as the most revolutionary of all in 1789 may diminish unjustifiably the significance of other events. Stress that each event occurred in a changing setting and within a flow of events and circumstances. The historian's judgement as to what the Revolution was about will determine the choice of the most important events. If the events are taken together, those of 1789 foreshadowed a radical remoulding of French society.

2 'Although the whole structure of the *ancien régime* was dismantled between 1789 and 1792, France failed to acquire strong and effective government.' How far do you consider this claim to be valid?

3 Why had France become a republic by 1792?

Question 2

'The Terror masked the achievements of the Committee of Public Safety.' How far is this claim valid?

Tackling the question

William Doyle has observed that a monopoly of violence and blood-letting should not be attributed to Revolutionary France in the closing years of the eighteenth century. While 30,000 people died in just under a year during the State Terror of 1793–4, Suvorov stormed the suburb of Praga on 4 November 1794 and killed between 10,000 and 20,000 Poles in a single day, he claims. Doyle adds for good measure that the deaths in France were 'far from the bloodiest episode in a murderous decade for Europe; the same number died in a matter of weeks in Ireland in 1798, in a country with one sixth of France's population'.

Notwithstanding these grim comparisons, it is the seemingly uncontrolled use of the guillotine that lends a peculiar horror to the killings in France. They reached a bizarre climax in 1794 when erstwhile allies fought each other and consigned each other to death by the guillotine. By that stage — when Danton, Desmoulins and others were executed in April 1794 – 'it seems', says Doyle, 'that they were struck down more for what they might do than for what they had done. Their execution … marked the beginning of a new phase in the Terror, when people would die for their potential as much as for specific crimes, and sometimes for their failure to match some ideal moral standard'. On Robespierre, whose name is inextricably linked to this kind of persecution, Doyle concludes that ultimately he seems to have believed 'that hardly anybody in public life could be relied on, and by saying so openly ensured that they could not. Men called him a dictator because they feared moral inflexibility in one who had power.' Robespierre believed that 'virtue' without 'terror' was 'impotent', suggesting that while he had a vision of an ideal society, if such a utopia was to be realised, actual and potential critics of it would need to be ruthlessly eliminated. Marat concurred – 'liberty must be established by violence'. By 1794 the violence was institutionalised – it was no longer the doings of a capricious and bloodthirsty mob – and used by Robespierre and his supporters to destroy rival Jacobin factions like the Hébertists and the Dantonists. The potentially endless picking off of members of the Convention, mooted by Robespierre, prompted the desperate members to destroy Robespierre himself, after which the Terror rapidly subsided.

Yet views on Robespierre remain polarised in France. Since the time of Jean Jaurès, socialists have sought his rehabilitation – they would endorse Mathiez's opinion that he was 'the incarnation of Revolutionary France in its most noble, most generous and most sincere aspects'. On the other hand, conservative opinion sees him as directly responsible for thousands of deaths and his temporary ascendancy in France as prefiguring twentieth-century rulers of totalitarian states. Today, official France has little to say in his favour. He did not figure in the bicentenary celebrations of 1989. While there may be many *rues Danton*, Robespierre is nowhere remembered in this way.

Answer

Begin by examining the circumstances that facilitated the creation of the Committee of Public Safety in 1793. What had the Committee achieved, albeit by using terror, by 1794? Why, ultimately, was its authority challenged?

When, in 1793, the Committee of Public Safety (CPS) was created to supervise all branches of the executive and to co-ordinate the policies of the Revolutionary government, France faced anarchy. A rift had developed between the Convention and the radical Paris sections, largely because the former would not sanction certain measures – like the control of grain prices – that the latter believed would relieve economic distress. The bitter rivalry between the Montagnards and the Girondins in the Convention was moving towards its climax. There was military defeat at Neerwinden (March 1793) followed by Dumouriez's desertion – events that weakened the Girondins' cause. The Vendéan revolt was spreading and capturing most of the region's towns. Draconian measures seemed unavoidable. The Terror authorised by the CPS in 1793 and 1794 produced the inflexible discipline that sustained the military fortunes of the Revolution both within France and on its frontiers. The enemy was driven beyond the Pyrenees (December 1793). When French armies entered Belgium, the Austrian Netherlands, France's fears of the foreigner sharply declined. As the *raison d'être* of the CPS lapsed, so its authority was challenged and its importance declined.

How did the Committee of Public Safety operate? How was administrative unity in France achieved?

The CPS was a twelve-man committee of the Convention. Although decisions were taken in common, the members rarely met together, for there was specialisation in the Committee and individuals were often absent on provincial missions. Robespierre and Barère alone remained in Paris. The CPS controlled other committees, ministers and commissions and also delegated its powers to *représentants en mission*, this last constituting the single most important element in organising the Terror. The *représentants*, the principal agents linking the departments of the Convention and the CPS, compelled local authorities to implement the decisions of the central government. Although initially the *représentants'* activities contributed to anarchic terror which stemmed largely from economic distress, France was obliged to accept uniformity as the government resolved to ensure that resources were available to feed townspeople and supply the armies.

Why was the Committee of Public Safety inexorably drawn towards the use of terror? Consider the significance of the activities of the Parisian *armée révolutionnaire*.

In the desperate circumstances of mid-1793, the Convention and the CPS were drawn away from moderation. Military defeat, counter-revolution and treason intensified popular pressure for ruthlessness towards the external foe, internal rebels and those who, in local government, weakened the authority of Paris. The pressure on government was shown when it permitted the formation of a Parisian *armée révolutionnaire* to act as an instrument of terror against the rebels. Thus, when Lyons fell to the

Republicans (October 1793), the CPS authorised brutal reprisals, including destruction of houses and mass executions.

The Terror is indissolubly linked with Robespierre. He was instrumental in reducing the influence of popular societies after 1793 and promoting centralisation so that the achievements of the Revolution could be protected. He supported fully the brake that the Convention put on the anarchic Terror and local initiatives by the law of Frimaire (14 December 1793). This prevented *représentants en mission* from delegating their powers without prior approval from Paris and abolished inspection of the national agents of the CPS and the Committee of General Security, the latter being tantamount to a ministry of Revolutionary Police. Moreover, levying taxes and loans at the local level was forbidden. Thus, France acquired a more rigorous and powerful bureaucracy than obtained during the eighteenth-century monarchy.

> What was Robespierre's achievement as a member of the Committee of Public Safety? What part did he play in checking anarchic terror and local autonomy in France at this time?

By late 1793 Robespierre, regarding the CPS and its Jacobin followers as custodians of the Revolution, resolved to purge those who were not unambiguously committed to the Revolution despite their earlier orthodoxy. Thus, the theory of the revolutionary élite developed. It may well have been that Robespierre sought political liberty and considered the Revolutionary dictatorship and its associated judicial terror as an expedient in an acute crisis. Yet when the *sans-culottes* demanded direct democracy, the CPS, its members all of bourgeois origin, abolished the Parisian *armée* (27 March 1794), seemingly acting against the Revolution itself. St Just's proposal that suspects' property should be confiscated by the state and the proceeds given to the poor was a political manoeuvre calculated to win back the loyalty of the *sans-culottes*. This weakened the authority of the CPS and soon there were divisions within the Committee.

> Consider Robespierre's acceptance of judicial terror in 1794. How did the Committee's handling of the *sans-culottes* weaken its authority?

That an invasion and conquest of France did not occur in 1793 was very much attributable to the vigour and disciplined resolve of the CPS. In those desperate times, its rule was essentially a war dictatorship, which created for the first time in modern history the phenomenon of a nation in arms. By 1794 France had 850,000 men in its armies. Under the CPS, generals like Bonaparte, Davoust and Augereau were discovered and tested. The victory of Fleurus (26 June 1794), followed by the occupation of Belgium, relaxed fears of the enemy. Indeed, it was this success that assisted in undermining the CPS's unity. Violent disagreements arose between Carnot and St Just, the latter supported by Robespierre, over the conduct of the war. There were divisions about the Law

> How did developments in France's wars weaken the authority of the Committee? Explain the divisions that emerged within the Committee.

of Suspects. Soon the CPS was being perceived as a personal dictatorship of Robespierre supported by St Just and Couthon. There was a growing atmosphere of suspicion and panic, reminiscent of the 'Great Fear' of 1789.

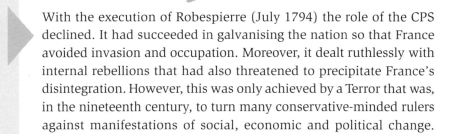

What were the achievements of the Committee of Public Safety because of, rather than despite, the use of the Terror?

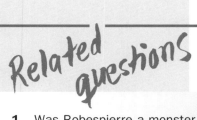

With the execution of Robespierre (July 1794) the role of the CPS declined. It had succeeded in galvanising the nation so that France avoided invasion and occupation. Moreover, it dealt ruthlessly with internal rebellions that had also threatened to precipitate France's disintegration. However, this was only achieved by a Terror that was, in the nineteenth century, to turn many conservative-minded rulers against manifestations of social, economic and political change. By 1794 the crisis had passed – the Terror seemed superfluous.

Related questions

1 Was Robespierre a monster or a saint?

Robespierre's personality and actions have been a subject of much controversy. Was he the embodiment of tyranny – foreshadowing that of twentieth-century totalitarian rulers – or was he 'the saint of democracy', 'the schoolmaster of democracy'? Explain the divided views of Marxists about him. Here is the substance for an initial paragraph, upon which you will expand in subsequent paragraphs. Consider the contribution made by Robespierre to saving Revolutionary France by 1794. What principles did he uphold and with what consequences? What do you think of his quest for a Republic of virtue prefaced by Terror? Why can he not be dismissed as a mere terrorist? Explain how in the early days of the Revolution he had acquired a reputation for promoting freedom. What did he mean by equality? Was he thinking purely in political terms and dismissing economic equality as irrelevant? What impact did Robespierre have upon the character of central government in France? In the final paragraph stress that Robespierre is too closely associated with the Terror to escape responsibility for its excesses. It may be argued that this austere character, who was unable to establish an enduring rapport with the *menu peuple* (humble people), personified the moral force of the Revolution, without which the Terror would have been merely the work of a government of national defence and intimidation. Thompson has called him a 'moral fanatic', who used means distasteful to himself to achieve ends that he valued more than public appeal. If he is to be considered as embodying some elements of saintliness, he cannot be seen as believing in an indulgent tolerance. Rather, he is indissolubly linked to a moral inflexibility which, in one who wielded power in practice, produced a regime indistinguishable from the brutalities of a dictatorship based on no readily identifiable principles.

2 Why and how did the Jacobins eventually ensure the fall of the Girondins?

3 Why had France become a republic by 1792?

Question 3

What part did the *sans-culottes* play in the French Revolution?

Tackling the question

Power was acquired by the people in the French Revolution, but how that power should be wielded was the subject of endless debate in assemblies and among the populace. The latter were often prepared to fight for their beliefs in the streets of towns and cities. The Constitution of 1791, which sanctioned a restricted franchise and gave an already discredited monarch a suspensive veto, did not appeal to the *sans-culottes*, organised in the 48 sections into which Paris was divided. They sought direct and popular participation in politics. They derived their thinking from Rousseau's teachings, which suggested to them that everybody – including the poorest and least educated – should be involved in day-to-day political activities. The *sans-culotte* movement played its part in securing the power of the Jacobins in 1793 and 1794 by providing the popular basis of Jacobin government. Historians have acknowledged the importance of the *sans-culottes* in a period when ideas – novel, ingenious and sometimes impractical – burst forth. Whilst the Revolutionary government could claim that it had popular support in 1794, Robespierre disbanded the Parisian *armée revolutionnaire* and, in the wake of his execution in July 1794, the *sans-culotte* movement was crushed.

Answer

Guidance notes

In the nineteenth century historians tended to regard the Parisian *sans-culottes* as the personification of either good or evil. More recently, Labrousse and Lefebvre have sought to see popular elements in the Revolution in human terms, while Rudé, using principally police records of the Archives Nationales, has investigated the composition of the revolutionary crowds without claiming to divine the motives that drew them together. The Revolution witnessed their becoming increasingly politicised by playing a part not only in facilitating the demise of absolute monarchy in 1789, but in radicalising the Revolution in 1792, their power harnessed by the Jacobins, who by 1794 had undermined the influence of the *sans-culottes*, fearful of the anarchic threat that they posed to the Committee of Public Safety.

How have the *sans-culottes* been viewed by historians? How did the movement influence the course of the Revolution? Why was their influence undermined by 1794?

Question 3

Explain the composition of the *sans-culotte* movement. How had such categories of people behaved before 1789?

Nine-tenths of the population of Paris in 1789, later to be called the *sans-culottes*, did not constitute a distinctive class. They comprised shopkeepers, tradesmen, craftsmen, journeymen, labourers and vagrants. Distinctions between categories of workers – like that between a wage-earning journeyman and an independent craftsman – were ill defined. In the past, despite their lack of coherence as a social class, they had used violence – as in 1775 – to express their social grievances, although in 1789 such distress may not have contributed decisively to the revolutionary temper.

How important was the role of the *sans-culottes* in 1789? How had they made known their grievances in 1789? In what dramatic way did they respond to the frustrations that they faced?

The people having articulated their complaints in *cahiers* (1789), their expectations were frustrated by the protracted procedural wrangles in the Estates-General, following its inaugural meeting (5 May 1789), and the intimidating presence of the King's troops around Paris. Necker's dismissal (11 July 1789) was the occasion for insurrection, manifesting itself in the storming of the Bastille (14 July 1789). This action by an estimated 900 Parisians was of little military importance, but it had profound political implications in that it did irreparable damage to the concept of monarchical absolutism.

Show how continued suspicions of the King's motives after the fall of the Bastille in July 1789 led to decisive action by the *sans-culottes* in October 1789 that severely restricted the King's freedom of action.

Yet suspicions of the King remained among Parisians. In residence at Versailles, he refused to consent to the Assembly's abolition of feudal rights (4 August 1789) or to the Declaration of the Rights of Man and the Citizen. The gains of July seemed precarious. It was the march of the people of Paris to Versailles (October 1789), ostensibly prompted by a bread crisis, which brought the King to Paris to be closely followed by the Assembly. Superficially, the constitutional monarchists were the beneficiaries of the people's action, but the members of the Assembly were conscious that the capacity of the *sans-culottes* for disorder could, in other circumstances, be directed against them.

Now consider the reasons for the social and political differences that led to the *sans-culottes* and the National Assembly being at odds with each other. Explain the *sans-culottes'* dissatisfaction with the 1791 Constitution. What was the significance of the 'massacre' on the Champs de Mar in July 1791?

Indeed, the economic and political objectives of the *sans-culottes* and the Assembly differed markedly. The former's demand for economic controls, including fixing prices to protect the people, accorded ill with the bourgeois emphasis on unrestricted private enterprise. Moreover, the *sans-culottes* sought political and social equality and believed in the duty of every citizen to participate in day-to-day politics. They were hostile to unchecked power even when in the hands of popularly elected representatives, for which there was limited provision in the Constitution of 1791. Soboul has claimed that *inter alia* they wanted legislation by referendum, a 'popular veto' and binding mandates for the people's delegates. This was a far cry from the content of the 1791 Constitution, which established a limited monarchy and a restricted franchise. The Assembly's retention of the King, discredited though he was by his failed attempt to flee from France (June 1791), merely intensified the chagrin of politically minded Parisians. The 'massacre' at the Champs de Mar (17 July 1791), where the *sans-culottes* were demanding revision of the Constitution, encouraged by the Cordelier and Jacobin clubs, highlighted the emerging breach between those who sought maintenance of the Constitution and those who strove for a republic.

In 1792 the *sans-culottes* played a decisive role in giving the Revolution a radical emphasis. While the Declaration of Pilnitz (27 August 1791) did not contemplate immediate armed intervention from abroad, it encouraged counter-revolution in France and assisted the Girondins in winning support for war, especially among political democrats and the *sans-culottes*. Distressed by inflation – aggravated by the effects of war after 1792 – rioters in Paris demanded an end to the royal veto (20 June 1792). Although no bloodshed occurred, the political crisis deepened with the inflammatory Brunswick Manifesto (25 July 1792), which threatened Paris with dire consequences if the city did not submit to Louis. Popular agitation culminated in a bloody attack on the Tuileries (10 August 1792), resulting in the King's immediate suspension from his office. In Soboul's words, the people were soon to be 'integrated in the nation' in 'the second revolution' with equal political rights.

> You are now poised to show how the *sans-culotte* movement was to a considerable degree responsible for ensuring that the Revolution was radicalised and the King's position rendered untenable.

The Jacobins then sought to harness the popular movement to promote their own political ambitions, while striving to prevent the leadership of the *sans-culottes* passing to the *enragés*. With the expulsion of the Girondins (May–June 1792), popular support for whom was to be eroded by their equivocation during the events of August 1792, the Jacobins were able to win that support by conceding the General Maximum (29 September 1792), which limited the prices of a range of vital goods and services. Thus, the Revolutionary government of Year Two seemed to be on a sure foundation with popular support.

> How did the Jacobins harness the support of the *sans-culottes* in 1792?

Yet the alliance proved not to be durable. Having created the *armées révolutionnaires* to facilitate links between the civil power and the army, Robespierre considered that the anarchy they caused threatened the authority of the Committee of Public Safety. Moreover, the wrath of the *sans-culottes* was turned against the government for its failure to implement the General Maximum. By March 1794 the Parisian *armée révolutionnaire* had been

> What were the reasons for the alliance between the *sans-culottes* and the Jacobins being undermined by 1794? What were the consequences of the rifts that developed between them?

disbanded, for Robespierre was unsympathetic towards their preoccupation with economic problems and impatient of their lack of commitment to his political theories. The disenchantment was mutual and divisions between them weakened both. Thus, when Robespierre was executed (28 July 1794) no effort was made by the *sans-culottes* to save him.

Finally, how were the *sans-culottes* brought to heel in 1795?

Thereafter, the *sans-culottes* faced a government resolved to remove the controls introduced by its predecessors, so that by 1794 the Maximum Laws had been abolished. This provoked agitation culminating in the insurrections of the *sans-culottes* of April–May 1795, ultimately crushed by military units. By this time, even the radical bourgeoisie had deserted them and their revolt had no hope of making political gain. Moreover, the *journée* of Vendémiaire (4–6 October 1795) brought the army into the capital and established an occupation which, under the Directory, paved the way for the rise of Bonaparte. After 1795 there was little that the revolutionary crowd could do to intimidate the government.

Related questions

1 'An unattractive, disreputable regime.' How far is this a fair verdict on the Directory?

In the initial paragraph, outline the traditional view of the Directory as corrupt and incompetent. It has long been insisted that it mismanaged the economy, embraced a provocative foreign policy, which was responsible for keeping France at war, and failed to maintain law and order at home. Contrast these unflattering views of the Directors with the more sympathetic assessments of recent French historians. They qualify the main allegations levelled against them. Their tentative conclusions indicate that, apart from Barras' conspicuous corruption, little compelling evidence can be levelled against the thirteen Directors who held office during the period 1795–9. The Directors did not mismanage France's finances, they claim. Rather, they initiated lasting fiscal reforms and presided over an economic recovery. By 1798, it is added, France's influence in Europe was virtually unchallenged. Perhaps it is the unsatisfactory way in which they received their appointments initially that has damaged their reputations – through their nomination by former members of the Convention, two-thirds of whom were re-elected to the new legislature. Roubell, responsible for foreign affairs, Neufchâteau, as minister of the interior, Tuilhard and Merlin are now considered constructive and able politicians.

The collapse of *assignats* in 1796 and the repudiation of two-thirds of the public debt in 1797 are now blamed on the miscalculations of the National Assembly of 1789–91. The new metallic currency introduced by the Directors soon restored France's finances and without much inflation. Their reforms of taxation are now admired. While it is conceded that the Directory sought peace, negotiations with England failed because the latter refused to surrender certain colonial conquests. On the other hand, the Directors' acceptance of the Treaty of Campo-Formio in 1797 effectively passed the initiative in foreign policy to Napoleon, who was determined upon expansion in Italy at the expense of the Directory's quest for natural frontiers. If there was a serious failure, it was in respect of the maintenance of law and order – the revival of royalism, the adoption of conscription in 1798, and the resulting brigandage of potential recruits practising evasion, aggravated the situation. You will need to examine every facet of the Directory's policies and decide to what extent the verdict of one French historian, Vandal, that the regime was 'lamentably incompetent', 'morally debased' and 'shameless' has any validity.

2   Examine the impact on French society of the French Revolution.

3   'It was the failures of the Directory that paved the way for the rise of Napoleon Bonaparte.' How far do you believe that this statement is just?

**'I am the Revolution.' To what extent was
Napoleon I's claim a valid one?**

Tackling the question

From 1799 to 1804, Napoleon Bonaparte styled himself First Consul. A decree of the Senate in May 1804 bestowed on him the title 'Emperor of the French'. He owed his military and political pre-eminence to the opportunities that the Revolution had given to the talented. The weaknesses of the Directory enabled him to gain power by a coup. He claimed that he was the heir to the Revolution, but while he endorsed the revolutionary changes made at the beginning of the Revolution, he detached himself from the doctrinaire policies of the Jacobins, which had been accompanied by increasing public disorder. Government, he believed, should be firm and unchallenged and able to enforce whatever policies were decreed by it. Under Napoleon, traces of the practices, influences and ethos of the *ancien régime* were blended with some of the ideas of the Revolution to produce a regime not classifiable with others. Like a twentieth-century dictator, he was skilled at manipulating public opinion by means of a controlled press and he took care to ensure that his personality was lionised for public consumption. Military success reinforced his acceptability to the French people, but he well knew that unlike other rulers who were exercising powers and privileges wielded by their predecessors, he, a parvenu, would lose all if his capacity for conquest deserted him.

Answer

Establish the aspects of the Revolution that Napoleon regarded as irreversible and those characteristics of it that he was prepared to abandon. The points raised will be discussed fully in the body of the essay.

After Brumaire, most Frenchmen acquiesced in Napoleon's imposition of a political, administrative and judicial system that fundamentally changed France's institutions. Nobody had gained more than himself from the Revolutionaries' promotion of 'the career open to the talents' and he resolutely preserved that principle. Certain crucial changes made by Revolutionaries were considered irreversible – equality before the law, the removal of seigniorial rights, the land settlement, restrictions imposed on the Roman Catholic Church and the alienation of its assets. However, he considered that the uncircumscribed exercise of political rights had produced irreconcilable disagreements which were responsible for recurrent political crises. He sought order and stability, linked with some of the accomplishments of the initial stages of the Revolution. If he personified the Revolution, it was as one who divested it of its Jacobin inheritance and consolidated and disciplined those aspects of it that he believed would promote an enduring strength for France.

Napoleon's claim to embody the General Will in his own person directly contradicted the fundamental principle of the Revolution – Rousseau's concept of popular sovereignty. He ensured that he avoided explicit statements of ideology and eschewed reference to *liberté*, *égalité* and *fraternité*. He merely paid lip service to representative institutions, whose powers were precisely defined and limited. Thus, the Tribunate – like the Legislative Body initially appointed and subsequently chosen from prescribed lists of candidates – could merely debate bills originating outside the chamber within limits decided by the government. The Legislative Body voted on, but did not debate, such bills. The Senate was an amenable body whose members were salaried to ensure co-operation. Such emasculated institutions were parallelled by a Council of State, an appointed body, which prescribed texts for the assemblies' consideration. Here alone, in secret, Napoleon permitted debate. However, he ensured that the reforms and codifications devised by the Council in its particular sections did not detract from his untrammelled powers of decision making.

> In what sense was Napoleon at odds with certain tenets of the Revolution? What was his attitude towards Rousseau's notion of the General Will? How did the representative institutions that he created and the Council of State reflect his view of decision making?

Napoleon appreciated that the divisive religious policies of the Revolution had encouraged sympathy for counter-revolution and sabotaged support for the ideals of 1789. Napoleon had no genuine religious convictions and considered the Catholic Church as important principally as a means of social control, required to instil morality and preach obedience to lawful authority. Thus, in the Concordat of 1802, the Pope was obliged to recognise that a regulated Gallican Church was effectively subordinated to the interests of the state. The Ultramontanism of the seventeenth and eighteenth centuries was finally defeated.

> How did Napoleon's religious policies affect the role of the Roman Catholic Church in France?

The codification of the law (1804) reflected Napoleon's resolve to trim the tenets of the Revolution by restoring some concepts embraced by the *ancien régime*. Although the Revolution's insistence on equality before the law was upheld by Napoleon, he reasserted the Roman Law concept of the absolute authority of the head of the family. Women, he deemed, were necessarily subordinated to men. Yet, like the Revolutionaries, he rejected primogeniture and insisted on equal division of property among heirs with the qualification that testators could dispose of a quarter of their property according to their wishes. Illegitimate

> To what extent was Napoleon's legal code consistent with the tenets of the Revolution? Note that traces of the legal practices of the *ancien régime* were reintroduced by Napoleon.

children, permitted by the Revolutionaries to inherit property, enjoyed no rights of inheritance under Napoleon. The departure from the liberalising tendencies of the revolutionary decade was accentuated by the provisions of his Criminal and Penal Codes (1808 and 1810), which revived the notorious *lettre de cachet*, rooted in the *ancien régime*.

How far did Napoleon depart from the fiscal policies of the Revolutionaries?

In his fiscal policies Napoleon distanced himself from the Revolution's egalitarian principles by restoring some practices of the *ancien régime*. A shift from direct to indirect taxation – by quadrupling taxes on tobacco, alcohol and salt (1806–12) – inordinately burdened the poor. Total taxes on consumer goods provided a quarter of government receipts in 1813. Stamp duties, registration taxes and customs revenue fell woefully short of expenditure. The failure of the Revolutionaries' *assignats* dissuaded Napoleon from creating paper money even when, after 1810, with a shortage of metallic currency and a flight of specie beyond France's frontiers, such issues would have been appropriate.

How far did he consolidate the educational policies of the Revolution?

While confirming the Convention's structural divisions of education into primary, secondary and higher levels, Napoleon did little to promote primary education, which was mainly limited to private and confessional schools to provide 'moral education'. He expended most of his energies on secondary education as a prelude to specialised studies for professional and administrative careers, but neglected technical education to the detriment of France's industrial development. The founding of the Imperial University (1806), with faculties of law, medicine, theology, letters and science, was essentially élitist in conception. He continued to sustain the recently formed *grandes écoles*, which provided advanced scientific education, and he had a special regard for the Polytechnic (founded 1794), which fostered engineering and was accessible to some poor families. Nevertheless, fees were payable after 1805 and it became an increasingly military institution. Thus Napoleon, who placed emphasis on training state functionaries, heavily qualified the idealistic educational tenets of the Revolution.

Conclude by assessing whether the degree of continuity with the work of Revolutionaries is sufficient for it to be claimed that he personified the Revolution. Do not omit reference to traces of Napoleon's indebtedness to the *ancien régime*.

The society that Napoleon created was a synthesis of concepts inherited from the Revolution and the *ancien régime*. He rigorously fashioned a social structure that had the pyramidal trappings of the *ancien régime*. Each class within the hierarchy was expected to be a zealous custodian of its own interests and willing to subordinate itself to the all-pervasive authority of the Emperor. Dissentients were checkmated by an assiduous secret police. Elements of the Revolution's legacy, indispensable to the maintenance of political stability, were judiciously consolidated in order to sustain the support of the peasantry and the bourgeoisie. Therefore, he personified a Revolution bereft of the tenets that, in practice, promoted disorder.

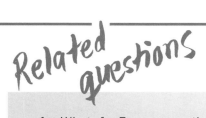

Related questions

1 What, for France, was the legacy of the rule of Napoleon I?

Napoleon I's autocratic rule ran directly contrary, in essence, to the fundamental concept of the Revolution – that of popular sovereignty derived from Rousseau's Social Contract. However, Napoleon considered some changes inspired by the Revolution as irreversible – the land settlement, equality before the law, the removal of seigniorial rights and the forfeiture of clerical privileges. Nor did he intend to abandon the notion of 'the career open to the talents', of which he was the most conspicuous beneficiary. Nevertheless, his concern for political stability persuaded him to abandon certain principles of the Revolution – like the concept of the sovereignty of the people, which he believed had burdened France with political instability during the 1790s. Thus, he modified or reversed reforms and actions of his immediate predecessors and bequeathed to France laws and institutions, some of which persist in modified form until this day. In the body of the essay, after the introduction, consider Napoleon's reforms and assess their longer-term impact on France. What were the consequences for France of Napoleon's distaste for representative institutions? What was the long-term impact of his land reforms? How may the Revolutionaries and Napoleon have jointly contributed to the relative decline of France's population after 1815 by their decisions relating to property? How lasting was Napoleon's policy towards the Roman Catholic Church? What long-term impact did Napoleon's reforms of local government have upon France? What durable legal reform did he initiate? How did the Revolution and Napoleon promote scope for the able and enterprising? What lasting impact did Napoleon have upon education in France? What damage did Napoleon do to France's long-term economic growth? Cumulatively, answers to these questions constitute his legacy to France.

2 'The economy of France stagnated under the Emperor Napoleon I.' Discuss the validity of this claim.

3 Account for the failure of the Continental System to achieve its objectives.

Question 5

Why did it take so long to defeat Napoleon I?

Tackling the question

In a recent book, Alastair Horne claimed that the political and economic stability of Napoleon I's empire was only as secure as his last victory. One battle would be followed by another, so that the victories early on at Austerlitz (1805), Jena and Auerstadt (1806) and Friedland (1807) led inexorably to Waterloo, fuelled by the self-destructiveness of Napoleon's ambitions. Indeed, he admitted as much when he observed that 'my power would fail were I not to support it by new glory and new victories. Conquest has made me what I am, and conquest alone can maintain me.' Wellington appreciated the implications of Napoleon's hunger for conquest – 'a conqueror, like a cannon ball, must go on; if he rebounds his career is over'. Napoleon crushed Austrian, Prussia and Russian armies between 1805 and 1809. Each state was coerced into joining the Continental System, which, he hoped, would isolate and finally defeat Britain. However, Talleyrand, who sought stability in Europe, disagreed and accurately perceived that the Continental System would bring not peace but war, which would not stop until Napoleon was defeated. Napoleon's resolve to humiliate the opponents he defeated precluded any lasting settlement. Moreover, in any consideration of the reasons for Napoleon's ultimate defeat there is, as Alastair Horne insists, the exercise of British sea power and maritime strategy together with the consequences of economic blockade.

In the end, Napoleon's genius for leading men – his ability, as he put it, to 'speak to the soul in order to electrify the man' – proved insufficient to save him. 'If the prolonged struggle over Napoleonic hegemony has any lesson or moral, it is perhaps the value of coalition. Muddled and inefficient as they may be, two World Wars and a Cold War show that, in the long run, they win wars – and possibly prevent them. Powers, however strong, that exist alone, isolated, are usually doomed', Horne concludes.

Answer

Outline the factors which ensured that it would be a long time before Napoleon could be defeated. What, ultimately, in 1813 turned the scales against him?

That it took so long to defeat Napoleon I was attributable to several factors. There was his unexampled genius as a leader of men in battle. Enjoying a monopoly of power in France, he was dependent on no vacillating government at home. He was able, until 1813, to ensure that no effective coalition of powers was formed against him. Britain's role, on Europe's periphery, was essentially defensive, at least until 1808 when it intervened on the Iberian peninsula – the importance of Britain arising from a command of the sea that frustrated Napoleon's quest for security. After defeat at Friedland (1807), Russia did not commit its armies against Napoleon again for five years. Memories of their armies being annihilated one by one induced caution among European powers in their dealings with Napoleon. Ultimately, when a grand coalition was formed (1813), Napoleon's defeat was attainable.

Although Napoleon was a military leader of exceptional resource-fulness, he was not a major military innovator. He benefited from French pioneering – in the late eighteenth century – of armies organised in autonomous mobile corps of 15,000–30,000 men, able to operate remote from France by living off the land, thus reducing the dangers arising from long lines of communication. As a master of his profession, Napoleon refined established techniques. At the critical point of a battle, he knew how to bring superior firepower and numerically superior manpower to bear to demoralise an outmanoeuvred opponent. His strategic and practical skills were incomparable. Nevertheless, as the army expanded with the growth of his empire, there was, after 1806, a deterioration in the quality of recruits and the thoroughness of their training. Yet at the time of the Treaty of Tilsit (1807), Napoleon seemed irresistible and for years afterwards his opponents were easily divided as to the wisdom of combining against him.

> What were the professional skills that Napoleon could bring to bear on his opponents, which deterred them from uniting against him?

Having reformed its armies on French lines after the débâcle at Austerlitz (1805), Austria was tempted prematurely to pit its armies against Napoleon in 1809 only to be heavily defeated at Wagram (July 1809), a French victory which, however, did not match the comprehensive defeat of Austria at Austerlitz. If the Peace of Schönbrunn (October 1809) may be considered a humil-iation for Austria, there was evidence that Napoleon was less commanding than in previous encounters, less flexible in his tactics than hitherto.

> Yet Napoleon was not invulnerable. How did Austria reveal a potential decline in Napoleon's fortunes in 1809?

The Prussians had experienced emphatic defeat at Jena and Auerstadt (October 1806) and they too were prepared to learn salutary lessons from the grim experience. Guided by Scharnhorst, Gneisnau and Clausewitz, the Prussians adapted Napoleon's skills to their local conditions. Promotion by merit within the officer corps, military service for all in order to dissociate service from serfdom, skilful evasion of clauses in the Treaty of Tilsit limiting the size of Prussia's army and, perhaps above all, fundamental social changes in Prussian society paved the way for the impor-tant role that Prussia was to play in the final stages of the conflict after its treaty with the Russians at Kalisch (February 1813).

> Reinforce the argument in the previous paragraph by considering how Prussia prepared itself after 1806 for a renewal of conflict with France.

Why was Russia a potential danger to Napoleon after 1807? How did Russia defy Napoleon's wishes? Why, when Napoleon was retreating from Russia in 1812, was Austria loath to join a coalition against him?

A similar ordeal was experienced by Russia after the defeat at Friedland (January 1807). Yet Russia enjoyed the boon of geographical remoteness, which meant that it could not be easily intimidated. Indeed, after Tilsit, Russia was confident that it could safely defy Napoleon, as it did by not implementing effectively Napoleon's Continental System, and by deftly ignoring Napoleon's wish that Russia should restrain Austria while France dealt with setbacks in Spain (1809). Austria, in particular, nursed fears that if a combination of powers challenged Napoleon successfully, France's hegemony in Europe might be replaced by Russia's. Thus, when Napoleon retreated from Russia (1812), Metternich's tardiness in committing Austrian armies to war was determined as much by his fear of Russia as by the dangers inherent in offering resistance to Napoleon.

How was Britain, complementing Russia, always a potential threat to Napoleon's security in Europe?

While it may be argued that Napoleon was at the height of his powers in 1807, Britain's obduracy and its naval ascendancy, confirmed at Trafalgar (October 1805), ensured that although Napoleon had command of much of the mainland, his writ did not run at sea. In consequence, Napoleon was never secure in Europe. His efforts to undermine Britain's economy after the Berlin Decrees (November 1806) were not successful, so that he could never emancipate himself from the vague, tantalisingly inaccessible menace across the Channel, just as on land there was the potential threat of Russia beyond the Grand Duchy of Warsaw.

Explain how Britain's military role in the Iberian peninsula played its part in paving the way for Napoleon's ultimate defeat.

Even when Britain did become directly involved in Europe by invading the Iberian peninsula (August 1808), it remained conceivable for a long time that Wellington's armies might be driven out. Nevertheless, Wellington's precarious foothold weakened Napoleon by forcing him to commit his ablest soldiers to the defence of France's southern flank. Ultimately, at a cost of 300,000 men, following Wellington's holding of the lines of Torres Vedras (1810–11), Napoleon failed to hold Spain. It was a war of attrition in which the bleak terrain reduced Napoleon's capacity to live off the land, thus gradually eroding France's military strength.

By this point it will be clear that the efficacy of coalition, despite Metternich's reservations, was proved in the final stages of the conflict with Napoleon.

Eventually, after Napoleon's retreat from Russia, Metternich overcame his indecision (1813) and so facilitated the formation of a coalition of all the major powers. Until the last, Metternich was loath to estrange himself from France and toyed with the idea of Napoleon maintaining his throne without his conquests, so that France would be a counterweight to Russia in the east. After the battles of Bautzen and Lützen (May 1813), Metternich deserted Napoleon, comforted by Tsar Alexander I's assurance that he did not seek to dominate Poland and Germany, and convinced that Wellington's victory at Vittoria (June 1813) would serve as a springboard for an invasion of France. The newly formed coalition defeated Napoleon at Leipzig (October 1813) and forced him to retreat into France itself, a prelude to his unconditional abdication (April 1814).

Related questions

1 'Napoleon I's invasion of Russia in 1812 sealed his fate.' Discuss the validity of this view.

In the introduction, outline the factors which contributed to the problems that Napoleon faced before he crossed the River Niemen in June 1812 and began his invasion of Russia – the resentment engendered by the workings of the Continental System; Russia's increasing disinclination to submit to Napoleon's dictation; the reshaping of Austrian and Prussian armies, which involved absorbing techniques that Napoleon had earlier used so effectively against them; Britain's seemingly impregnable insularity. When these factors combined to persuade the powers to form a coalition – albeit not without hesitation, but encouraged by the retreat of the beleaguered French armies from Russian soil – the likelihood of Napoleon's defeat was much enhanced.

Having made these points initially, proceed to examine them in detail, devoting single paragraphs to each. How had the continental states endangered Napoleon's interests? Why was Russia increasingly reluctant to submit to Napoleon's dictation? How were the individual strengths of his potential enemies increased by 1812? Once Napoleon was obliged to retreat from Russia, discuss the significance of Prussia's willingness to sign the Treaty of Kalisch with Russia in February 1813. Then explain why Austria moved more slowly to join the fight against Napoleon. What ultimately persuaded Metternich to join the coalition? What were the consequences for Napoleon of the formation of the coalition against him? – the 'Battle of the Nations' at Leipzig, and the invasion of France from the Iberian peninsula after the battle of Vittoria in June 1813. Conclude by stressing that invasions of Russia are replete with risk. The sheer size of the country and its long, bleak winters bode ill for the unwelcome intruder. The traditional Russian practice of conceding land to opponents extends their lines of communication, which become increasingly precarious with the onset of winter. The unfamiliar spectacle of Napoleon's battered armies in ignominious retreat, together with the pent-up hatred of uncomfortable subordination to France, from which it was now possible to think of being freed permanently, persuaded the powers, in combination, to make the supreme effort needed to ensure the Emperor's defeat.

2 Account for the failure of Napoleon I's Continental System to achieve its objectives.

3 Assess the part played by the Peninsular War in the defeat of Napoleon I.

'Giving satisfaction to nationalist sentiment was not an objective of the peacemakers at Vienna (1814–15).' Discuss the truth of this statement.

Tackling the question

All the powers that had joined in coalition to defeat Napoleon I in 1814 and 1815 were anxious to avoid future political and social strife on the scale that they had been forced to experience since 1792. When they redrew the map of Europe's frontiers at Vienna, they sought territorial changes that they believed would promote political stability. Instability would recur, they believed, if France was tempted to look for revenge after its defeat. For Austria there was the additional fear that Russia might destabilise central Europe by expanding westward. With the exception of Britain, the victorious powers were determined to nip in the bud any manifestation in any country of political change that was threatening to the existing ruler. That the settlement of 1814–15 was little disturbed before 1860 would suggest that the decisions that they made were sound.

The restoration of legitimacy, the preference for the old order and existing rights, was at a price. The nationalist sentiment aroused by the French Revolution, provoked by hostility to Napoleon's conquests and encouraged by the imposition of Napoleon's unifying administrative and legal reforms, was virtually ignored. So too was the impetus given to liberalism by the French Revolution both in its political and economic aspects, weakened by the conservatism for which Metternich in particular stood. In any case, the particularism so much in evidence in Germany and Italy after 1815 lent some justification to the view that the time had not yet come when measures to accommodate nationalist feeling were appropriate. Nor was it likely that the autocratic rulers of continental Europe would sympathise with liberalism, which, besides advocating the removal of barriers to economic enterprise, preached constitutional government. For them the attempts between 1789 and 1791 to make Louis XVI a constitutional ruler had served as the prelude to the Terror of 1793–4 and the onset of the Revolutionary and Napoleonic Wars. Understandably, if not with justification, continental rulers were sensitive to what might be the dire consequences of tolerating any political change that was challenging to existing rulers. According to their lights, therefore, the settlement they made was prudent – it was 'carried out with the scrupulous nicety of a grocer weighing out his wares, or of a banker balancing his accounts', as it has famously been put. France was not treated ungenerously and every effort was made to contain the radicalism that in their view had given Europe a quarter of a century of virtually uninterrupted turmoil.

Answer

The overriding purpose of the peacemakers in 1814–15 was to devise a settlement that would prevent any recurrence of French hegemony in Europe. Associated with this was the aim of suppressing political and social revolutionary attitudes identified with recent French aggrandisement. While it was evident that national sentiment had been aroused during the Revolutionary and Napoleonic Wars, the peacemakers chose not to appease it in the details of the settlement. The restoration of legitimacy, insofar as that could be achieved, seemed to be – in the defensive mood of 1814–15 – the best insurance against a recrudescence of European havoc. This approach ran counter to any promotion of the concept of the nation state.

Make clear the objectives of the peacemakers at Vienna and explain concisely why they restored legitimacy rather than sought the promotion of nationalism.

The French revolutionaries had asserted, in a literal sense, the sovereignty of the nation, not that of the prince. In the traumas after 1792, this concept awakened latent feelings of national identity in much of Europe. This realisation of separateness was achieved by imitation of France's domestic achievements and a resistance to French aggression. Thus, if Italians and Germans welcomed French ideas and gained from administrative efficiency and the legal practices of Napoleonic France, in part derived from the Revolution, they were hostile to the oppressive presence of French armies and rapacious French tax collectors. In resenting Napoleon's attempt to subordinate their economies to France, nationalist sentiment was stirred. Yet, in 1814–15, the concept of the 'nation' – based on the consciousness of a common language, culture and religion, and geographical propinquity – was incoherently expressed.

To what extent had nationalist sentiment been aroused in Europe by 1815? How had Napoleon given an impetus to the expression of nationalist feeling?

Metternich had claimed, with more than a vestige of truth, that Italy was 'a mere geographical expression'. Certainly, some of the educated middle classes nurtured ideas of nationhood, but the vast majority of the illiterate peasantry was politically indifferent. Moreover, attempted revolutions in Piedmont, Naples and Sicily (1820) were parochial rather than nationalistic. In Naples the Constitutionalists gave assurances that they had no ambitions beyond their existing frontiers. Thus, nationalism was not an irresistible force in Italy. In the circumstances, the powers could, without compunction, establish nine separate units, make complex arrangements for the lesser states like Modena, Parma, Lucca and Tuscany, and unite the two separate kingdoms of Naples and Sicily under the Bourbon, Ferdinand I. For years to come the Austrians were to ensure that any manifestation of discontent in the peninsula was swiftly suppressed.

Take Italy as an example of a region where there were some signs of nationalist feeling. But how far had nationalist ambitions been aroused? In the light of the circumstances that they faced, how did the peacemakers settle the problem of Italy?

Now consider Germany. Examine the settlement made in the Federative Act of 1815. What did Metternich seek in Germany? What would have been an impediment to the establishment of a German state in 1815? However, in what sense had the peacemakers begun to lay the foundations for the ultimate unification of Germany under the auspices of Prussia?

Similarly, in Germany, in the wake of the Federative Act (1815), there were to be 39 independent states, their policies to be co-ordinated by a Federal Diet at Frankfurt. The voting arrangements in the Diet were intended by Metternich, to whom nationalism and constitutionalism were anathema, to thwart the imposition of any single will and to ensure Austria's overriding influence. While particularism was common among restored princes who were resolved to govern their own territories, there was an incipient demand among educated opinion for a united Germany, justified by a common language and culture and the mystique of 'race'. Although it was too early to set geographical boundaries to reflect this sentiment, the peacemakers unwittingly gave an impetus to ultimate unity by ceding Westphalia, Swedish Pomerania, Posen and part of Saxony to Prussia, so that it was no longer almost exclusively an east but also a west German state. The cessions were intended to enable Prussia to play a crucial role in the containment of France, but in the event marked the beginning of a slow process by which Prussia gained an overriding influence in Germany, reinforced after the 1830s by an economic ascendancy derived from its establishment and control of the Zollverein.

How did the peacemakers handle Polish nationalism in 1815 and with what consequences?

Because of its predatory neighbours, a deeply ingrained and febrile nationalism in Poland, which until 1795 had expression in an independent state, albeit an increasingly attenuated one, remained unsatisfied after 1815. The most that was secured for Poles was a constitution granting a measure of autonomy under Russian suzerainty. It was indicative of Poland's vulnerable geographical setting that – strictly in violation of the 1815 settlement – its capacity for self-rule was undermined by Russia after 1825. Thereafter, efforts to throw off the Russian yoke in 1830 and 1863 proved unavailing.

Why, in 1815, did the victorious powers choose to ignore the separate identities of Belgium and Holland? What were the consequences?

The separation of Belgium and Holland in 1830 was testimony of the unwisdom, in 1815, of authorising the uniting of two peoples with irreconcilable cultural, linguistic and religious differences. The initial acquiescence in a denial of their separate identities was inspired by Castlereagh's conviction that, united, the new entity, assisted by financial help to fortify its frontier against France, would constitute a more effective barrier against any attempt by France to change its frontiers. However, its failure served to encourage peoples elsewhere to believe that independent statehood could be achieved by struggle.

The peacemakers chose to give short shrift to gathering nationalist sentiment in 1815. After 25 years of almost unbroken military strife, engendered very largely by a clash of ideologies, they were unmoved by ideas. Their approach was essentially pragmatic, evidenced in a prudent lenience towards France and, as it has been observed, in the adjustment of frontiers 'with the scrupulous nicety of a grocer weighing out his wares'. Their novel attempt to pre-empt future troubles by meetings of the powers at fixed periods thereafter, to discuss matters of common interest, may have foundered by 1822, but it spawned the *ad hoc* conference diplomacy that dealt successfully with international crises before the Crimean War (1854–6). Notwithstanding their indifference to nationalist aspirations, their efforts in 1814–15 secured 40 years of relative peace.

Emphasise the pragmatism that informed the decision making of the victorious powers. What was to be the effect of setting up the so-called Congress System after 1815?

Related questions

1 Why did the Congress System, established in 1815, collapse by the mid-1820s?

The Quadruple Alliance of 20 November 1815, which created the Congress System, was established mainly to uphold the Vienna Settlement. From the outset Britain and Russia contended for the leadership of it, so that there was much argument as to its character and purpose. Such debate raised the vexed question of how the powers should respond to revolutionary insurrections in small states. By the early 1820s turbulence within the Ottoman Empire was causing tensions in Austro-Russian relations. The interaction of the cumulative burden of these issues paved the way for the demise of the Congress System after the Congress of Verona in 1822 and the end of the novel idea – in Article VI of the Treaty of November 1815 – of occasional meetings to discuss matters of common interest and to consider measures appropriate for the maintenance of European peace. Here is the content and analysis for your introduction.

Now explain how Castlereagh and Metternich were anxious that Russia should not penetrate further into eastern Europe, although they counted on the Tsar's fears of revolution to keep Russia loyal to the alliance. How did Russia seek to weaken Anglo-Austrian relations? Nevertheless stress that Russia shared the common resolve of all the victorious powers to prevent any resurgence of French power in Europe. Now consider the Congresses that were held periodically. What was the outcome of the first Congress held at Aix-la-Chapelle in 1818? How was a semblance of unity maintained? What was the immediate impact of the rebellions that broke out in 1820? What were the differences between Britain and Austria as exemplified in Castlereagh's State Paper of May 1820 and Metternich's Preliminary Protocol of November 1821? How did the differences affect Anglo-Austrian relations at the Congress of Troppau in 1820? What were the consequences of rebellion in Greece, beginning in February 1821? What scope might there have been for improving Anglo-Austrian relations over this particular issue?

What grounds might there have been for believing that Austria and Britain would be able to co-ordinate their policies in Spain, where revolution had begun in 1820? What was Russia's response to this possibility? Before drawing your conclusions, examine the significance of the Congress of Verona (October–December 1822). The Congress System collapsed after the Congress of Verona. Co-operation among the powers continued as necessity dictated. There developed the practice of convening *ad hoc* conferences, comprising powers directly involved in seeking solutions to specific disputes – the Treaty of London (1827) and the Straits Convention (1841) are two examples. This pragmatic approach proved to be more helpful than the conferences of all the major powers, held at intervals to discuss a variety of issues where little common ground existed.

2 'An admirable and enlightened example of international co-operation.' How far do you agree with this assessment of the Congress System (1815–25)?

3 'The Concert of Europe long outlived the Congress System established in 1815.' Discuss the truth of this statement in relation to the period 1815–50.

Question 7

How did the revolutions of 1830 affect relationships among the major powers?

Tackling the question

The 1830 revolutions were prompted by dissatisfaction with specific aspects of the peace settlement of 1814–15. Liberals and nationalists took little comfort from the terms imposed by the victorious powers. In the event, revolts in Poland, Italy and Belgium were easily contained. That the powers would have been appalled had France become a republic meant that they soon accepted that an Orleanist should succeed a Bourbon as king, provided that he was ready to accept the existing order in Europe. More important than the local upheavals that had taken place in 1830 were the conflicting ideas that were intensified by the unsuccessful attempts to overcome what liberal nationalists considered to be an old order of autocratic rulers, who were deaf to the needs and wishes of the peoples of Europe. Despite the setbacks of 1830, they were confident that eventually the notion of the dynastic rights of states and the existence of binding treaties would be undermined.

The occasion for the realisation of liberal nationalist aspirations appeared to come in 1848 when much of Europe was in revolutionary turmoil. However, the co-operation of workers, artisans, students and those members of the middle classes who gave the riots political direction proved to be merely temporary. In the Frankfurt Assembly (1848–9), German liberals were indecisive and bickered endlessly about the niceties of constitution making, insensitive to the material concerns of the mass of the people. As in 1830, reaction triumphed after a brief interval of confusion. The opportunity for liberal nationalists to assert themselves was not to recur in Germany. Indeed, thereafter, with the breakdown of the relatively orderly pattern of international diplomacy that had existed since 1815 – described as the Concert of Europe – there was ample scope for a master of *realpolitik* and a consummate opportunist like Bismarck to wrest the promotion of nationalism from the liberals and by 'iron and blood' establish the German Empire in 1871. Liberalism had become detached from nationalism, the latter now in alliance with conservatism and militarism.

Answer

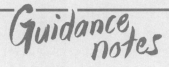

Guidance notes

The peace settlements (1814–15) which, after 25 years of strife, attempted to re-establish legitimacy in Europe, were attacked by liberals and nationalists alike for failing to accommodate the aspirations of many peoples in Europe. While the powers had succeeded in controlling the revolutions of 1830, all of which were

> Explain concisely the longer-term consequences of the 1830 revolutions.

revolts against specific parts of the peace settlements, within less than four decades few vestiges of the Vienna settlement remained. Ironically, liberal nationalists, who had anticipated that the will of the peoples would be satisfied in the long run by the espousal of liberal nationalism, were to be outmanoeuvred by conservative monarchies in the 1850s and 1860s, which separated liberalism from nationalism and appealed directly to their people, ignoring middle-class liberal opinion.

How did the three eastern European powers manage to maintain a degree of co-operation during the upheavals that began in 1830? What differences did Prussia and Austria have with Russia over the Balkans? What was Russia's response to Austria's anxieties in the Balkans? Above all, what persuaded Prussia and Austria to remain on good terms with Russia?

By 1830 relations among the three major eastern European powers seemed in disarray. Prussia and Austria were opposed to Russia's policies in the Balkans, especially when the problem of Greece was resolved by Russia's co-operation with Britain and France. Nevertheless, the 'Holy Alliance' (1816) survived, Russia careful not to threaten Austria's crucial interests in the Balkans. Prussia and Austria were conscious of the need to cultivate Russia's goodwill in case of a resurgence of France. In the Chiffon de Carlsbad (August 1830) they reaffirmed their resolve to maintain the 1815 settlement and reminded Louis-Philippe that he should not seek to subvert it, although they appreciated that they were powerless to prevent the revolution in France (1830), resolved though they were that its example should not spread.

Now explain the nature of the relationship between Russia on the one hand and Britain and France on the other. Why were Prussia and Austria satisfied with poor Franco-Russian relations after Louis-Philippe's usurpation of the French throne in 1830? Even though France and Britain had common apprehensions about Russia – give examples – Britain retained a common front with all the powers on one important matter. Explain.

Russia, most distant from the potential danger of France, did not recognise Louis-Philippe's usurpation until 1831. That Franco-Russian relations remained cool until after the Crimean War comforted Austria and Prussia in their resolve not to tolerate modifications to the 1815 settlement. Moreover, France and Britain were concerned that Russia might exploit Turkey's declining power in the Balkans. They were critical of absolutism and of Russia's brutal crushing of the Polish revolt (1830). Nevertheless, Britain had no wish to see France's borders revised, and France, anxious to avoid isolation, in the meantime did not press for border changes. Thus, while Britain was concerned at Russian ambitions in the Balkans, it shared the concern of all the powers at signs of French expansionism.

You are now ready to explain how Britain managed its relationship with France during the Belgian crisis. How was France obliged to forfeit any claim to Belgian territory? What had been Britain's key concern regarding Belgium?

Britain's ambivalent position was clear during the Belgian crisis (1830–1). Once the Belgian revolt broke out against the joint kingdom in August 1830, the prospect of Prussian intervention to help the Dutch, intimated by the legitimate military occupation of Luxembourg, raised the prospect of a French invasion of Belgium. The London Conference, convened in November 1830, with France present, dispelled that risk by establishing an independent state and accompanying that with a solemn promise that none of the signatories would make claims to Belgian territory. The basis was laid for Belgium's neutrality, and France committed itself to remaining within its established boundaries. Dutch resistance to the agreement endangered the agreement because it gave France an excuse to intervene in Belgium, but ultimately Britain insisted that France should withdraw, so that Britain's security was not jeopardised.

In Italy, however, where revolution occurred in the Papal States, Parma and Modena against the Austrian ascendancy, France, exploiting Metternich's distaste for the Orleanist succession, was prepared to exercise its influence as a Roman Catholic power. It was not a matter of France risking war to gain territorial revision there, but a quest by France for a diplomatic success at a time when Austria seemed isolated. Moreover, Russia was preoccupied with revolt in Poland, and Britain had, since 1815, shown little sympathy for Austria's heavy-handed interventions in Italy to contain resistance to the absolutism of minor princes. In response to Austria's invasion of the Papal States, France occupied the naval port of Ancona until 1838, although meanwhile Metternich had crushed rebellion as effectively as he had done earlier revolts in Italy. In that France had sought to sustain rebels against the conservatism of rulers who were dependent on Austrian support, it encouraged the solidarity and aroused the deepest suspicions of the three eastern European powers.

> Explain the impact that the revolt in Italy (1830–1) had upon Austro-French relations. How did France arouse the apprehensions of the 'Holy Alliance' powers by its conduct in Italy at this time?

Similarly, although at a distance, the Orleanists professed their sympathy for the Poles, who in November 1830 initiated a rebellion against their Russian suzerain. France condemned the treatment of the Poles by Russia, which had paid scant attention to the autonomy granted to them in the Vienna settlement. In that sense, Poles – like Frenchmen – were dissatisfied with the settlement of 1815. Tsar Nicholas I's distaste for France was deepened. The Poles, uncomfortably placed in Russia's political sphere of influence, might have the sympathy of France and Britain, but neither of the western powers had the capacity to render practical assistance to them.

> Now consider how Britain and France responded to Russia's crushing of the Polish revolt in 1830. Why was neither Britain nor France able to proffer any assistance to the Poles when the limited autonomy granted to them in 1815 was ignored by Russia?

In 1830 there was little scope within European diplomacy for effecting modifications in the way that smaller states were despotically governed. Small Italian states, subject to absolutist rule, were secure under the wing of an Austrian ascendancy affirmed by the 1815 settlement. The physical closeness of Russia to Poland ensured that the concept of an autonomous Poland would not be

> Finally, explain why the Belgian crisis alone provided scope for a modification of the 1815 settlement. Why were Britain, Prussia, Austria and Russia able to find common ground in

modifying the Vienna settlement in respect of the Netherlands?

sustainable if Russia chose not to respect it. Belgian independence was an exception to the general rule. The willingness of the major powers to accept a modification of the Vienna settlement and create an independent Belgium arose from their consciousness that a disrupted Belgium might tempt France, its neighbour, to push back its borders and thus raise the fear of a resurgent France, which had been consistently held back by the victors of 1815.

Related questions

1 How did the Greek Question affect relationships among the major powers?

Begin by emphasising that after 1815 the overriding purpose of the peacemakers was to ensure the future containment of France. With the exception of Britain, they also sought to suppress what they perceived to be revolutionary intent, wherever it showed itself. The restoration of legitimacy in 1815 was a rebuff to emerging liberal nationalist sentiment. Over the Greek rebellion, however, rapport among Russia, Austria and Prussia was threatened. Why was this so? What did France and Britain have in common with Prussia and Austria over the Greek rebellion?

Having established the arguments at the start of the essay, first consider in detail the anxieties of the powers at the perceived potential danger of Russian expansion in the Balkans. Before considering the tensions among the powers as the steps were taken that gave Greece its independence by 1831, explain the development of Greek nationalism prior to the outbreak of rebellion in 1821. Note Greek exposure to western European influence because of the thriving commerce abroad and because Greeks educated in the West not only imbibed French revolutionary ideas, but became very conscious that Ancient Greek civilisation was venerated abroad. Finally, that Greek independence was anathema to Prussia and Austria underlined the fluidity of relations among the powers. Alignments were not reliable. Russia's Treaty of Unkiar Skelessi with Turkey in 1833 aggravated still further Russia's relations with all major powers. However, the Austro-Russian Treaty of Münchengrätz (1833), guaranteeing the maintenance of Turkey, reduced tension and prevented collective protest directed towards the Treaty of Unkiar Skelessi. France had unsuccessfully sought to exploit the Greek crisis by intimating to Russia that it would accept extensive Russian gains at Turkey's expense, in return for French gains at the expense of the United Netherlands, soon to be divided. Thereafter, France intrigued in north Africa, occupying Algiers and thus aggravating Britain's fear that its supremacy in the Mediterranean was at risk. Later, further French intriguing with Mehemet Ali, encouraging him to defy his Sultan in 1839, not only persuaded the powers to support the Ottoman Empire's integrity in the Straits Convention of 1841, but reinforced their determination to uphold collectively the Vienna Settlement against any threat from France.

2 What was the significance of the revolutions of 1830?

3 What factors led to the establishment of a lasting Belgian state during the 1830s?

Why was the Eastern Question important in European affairs between 1815 and 1841?

Tackling the question

The terms of the Treaty of Vienna (1814–15) did not refer to the Ottoman Empire in Europe. It was a subject about which there were serious differences among the major powers. They were all painfully conscious of the decline of the Empire, aware that the Turks treated their Christian subjects brutally, and concerned that central government was unable to exercise much authority in the remoter provinces in Europe. Throughout the nineteenth century there was to be an Eastern Question because the major powers were unable to agree how to handle Turkey's problems. It became a common occurrence to do no more than improvise reactions, usually anxiously and in some disarray, whenever Turkey's difficulties became particularly acute. The exception was in the 1850s when Napoleon III sought a diplomatic victory over Russia because he believed that the Tsar's hostility to France was an attempt to revive the unity of the 'Holy Alliance'. Certainly, France outmanoeuvred the Russians over the keys to the Holy Places, but its success proved to be the prelude to a military conflict beginning in 1854. The terms imposed on the defeated Russia at the Congress of Paris in 1856 proved to be unenforceable. There was to be no solution to the Eastern Question between 1856 and 1914, although between 1856 and 1871 tensions in the Balkans were upstaged by dramatic developments in central Europe as Italy gained its independence and Bismarck secured the creation of the German Empire. Nevertheless, until the outbreak of the First World War in 1914, the Eastern Question constantly concentrated the minds of all powers and occasionally threatened to sour relationships and raise the spectre of a major conflict.

Answer

Guidance notes

The inexorable decline of the Ottoman Empire in the nineteenth century preoccupied the major powers. None of them relished the prospect of its collapse because there was no agreement as to what should fill the political vacuum arising from the Sultan's demise. There was a recurring anxiety that Russia – since the Treaty of Kuchuk-Kainardji (1774) frequently claiming that, as custodian of the interests of the Sultan's Slav subjects, it was entitled to act on their behalf – might change the balance of power in south-east Europe and the Mediterranean to its advantage if

Explain the concerns of the powers at the plight of the Ottoman Empire between 1815 and 1841. Note their fear of Russia, arising from disarray in the Balkans, and also their concern that France might fish in troubled waters if the Sultan's empire threatened to collapse utterly.

the Sultan's power collapsed. Moreover, all powers feared that complete disarray in the Balkans would encourage France, dissatisfied with the peace settlement of 1815, to secure revision of its terms and thus facilitate a resurgence of its power, so recently contained at great cost. The steps taken by the powers between 1815 and 1841 to resolve the Sultan's internal problems were characterised by an underlying distrust of each other's motives and by an awareness that failure in the task would unleash unpredictable, probably catastrophic, consequences for Europe.

Distinguish between Britain's and Austria's anxieties in regard to the fragility of the Ottoman Empire.

Both Britain and Austria were acutely suspicious of Russia's intentions in the Balkans. For Britain there seemed to be an abiding threat to the direct route through the Mediterranean to its Indian Empire. Britain sought to counter this by supporting Turkey, but was hampered by the latter's weakness and the growing nationalism in the Balkans, which looked to Russia for sustenance. If any part of the Ottoman Empire was to secede, Britain was determined that a newly independent state would be subject to a European guarantee. Austria was concerned that burgeoning nationalism in the Balkans would provide a focal point for the Slavs within the Habsburg lands to seek their freedom. Metternich was convinced that a collapse of the Sultan's authority would presage the disintegration of Austria's polyglot empire.

Why did the Greek revolt after 1821 arouse fears about Russia's intentions in the Balkans? Explain Metternich's attitude towards the Greek rebels.

The powers' handling of the Greek Question illustrates their realisation that their mutual co-operation was necessary. Philhellenism in western Europe was paralleled by the subjugated Greeks, conscious of their cultural inheritance, yearning to be free. When the Greeks rose in revolt after Ypsilanti's abortive rebellion (1821), sympathy for Greek suffering was won in western Europe. The powers were concerned that Russia should not benefit from the Greeks' predicament. In vain, Metternich insisted that the principles of the 'Holy Alliance' dictated that the Turks should be allowed to crush their rebels. When the Sultan, aided by his able vassal, Mehemet Ali, subdued the Greeks, Russia's resolve to assist them was viewed by the powers as essentially politically motivated.

How far was fear of Russian intentions allayed by the steps taken to resolve the Greek problem? Explain how Russia had co-operated with other powers so that the Greeks could be freed from Turkish control. Even so why did suspicions of Russia remain?

Russia was aware of the danger of a coalition of the powers against it and was therefore ready to be conciliatory. By 1826 there was an Anglo-Russian agreement in the St Petersburg Protocol to mediate between the Greeks and Turkey with the aim of securing Greek autonomy under Turkish suzerainty. By the Treaty of London (1827), Britain, Russia and France agreed to give joint active support to the Greeks if Turkey refused an armistice. This conditional promise was consummated in the naval battle of

Navarino (1827). Nevertheless, Britain and France remained wary of Russia's motives when a Russo-Turkish war broke out (1828), ostensibly because of a Turkish violation of the Treaty of Akerman (1826). That Russia gained a protectorate over Wallachia and Moldavia by the Treaty of Adrianople (1829) seemed an indication of its expansionist aims. Nevertheless, this did not prevent the establishment of an independent Greece by 1830 under the auspices of the powers.

The feebleness of the Sultan was demonstrated by the ease with which Mehemet Ali, dissatisfied with the reward for his part in the Greek troubles, declared war on his overlord and defeated him at Koniah (1832). While the Russo-Turkish Treaty of Unkiar Skelessi (1833) – secret in its terms – secured for Russia the closure of the Straits in wartime, it did not permit Russia to enter the Mediterranean. Notwithstanding, although Russia preferred the preservation of the status quo, the powers were alarmed at Turkey's dependence on Russia. However, the Austro-Russian Treaty of Münchengrätz (1833), guaranteeing the maintenance of Turkey, reduced the tension and prevented collective protest at the Treaty of Unkiar Skelessi.

Now explain the consequences of the Sultan's failure to control his vassal, Mehemet Ali, in the early 1830s. How was the Sultan's powerlessness demonstrated in 1832? How was the tension in the region aggravated in 1833, but in the same year diminished?

Yet by 1839, Mehemet Ali, encouraged by France, was again defying the Sultan and meting out a defeat on him at Nezib. Once again Turkey seemed in total disarray. On this occasion Britain, Russia, Austria and Prussia agreed, in the Treaty of London (1840), to force Mehemet Ali to accept a settlement. France's support for him was seen as a transparent attempt to cause the kind of disarray in the region favourable for France to press for revision of the peace settlement (1815). In the event France relented, although military and naval intervention by the powers was needed to subdue Mehemet Ali. It was to secure greater stability in the Sultan's empire that the powers signed the Straits Convention (1841), by which the Straits were permanently closed to foreign warships in peacetime and Russia forfeited the special terms it had negotiated with the Sultan in 1833.

How did the powers react to a further demonstration of the Sultan's weakness in dealing with Mehemet Ali in 1839? What was the purpose of the Treaty of London of 1840? In what sense was French foreign policy mischievous at this time? How did the Straits Convention of 1841 contain the tensions that had been generated?

Thus, temporarily, the problem of the Ottoman Empire was stabilised. Despite the fluidity of relations among the powers preventing lasting and coherent alignments, for years after 1815 the major powers often sought to resolve specific problems by limited conference diplomacy. Common to all powers was the fear that disarray among them might enable France to break free of the restrictions imposed on it in 1815. The Straits Convention (1841) was yet another manifestation of interested powers acting

Why were the powers prepared to use conference diplomacy to deal with problems arising from the weakness of the Ottoman Empire? Under what circumstances was diplomacy found wanting and with what results?

together to deal with a particular crisis. However, if they combined to preserve the Sultan from the consequences of his own weaknesses, diplomacy offered no solution when one of their number went to war with the Sultan, as Russia did in 1854. The main effect of the Crimean War (1854–6) was to be the collapse of the European settlement of 1815.

Related questions

1 Examine the view that the Crimean War of 1854–6 was unnecessary but highly significant.

Periodically, diplomacy fails to prevent the outbreak of war. Sometimes an event – or events – precipitate conflict because, in a highly charged contest, the spirit of compromise is absent. It has long been debated whether it was necessary for Britain and France to declare war on Russia after the sinking of a Turkish naval squadron at Sinope in November 1853. Some historians have not been convinced that Tsar Nicholas I was seeking such an extension of Russia's influence in the Balkans that there was bound to be a detrimental effect on the interests of Britain and France in the Mediterranean. Russia had accepted that its forces should withdraw from the Principalities so that they could be occupied by the Austrian army, thus precluding Russia from endangering European Turkey. The war was to continue until 1856 mainly, it would seem, as an ideological conflict between Britain, France and Piedmont – advocates of constitutional government – and Russia, which was committed to autocracy.

Even if this squalidly fought war may have seemed to be unnecessary, it was certainly not without important repercussions for participants and non-participants alike. It prompted Austria's diplomatic isolation in the late 1850s, which prefaced its withdrawal from Italy and its humiliation at Prussia's hands in 1866. The Crimean War exposed the bankruptcy, material and spiritual, of the unreformed Tsarist Empire and caused Tsar Alexander II to carry out wide-ranging reforms, beginning with the Edict of Emancipation in 1861. The war was a further encouragement to Balkan nationalism and increased the restiveness of the subjects of the Habsburg Emperor. It encouraged Russia to begin to look to the Far East (Vladivostok was established in 1860) – a policy which culminated in the humiliation of Russian defeat in war against Japan (1904–5). Emerging Piedmont, a minor participant in the Crimean War, sought to further its cause in the Italian peninsula by attending the peace making in Paris in 1856. Indirectly, the Crimean War paved the way for a fundamental change in the balance of power in Europe by facilitating the development of a Prussian-dominated German Empire in central Europe.

2 How seriously did the Eastern Question threaten the peace of Europe between 1821 and 1841?

3 What were the consequences for the peoples of the Balkans and for the major powers of the Treaty of Paris of 1856?

Why were there revolutions in the Habsburg Empire in 1848 and 1849, and why were they rapidly undermined?

Tackling the question

After 1815 the Habsburg Empire – without ethnic, cultural, economic or linguistic unity – was susceptible to increasingly pressing demands of nationality. Centrifugal forces, where each group sought concessions from autonomy within to independence of the empire, boded ill for the empire's continuance. Moreover, the challenge of liberalism, closely linked to nationalist aspirations before 1848, threatened an autocracy ruled on the Emperor's behalf by a privileged aristocracy of bureaucrats, soldiers and ecclesiastical leaders. In this context Metternich endeavoured to maintain the plenitude of monarchical power, although he remained pessimistic of his capacity to buttress an empire which, in his words, 'resembles a worm-eaten house. If one part is removed, nobody can tell how much will fall.' He always resisted federation in Austria, believing that it would merely sponsor constitutional changes that facilitated the emergence of strengthened representative bodies, anathema to one who considered liberalism as an 'accomplice of demagogy'. For years he doggedly and gloomily repelled challenges to imperial authority. Prophetically, he was convinced that, should the Ottoman Empire collapse, the Habsburg Empire would quickly follow it into oblivion. By 1848, with the empire vulnerable to insurrection, not only was he the target of proponents of liberalism and nationalism, but he was abandoned by his conservative colleagues and forced into exile. Nevertheless, the deep crisis for the Habsburg Empire in 1848 and 1849 was survived – reaction was able to reassert itself.

Answer

Guidance notes

Metternich's resignation (13 March 1848) was engineered by those opposed to him within the Habsburg Court, who were alarmed by clamorous demands for political reform inspired by revolutionary example in Paris. That the symbol of order and stability was removed from office played a part in temporarily unnerving the ruling power. European economic depression after 1845–6 was particularly burdensome to the burgeoning peasant population and in cities, like Vienna, where immigration from the countryside aggravated existing social tensions arising from industrialisation. Moreover – and above all – the polyglot Habsburg Empire

Analyse concisely both aspects of the question set.

was stirred by nationalistic sentiment most conspicuously in Italy and Hungary, which inspired middle-class liberalism long-offended by Metternich's hostility towards constitutionalism. Yet revolutionary success was short lived. Government was merely temporarily disorientated and the army was not susceptible to notions of revolutionary change. Early political concessions soon undermined the unity of the constitutionalists and radicals. Once the army successfully initiated counter-revolution (June 1848), manifestations of nationalism were systematically crushed and autocratic rule was re-established.

What was the immediate effect of Metternich's fall from power?

It was plain that Metternich's departure had left a political vacuum. The demands of the Diet of Lower Austria for reforms – the abolition of censorship and the promise of steps being taken to introduce a constitution – were nervously conceded in April 1848 in German parts of the empire and in Bohemia, Moravia and Galicia. The flight of the incompetent Emperor Francis and his Court to Innsbruck emphasised the dynasty's disarray (May 1848).

Examine the most insistent demand in the Habsburg lands for national self-determination with special emphasis on Hungary. What effect did political concessions to the Hungarians have upon the position of Slav minorities and Romanians inside Hungary?

The most insistent demands in 1848 in the Habsburg lands were for national self-determination – a notion embraced by students, academics and members of the professions, and percolating through to the masses of subject peoples. Kossuth not only vigorously prosecuted Hungary's aspirations for independence, but persuasively proclaimed liberal sentiments – *inter alia*, responsible government and political and religious equality before the law – which inspired liberals throughout the empire. Hungary's autonomy was endorsed in its Diet's March Laws, sanctioned by the Emperor. The *robot* was abolished and provision made for a restricted property franchise to elect a parliament. However, the emphasis on the Magyar language meant that Slav minorities and Romanians within the part of the empire comprising Hungary would merely find that their subjection to Austrian control was replaced by political subordination to the Magyar nobility and the gentry.

How did Czech nationalism differ from Hungarian nationalism? Explain the concept of Austro-Slavism. What were the demographic circumstances of Bohemia that made independence for Slavs there unlikely?

Czech nationalism was of a different order from Hungarian nationalism. While the Bohemian nobility nurtured ideas of independence from Vienna, the movement was mainly inspired by the intelligentsia, expressed by Palacky and others, who, although seeking radical social reform, were anxious to remain within the Austrian Empire. They wanted autonomy and a policy of Austro-Slavism, concerned that Austria alone could protect Slav minorities from potential threats from Russia. In any case, 70% of the

Bohemian population was German and they comprised most of the urban middle classes, while Czech and other Slav groups were mainly restricted to menial occupations in town and country. Thus, demographic circumstances precluded independence for Slav groups.

By May 1848, revolution appeared triumphant throughout the empire. Imperial power was ostensibly crumbling peacefully. However, neither the civil service nor the army was influenced by revolutionaries while the revolution held sway. In Italy, Radetsky's armies had merely retired to the formidable Quadrilateral. Indeed, military action spearheaded the restoration of imperial authority. Once the soldiers exercised their capacity to challenge the revolution, the revolutionaries – except, perhaps, the Hungarians – faced inevitable defeat. When students rebelled in Prague, where a Slav Congress was in progress, Windischgrätz's bombardment crushed the Czech revolution and began the Habsburg revival. Radetsky's victory at Custozza (July 1848) and the Piedmontese withdrawal from Lombardy augured ill for revolutionary activity elsewhere in the empire.

Why were revolutionary successes precarious despite appearances? How was order rapidly restored in much of the Habsburg Empire?

If the earliest triumphs of the revolution were in Vienna, once the Emperor had granted the election of a Constituent Assembly, the divergent interests of the revolutionaries became apparent. While some lawyers, civil servants and other middle-class elements advocated constitutionalism, radical students embraced more democratic ideas, although both groups feared the workers' potential for disorder and were unmoved when the National Guard dispersed a workers' demonstration (August 1848). Middle-class *laissez-faire* sentiments considered social policies as impediments to economic growth, while radicals were ready to restrict growth in order to facilitate social reforms. Moreover, the Constituent Assembly, although securing the abolition of the hated *robot*, did not seek to oppose the monarchy, mindful that the latter's authority was needed to assure Austrian ascendancy over the Magyars and the Slavs. When students objected to the army's preparations to crush the Hungarian revolt, Windischgrätz bombarded Vienna and established martial law, effectively completing the counter-revolution in the Empire. Ferdinand's abdication and the succession of Franz Josef were further proof of the regime's restored confidence (December 1848).

Why, in Vienna, where the revolution was initially successful, did divisions emerge among those who sought change? What factors enabled the beleaguered regime to mount a counter-offensive?

The Hungarians were not so easily crushed. A Hungarian army was speedily assembled and was able to hold out against Schwartzenburg's armies, which had been reinforced by the

How, eventually, was the Hungarian revolt overcome by the established authorities?

imperial government's use of incipient Slav nationalism as an ally against Magyar nationalism. With Kossuth's declaration of an independent republic (April 1849), Hungary alone resisted the resurgence of Habsburg power. Schwartzenburg's decision to recruit the help of the Russians, themselves concerned that revolutionary sentiment might spread to Poland, ensured the crushing of the Hungarian revolt. It was now possible to restore the absolute nature of the power exercised by the Emperor, his ministers, the bureaucracy and the army.

Conclude by emphasising that liberal nationalism had been found wanting and that in future nationalist ambitions in central Europe would be in the hands of conservatives who were altogether tougher in the way that they secured their objectives.

If within the Habsburg Empire nationalism was the principle motivation for change, it had been found wanting. After 1848 nationalism would change its character. The army was much too powerful to be resisted effectively, even though the regime was incoherent and prey to centrifugal pressures. The new nationalism of central Europe would be essentially German, illiberal and aggressive, in the hands of conservative politicians who were unafraid to wage war to achieve their ends.

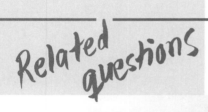

Related questions

1 Examine the course of the revolutionary disturbances in Germany in 1848 and explain why the traditional forces of law and order were able to reassert themselves.

In 1848 Germany was a collection of nearly 40 states, in which revolutionary disturbances followed different patterns. Nevertheless, whether it was in Bavaria in the south or Prussia in the north, liberalism seemed a potentially unifying theme. Yet, as in the Austrian Empire, established authority in Prussia, the leading German state, which was temporarily unnerved by liberal demands in 1848, soon reasserted itself. It was encouraged in this by the indecision of the Frankfurt Assembly, which was elected by a restricted franchise, and the irreconcilable differences that became increasingly apparent between middle-class liberals, who were overwhelmingly dominant in the Assembly and preoccupied with constitutional issues, and the mass of the people, who were concerned primarily about the material effects of industrialisation upon their livelihoods. These points should be established in the first paragraph.

Then consider in detail the character of the Frankfurt Assembly. What divisions emerged between the Frankfurt Assembly and the mass of industrial workers? What divisions of opinion on constitutional matters arose within the Assembly, and how did a growing split with Prussia reveal itself? What inhibited the prospect of a genuine revolution in Prussia, even though liberal ministers had been appointed by the King and there had been an announcement that a constituent assembly would meet to draft a constitution? How were serious differences between the King of Prussia and the Frankfurt Assembly exposed by the handling of the Schleswig-

Holstein crisis? What occasioned the collapse of the Frankfurt Assembly? If the rivalry between Austria and Prussia for ascendancy in Germany was, for the present, still unresolved, it was clear that liberal nationalism had failed. Firstly, the Frankfurt Assembly had amply demonstrated that there were stark differences between elements pressing for change – middle-class liberals sought German unity governed by principles of economic and political liberalism, while the mass of workers were making demands consistent with their difficult, even desperate, material circumstances. Secondly, the Assembly's dependence on the monarchs meant that it was incapable of wresting power from them.

2   Why were there revolutions in Europe in 1848?

3   'The revolutionaries in the Habsburg Empire were responsible for their own failures in 1848 and 1849.' How far is this statement valid?

Question 10

To what extent was there a development of national feeling in Italy between 1815 and 1849?

Tackling the question

States claim sovereignty within their territorial limits. There they have exclusive control of law and order. Their statutes are recognised in international law. Only states may sign treaties or wage war. Necessarily, statehood has to be defined for the purposes of domestic and international law. However, nationhood is not a legal concept. Rather, it is a subjective one. A nation is a group of people who claim a common descent and share the same culture and language. A common religion may also be an attribute of nationhood. Since medieval times there has been a recognition of nations and national differences. The creation of nations has owed much to states. Monarchies suppressed rival sources of power and imposed legal and fiscal systems that formed nations – such as the English, French and Spanish. Elsewhere in Europe, however, while there were Germans and Italians, politically there was no German or Italian state.

Many political concepts have been derived from the American and French revolutions as well as from the Napoleonic era. Thereafter, states recognised that they would need to increase the demands that they made on their respective peoples – direct taxation would need to be increased and it might well be necessary to oblige them to give military service to the state. Such requirements would be more readily accepted, it was believed, if the state's legitimacy was perceived to be derived from the nation. Thus, the nation state became an acceptable ingredient within the wider political arena. However, if the nation state was to be regarded as a means of enhancing security and general well-being, those nations that had not yet achieved the status of a state would understandably seek to achieve it – hence the quest for German and Italian unification during the nineteenth century. Moreover, nations that were conscious of their nationhood but were subject to a polyglot or multinational empire like the Habsburg Empire – Poles, Czechs and Magyars, for example – also wished to establish nation states. This essay seeks to gauge the degree to which national feeling developed in Italy before 1850.

Answer

How was Austria able to thwart the growth of Italian nationalism after 1815? How, ultimately, was the Italian state created?

Although Napoleon's control of much of Italy before 1815 had weakened acceptance of the earlier political divisions of the peninsula, particularly among the educated, after his fall from power particularism reasserted itself, earning Metternich's contemptuous judgement that Italy was merely 'a geographical expression'.

Austria, with military control based upon the formidable Quadrilateral in Lombardy, was always ready and able to thwart what it perceived to be potentially revolutionary discontent within the nine states of Italy. Repeated humiliations at the hands of the Austrians (in 1820–1 and 1831–2) eventually encouraged consideration of alternative modes of thought and action. Mazzini had faith in a unified republic achieved through insurrection. Gioberti sought a federation under the Pope. There was also the concept of an independent Italy under the auspices of Piedmont. It was this last which survived the brutal reassertion of Austrian control of Italy in 1848–9. From this débâcle, Piedmont emerged with its constitution intact. It became the base from which Cavour, in the 1850s, was able to fashion, with foreign help, an Italy emancipated from Austrian control, and to accept, albeit reluctantly, the virtual unification of the whole peninsula by 1861.

Before 1815, although Napoleon's rule had incurred the hatred of many Italians towards alien predominance in the peninsula, the techniques employed to produce efficient administration also intensified criticism of conducting government in a variety of separate states. Moreover, the French Revolution had done much to disseminate the idea of the nation state and to encourage national sentiment. Yet such notions were the preserve of a small educated minority in Italy. As early as 1796, Buonarotti was the first to advocate a united Italian republic and secret societies, like the Carbonari, although differing in character from one region to another, also encouraged patriotic feeling. However, most of the populace, poverty-stricken and illiterate, remained attached to their traditional local loyalties.

> Who were Italian nationalists by 1815? And who were not?

Despite Italian historians seeing the unification of Italy as the culmination of a national revival, or Risorgimento, originating in the eighteenth century, parochialism in public affairs persisted. Regional loyalties were strong in the reconstituted states after 1815 – nine in 1815, seven by 1847. The Papacy and its possessions straddled the peninsula, effectively dividing it in two. The disparate territories, in thrall to Austria's capacity to interfere by force in their affairs, seemed to have little inclination for political change that had application beyond their immediate frontiers.

> Explain the continuation of Italian parochialism after 1815.

After 1815 the oppressive control of Austria, insisted upon by Metternich, was prepared to give short shrift to any manifestations of constitutional change within an Italian state because it was seen as potentially disruptive of European stability. An attempt to institute a constitution in Naples, complicated by a

> What impact did Austria's political ascendancy in Italy after 1815 have upon the development of Italian national sentiment by the 1830s?

revolt in Sicily that the Neapolitans were resolved to destroy, was subjugated by the Austrians at the time of the Congress of Laibach (January 1821). Similarly, efforts by the Piedmontese to introduce the 1812 Spanish constitution were successfully opposed by Austria. In the aftermath of the July Revolution (1830), vaguely constitutionalist uprisings occurred in Modena, Parma and the Papal States (1831–2), but these were crushed by Austrian intervention after achieving virtually nothing. In none of these revolts did the rebels' intentions go beyond the securing of changes within an individual state. Such objectives were without hope, given Austria's military supremacy.

What new ideas were developing in the 1830s that gave an impetus to the spread of national sentiment?

By the 1830s, therefore, other ways were being considered for removing the incubus of Austrian domination. Firstly, there were those who sought a revolutionary unified republic. Mazzini, their most influential prophet, articulated for the first time a coherent Italian nationalism that attempted, through his secret society, *La Giovine Italia*, to reconcile liberalism and nationalism and to utilise religion in the service of the state. Secondly, there was Gioberti's idea, rejecting revolutionary means, that the Italian princes should unite in a federation under the Pope. Thirdly, Balbo and d'Azeglio, revolutionary in character, insisted on the need to displace the Austrians and advocated that Piedmont should play the role of leader of Italy, but they displayed no faith in unification.

What was the significance of the actions of Pope Pius IX after 1846?

The freedoms embraced unexpectedly by Pope Pius IX after 1846 – judicial, fiscal, political and economic – suggested that Gioberti's vision might prevail. Hostility to Austria's ascendancy manifested itself when revolutions broke out all over Europe – including Austria itself – in 1848. Constitutions were granted by rulers of Italian states, including the Pope. Piedmont was encouraged to wage war on Austria, and for a short period Lombardy, Venetia, Modena and Parma were merged into one state with Piedmont. When Austria recovered its nerve and routed Piedmont's forces at Custozza (July 1848), a reassertion of the Austrian ascendancy meant the collapse of the recently bestowed constitutions, except that of Piedmont. It was the republicanism of Rome and Venetia that held out the longest. In Rome, Garibaldi gallantly resisted the combined forces of Austria and France until July 1849, while Manin resisted in Venetia until August 1849.

Why did revolution in Italy collapse by 1849? Stress the continued importance of local loyalties at this time.

Despite individual states adopting constitutions in 1848, there was a measure of co-operation between states. The creation of the short-lived Kingdom of North Italy was a precedent for later change. Yet there remained disputes between states and much distrust that tended to nullify the advance of incipient nationalism. At war in 1848, Tuscany pursued a border dispute with Modena. Tuscany in turn distanced itself from the Roman Republic. Except in Sicily, the peasantry everywhere generally adhered to the old regimes. The returning Austrians were able to exploit this prevailing parochialism, so that the revolutions of 1848 in Italy in practice did little to advance the cause of a nation state. The crucial lesson of failure was that, even though national sentiment was slowly emerging, it counted for little if Austrian hegemony remained in the peninsula. The most encouraging development after 1849 was that Piedmont, although defeated comprehensively at Novara (1849), retained its independence and was equipped with a constitution.

Related questions

1 By what means and with what results did Metternich seek to maintain the Habsburg Empire after 1815?

After 1815 the Habsburg Empire – without ethnic, cultural, economic or linguistic unity – was vulnerable to increasingly pressing demands of nationality. Centrifugal forces, where each group sought concessions from autonomy within to independence of the empire, boded ill for the empire's continuance. In addition, the challenge of liberalism, closely linked to nationalist aspirations, threatened an autocracy ruled, on the Emperor's behalf, by a privileged autocracy of bureaucrats, soldiers and ecclesiastical leaders. In this context, Metternich endeavoured to maintain the fullness of monarchical power, although he was pessimistic of his capacity to sustain an empire that 'resembles a worm-eaten house. If one part is removed, nobody can tell how much will fall'. What policies did he pursue to preserve the Habsburg Empire? How did he maintain Austria's ascendancy in Italy? How did Metternich seek to maintain Austria's ascendancy in Germany? How did Prussia mount a challenge to Austria's ascendancy in Germany by the 1840s? Explain his policy of 'divide and rule' within the empire when dealing with the well-established rivalries between Magyars and Czechs, and Magyars and Germans, as well as the hostility between Croats and Romanians on the one hand and Magyars on the other. By the 1840s Magyar had been conceded as a language for official purposes, by which time Metternich's determination to resist expressions of nationalist and liberal feeling was being weakened by the emergence of Kossuth, who argued tirelessly and persuasively for a Hungary independent of the empire. Until his fall in 1848, Metternich was determined to resist challenges to imperial authority. He was convinced that, if the Ottoman Empire collapsed, the Habsburg Empire would quickly follow.

2 How justified was Metternich in dismissing Italy as a 'mere geographical expression'?

3 'A ramshackle empire.' How far is this view of the Habsburg Empire in the period 1867 to 1914 justified?

'The unification of Italy was achieved despite rather than because of Cavour's leadership.' How far may this claim be regarded as valid?

Tackling the question

L ord Clarendon described Cavour in 1856 as 'an excellent colleague and one of the few foreigners I know who is like a practical well-educated English gentleman ... one of the most moderate but at the same time most practical men I have ever had to do with'. On the other hand, Lord Cowley in 1859 described him 'as unprincipled a politician as ever existed', one whose word could never be trusted and who had 'ruined himself in the opinion of every honest man'. They were both speaking of the man who shares with Mazzini and Garibaldi – both of whom Cavour viewed with distaste and fear – the credit for having secured Italian unity. Yet he spoke French more fluently than he did Italian and according to Mack Smith, his most recent biographer, he 'had no thought at all of Italian unity unless and until he could discover whether the idea was practicable and well supported'. He was passionately hostile to revolutionaries and was resolved that Italy should not be governed by them. It may be argued that it was to Cavour's credit that the independent Italy that emerged in 1861 was a centralised monarchy rather than a republic or a loose federation. Mack Smith insists that it was Cavour's vision that eventually triumphed – 'a success story', he claims.

Some historians may be inclined to question this verdict. It was still necessary to 'make Italians', in d'Azeglio's words, after 1861. It always remained a seriously divided country – the south remained desperately impoverished, isolated from progressive developments in the north. For millions after 1861 the concept of Italy had little meaning, as the only reality for them was the locality. Loyalties to collapsed dynasties persisted. The so-called liberal central government depended from the start on fraud and petty venality. Thus, the new Italy was enduringly weaker than other major powers; its military defeats on its own soil at the hands of Austria-Hungary in the First World War were testimony of that. That it felt short changed when the peace settlements were made after 1918 reflected its political weightlessness at the conference table and played its part in hastening the rise of Mussolini.

Answer

Explain that there are divisions of opinion as to Cavour's ultimate ambitions for the Italian peninsula. Why was he unable to prevent

The achievement of the unification of virtually all of the Italian peninsula has been largely attributed to the political and diplomatic skills of Cavour, Prime Minister of Piedmont during most of the 1850s. Yet Mack Smith, Cavour's biographer, has cast doubt on Cavour's enthusiasm for a united peninsula. Rather, he claims, Cavour's concept of an Italian nation was restricted to regions in the north that had comprised Napoleon's 'Kingdom of Italy'. He had no wish that his own ideas for Italy should be confused with the cause of Italian patriotism, pre-empted by Mazzini and other revolutionaries who were striving, in vain, for a united republican Italy. Initially, Cavour sought to free Italy from Austrian control – an objective that seems to have been his main concern as late as 1860. Salmour, his confidant, recalled that he always spoke of 'emancipation' rather than 'unification'. He would have wished to prevent Garibaldi's expedition to Sicily as likely to frustrate his diplomacy, but Garibaldi's popularity and legendary valour made that impossible.

Garibaldi's invasion of Sicily in 1860?

From the time he became Prime Minister (1852), Cavour resolved that a robust Piedmont, still free after Austria's restoration of its own authority (1849), would be a prerequisite for the task of freeing Italy. During the 1850s he was instrumental in advancing Piedmont's economic and commercial prosperity. An effective railway network was developed and commerce was expanded by free trade treaties with Britain, France, Holland, Belgium and the Zollverein. Cavour carried through fiscal reforms, placed strict controls on Piedmont's government expenditure and reformed the army and the administration. It was much to his advantage that by 1852 Piedmont already had a system of parliamentary government, so that, without the need to give priority to constitution making, there was little scope for advocates of republicanism. The rejuvenation of Piedmont was, in Cavour's view, an essential prelude to achieving the creation of some kind of Italian kingdom by means of the expansion of Piedmont.

Why and how did Cavour ensure the strengthening of Piedmont during the 1850s? Stress economic and commercial prosperity, fiscal reforms and the establishment of constitutional government.

Even a strong Piedmont could not alone expel the Austrians from Italy. Piedmont's participation in the Crimean War (1854–6) improved its standing internationally, but it gained more from Austria's isolation following the latter's neutrality in the Crimean War. Even so, Austria could not be challenged successfully alone. It was French help that Cavour needed, but Napoleon III was unpredictable. His demand, in 1858, that Piedmont should institute more rigorous controls to undermine revolutionaries in Piedmont, following the attempt on his life by Orsini, a Piedmontese, did not suggest that he was about to play a positive part in Italy's affairs to Piedmont's advantage.

Explain how Cavour realised that Piedmont could not alone expel Austria. Why, initially, did it not seem likely that he would be able to rely on French assistance?

If Cavour merely sought the establishment of a united kingdom of north Italy, excluding central and southern Italy, his agreement

Now consider France's involvement in Italy from 1858

onwards. What were the consequences of the Plombières agreement of July 1858? How was it that France was to become involved in war with Austria? What did Cavour seek to achieve by war with Austria? Trace the unpredictability of Napoleon III's involvement in Italy, including the revised agreement in 1860, which, for the price of Nice and Savoy, would enable Piedmont to control all of Italy north of the Papal States, except for Venetia.

with Napoleon III at Plombières (July 1858) appeared to illustrate that aim. Provided that France could not be held responsible for initiating war, it was prepared to wage war against Austria with a view to establishing a kingdom of Upper Italy and an independent kingdom of Central Italy in return for the cession to France of Savoy and Nice. When war came (May 1859), it was abruptly terminated after the battle of Solferino when Napoleon, without consulting Cavour, made a truce with Austria at Villafranca (July 1859). Initially angered, Cavour was later to say, 'How many times have I not exclaimed, "Blessed be the peace of Villafranca"?' because within a year, Napoleon, having gained nothing territorially, was ready to make another agreement with Cavour, by which he gave his support for Tuscany to be absorbed into a kingdom of Northern Italy, thus bringing all of Italy north of the Papal States, except Venetia, under Piedmont's control (January 1860). In return, Nice, Garibaldi's birthplace, and Savoy, the ancestral home of the kings of Piedmont, were to be annexed by France.

Why, and with what consequences, did Cavour acquiesce in Garibaldi's invasion of Sicily in 1860? In your analysis, trace the course of events that culminated in Garibaldi surrendering his conquests to Victor Emmanuel.

Until 1860, despite the vicissitudes of co-operation with Napoleon III, Cavour had retained the political initiative. Suddenly, however, he found himself faced by a challenge from Garibaldi, whose quixotic gesture of an invasion of Sicily with 1,000 men seemed to threaten the success of Cavour's calculating diplomacy. Like Napoleon III, Cavour had a distaste for a Mazzinian republican movement gaining control of Italy. Moreover, Cavour was always conscious that the absorption of southern Italy would face a united Italy with potentially insoluble economic and social problems. Garibaldi's success in setting up a provisional government in Palermo before crossing to the mainland, his following burgeoning as he advanced, threatened foreign intervention – possibly from Austria and France – should he seek to enter Rome. When Cavour ordered the invasion of the Papal States, he may well have been most conscious of the danger to the Piedmontese dynasty and army of the growing prestige of Garibaldi. It was remarkable and unexpected that Garibaldi should surrender his conquests to Victor Emmanuel and oblige Cavour to acquiesce reluctantly in the unification of the whole peninsula, much as did Mazzini, but for the reason that the new Italy was not to be a republic.

What was the nature of Cavour's achievement?

Cavour's untimely death (June 1861) was to deprive Italy of the one person who might have been able to 'make Italians', in d'Azeglio's words, now that Italy was unified. In the event, Italy did not prove to be an effective major power. Venetia and Rome were gained in 1866 and 1870 respectively, but none of Cavour's successors as Prime Minister – six in the 1860s alone – had the vision, courage or strength of character of their illustrious predecessor, or his financial acumen. Whether or not Cavour desired the unification of the peninsula, he had masterminded the diplomacy that made it possible. Ultimately, he was able to exploit Garibaldi's success and ensure that a united Italy was not republican. Thus, Cavour's contribution to unification was indispensable, whatever reservations he may have had about the absorption of the whole peninsula.

Related questions

1 Assess Garibaldi's contribution to the cause of Italian unification.

It was a precondition of Garibaldi's extraordinary conquests in Sicily and Naples in 1860, which precipitated the unification of most of the peninsula of Italy, that Austria had not only been defeated in Italy, but would be unlikely to resume conflict there. The astute diplomacy of Cavour, who may not have had any real intention of establishing more than a kingdom of northern Italy, had achieved that. With some reluctance, Cavour was obliged by events to accept the inclusion of Naples and Sicily in the united kingdom. Although Cavour's and Garibaldi's efforts appear to have been complementary, they were usually ideologically at odds with each other. Garibaldi, a legendary and inspirational figure, enabled those Italians who sought an independent state to feel that at least in the final stages of their struggle it was achieved without foreign intervention. However, after 1860, Garibaldi's military flair had little scope. He became speedily disillusioned by the conduct of the constitutional monarchy and, by the 1870s, was reaffirming his belief in republicanism.

All the points raised so far should be examined in depth in the body of the essay. Contrast Cavour, the consummate politician, schooled in parliamentary methods, and Garibaldi, the demagogue who appealed directly to the people, impatient of the niceties of political compromise. How had Garibaldi become a legendary figure in the cause of Italian unification? Examine closely the context in which he was able to achieve the virtual unification of Italy. Why, despite the triumphant outcome of his expedition to Sicily in 1860, did he achieve so little thereafter? In the mid-1850s Garibaldi had claimed that monarchists and republicans should 'amalgamate and join whoever is the strongest among them'. This led to his acceptance of an Italy under Victor Emmanuel's monarchical and constitutional auspices. After 1860, without Garibaldi's assistance, unification was completed when Austria ceded Venetia to Italy in 1866 as the price of defeat at Prussia's hands, and France yielded Rome to the new state at the outset of the Franco-Prussian War in 1870.

2 Assess the contribution made to the cause of Italian unification by Mazzini.

3 'Foreign intervention did more to help than to hinder the cause of Italian unification between 1848 and 1870.' How far is this claim valid?

'A sphinx without a riddle.' 'Napoleon III le Petit.'
Consider whether it is appropriate that the Emperor
should be dismissed so contemptuously.

Tackling the question

Was Napoleon III a despot or a liberal? If despotism means rule by whim and is a mere manifestation of self-will, Napoleon III was no despot. On the other hand, he did believe in firm and efficient government where a representative body sanctioned proposed legislation presented to it and where he, a man above party, could seek a plebiscitary mandate from the people in order to endorse his personal policies. In that sense he was authoritarian. Nevertheless, during the 1860s he did progressively relax restrictions on the power of the legislature. Even so, he was disinclined to accept parliamentary sovereignty, parliament's capacity to accept or reject proposed legislation put before it and its ability to determine the composition of ministries. Politically, therefore, he was no liberal, although he was prepared to relax his methods of government. In his quest for free trade he was associated with economic liberalism.

At the end of his reign, he insisted that sovereignty was beyond the remit of parliament, but he did not close his mind to limited constitutional changes. Although he secured a sure majority in the election of 1869, mindful of pressure for further constitutional change, he permitted the Legislative Body to formulate its own proposals for change. Apparently without demur, he accepted its demands for ministerial responsibility and asked Ollivier to form a ministry responsible to parliament and to himself. Dual sovereignty was Napoleon's questionable way of preventing the reality of parliamentary sovereignty. Moreover, Napoleon did not preclude resorting to plebiscites as a means of interpreting the people's will. That these constitutional changes were accepted resoundingly in a plebiscite in May 1870 seemed to restore the Emperor's authority, although they weakened the capacity of Ollivier's ministry.

It may be argued that, before the crisis of the Hohenzollern candidacy in July 1870, Napoleon's regime was already disintegrating. Gambetta was already regarding the political situation in 1870 as 'a bridge between the Republic of 1848 and the Republic of the future'. For his part, Napoleon III had gradually relinquished his capacity to be authoritarian without agreeing to forfeit, at the time of his fall, his right to appeal to the French people by means of the plebiscite, in order to endorse his decisions, if necessary, in defiance of the elected Legislative Body.

Answer

What were the potential implications of Napoleon I and Napoleon III being outsiders?

Napoleon I once lamented to his father-in-law, Francis II, the Habsburg Emperor, that while the latter could survive defeat, he, Napoleon I, could not. He was painfully conscious of his parvenu origins. His spectacular military victories and his role as custodian of certain aspects of the legacy of the French Revolution ensured some nostalgia for and indebtedness towards Bonapartism in France after 1815. Fortuitously – as a result of the deaths of his cousin 'Napoleon II', his elder brother and his uncle, the ex-King of Spain – Louis Napoleon became the Bonapartist heir. Having secured imperial power (December 1852), like his distinguished forebear he ultimately could not survive comprehensive military defeat. In the 1850s his authoritarian rule was accompanied by economic and commercial expansion and diplomatic prestige. In the 1860s liberalisation of his regime won few plaudits as his foreign policy was dogged by damaging reverses and eventually by humiliating military defeat. Again, the parvenu could not survive such disaster. The verdicts of his contemporaries Bismarck and Hugo, quoted in the question, have proved durable. It is arguable that these verdicts are unjustifiable.

His earlier years resembled *opéra bouffe*. Doubts linger as to whether he was the legitimate son of Louis Napoleon, Napoleon I's brother, and Hortense de Beauharnais. Footloose in his early adulthood, he plotted revolution against the Austrians in the Papal States (1831), planned an abortive coup in Strasbourg (1836) and another at Boulogne (1840), this last punished by six years' imprisonment at Hamm. The same conspiratorial urge informed his *coup d'état* against the Orleanist Chamber when he was already President of the Republic. Clandestine ways were reflected in a diffident demeanour – he listened apparently intently, but rarely spoke. Queen Victoria, while admitting his 'great qualities', regarded him as 'mysterious'. Some considered him a profound thinker; others suspected mental vacuity. Bismarck and Hugo inclined to the latter viewpoint. France's traditional ruling élites suffered him only if he was successful.

Consider the bizarre character of Napoleon III's early years – his penchant for conspiracy, which led him to ludicrous and disastrous adventures. How was his diffidence regarded by others, including Bismarck and Hugo?

Initially, the Second Empire enjoyed some prosperity, but this coincided with a general expansion of European economies. France's railway network developed rapidly. Napoleon's Crédit Mobilier facilitated investment in worthwhile commercial projects. Thus, an impetus was given to France's rapid industrialisation. He embraced free trade, as evidenced in the Cobden Treaty (1860), with almost Peelite resolve. His Saint-Simonian interventionism seemingly worked and was grudgingly accepted by earlier beneficiaries of Orleanism, who considered him to be an adventurer and

By explaining his achievements, you will be doing something to counter the dismissive views of him from Bismarck and Hugo.

of dubious provenance. Abroad, he consolidated French power in Algeria and established a French presence in Indo-China. Under Napoleon III's auspices, France provided most of the capital for the Suez Canal (opened 1869). Paris, rebuilt by Haussman, is a durable monument to Napoleon's rule whatever his motives may have been. France enjoyed a dash of diplomatic prestige at the Congress of Paris (1856) as Napoleon, who professed *'L'Empire c'est la paix'* (1852) to reassure a nervous Europe, sought the means – at the time *rapprochement* with Britain – to dismantle the 1815 settlement peacefully.

Notwithstanding his various successes in office, he made political enemies. Who were they?

Despite his early political, commercial and diplomatic successes, many were unreconciled to his regime. Besides the traditional ruling élites, republicanism continued to flourish in major industrial towns. Many parliamentarians opposed free trade policies. Others deplored the offence given to the Papacy by Napoleon's promotion of Italian unification. Once controls imposed on the Senate and the Legislative Body were relaxed after 1860, it required deft parliamentary management by de Morny to sustain government majorities. His death (1865) made that task the more difficult.

Assess whether the political concessions made in the 1860s by Napoleon III stemmed from his weakness or his convictions. Why did he develop the concept of dual sovereignty?

There is no consensus as to whether the Emperor's political concessions stemmed from weakness or conviction. After 1860 the Senate and the Legislative Body could discuss and vote an address, and the latter could question ministers without portfolio about policy. In 1861 Napoleon surrendered his institutional right to authorise supplementary budget credits when the Legislative Body was not in session. By 1867 not only had he relaxed the laws controlling the press and public meetings, measures which encouraged rather than reduced virulent criticism of the regime, but he had granted the right of interpellation to the Legislative Body, thus reinforcing its independence. Electoral majorities for Napoleon were not wanting – as in 1869 – but pressure for constitutional change persuaded him to accept demands for ministerial responsibility. This was qualified by the authoritarianism implied in a dual sovereignty which enabled him, if he wished, to resort to plebiscites (often favoured by autocrats) in order to ascertain the people's will. Superficially at least, these constitutional changes were vindicated and his authority was consolidated in the plebiscite (1870).

Discuss the errors of judgement in his foreign policy and the implications for his reputation.

It may well be argued that a catalogue of disasters in foreign policy prompted pressure at home to relax his authoritarian rule. If there was scope for Bismarck's and Hugo's scathing denigration of

Napoleon, it was in respect of foreign policy, Bismarck having been a vastly successful beneficiary of the Emperor's miscalculations and inconsistencies. His erratic support for Piedmont, which contributed ultimately to the unification of Italy, offended much Catholic opinion in France. The débâcle of military intervention in Mexico was compounded by the ignominy of the execution of Napoleon's protégé, the Emperor Maximilian (1866). Despite his diplomatic isolation, caused by his capacity for fishing in troubled waters, he recklessly sought rectification of France's eastern frontier after 1866, despite the strategic and diplomatic advantage having passed to Prussia. It was inopportune to be pressing for the French acquisition of Luxembourg or expressing an ill-judged interest in Belgium to Bismarck when, in practice, France was as much a loser as Austria by Prussia's victories in 1866. Napoleon's inept diplomacy played into Bismarck's hands as he sought German unification. Although Napoleon may have reluctantly engaged in war (1870), such an indiscretion was consistent with past blunderings.

Namier, author of the essay 'The First Mountebank Dictator', and other historians have largely endorsed the verdict of Bismarck and Hugo. Yet others have engaged unpersuasively in panegyric. No political buffoon could have survived for twenty years. His domestic policies and constitutional experiments would not alone have doomed him and, indeed, were not without merit. Foreign policy was his Achilles' heel and the scale of the humiliation it brought to France eclipsed any value attributable to his domestic policies and lent credibility to the scurrility of Bismarck's and Hugo's verdicts.

> How valid were the verdicts of Bismarck and Hugo?

Related questions

1 Military defeat by itself did not bring about the collapse of the Second French Empire.' To what extent do you agree with this verdict?

There is no denying that Napoleon III's armies were emphatically defeated in the Franco-Prussian War. In August 1870 the stunning impact of military humiliation persuaded the *Corps Législatif* to agree to the declaration of a republic as the best way of averting insurrection in Paris. The imperial regime had always faced some implacable opposition. Inflation in the 1860s outpaced increases in nominal wages, thus alienating the urban proletariat. Napoleon III contributed to the erosion of his own authority by concessions that liberalised France's political institutions. However, these changes not only were insufficient to satisfy republicans, but did not meet wholly the demands of those not unfavourably disposed towards the regime. Thus, he had problems at home. Added to this, miscalculations in his diplomacy abroad increased pressures on him at home, and aroused to such an extent traditionally held fears about France's capacity for expansion among other countries that in 1870 the Second Empire was isolated in the face of Prussia's military might. These are points that you may explain concisely in your opening paragraph.

Show how Napoleon's shortsighted diplomacy during the 1860s ensured his diplomatic isolation in 1870, and that in any case France was ill prepared for war when it came. What was the immediate effect of military defeat on France's political circumstances in 1870? Show how declining political support for the government by 1863 persuaded Napoleon III to make political concessions. How did the *Corps Législatif* react to the government's wish to re-equip and reorganise an enlarged army after 1866? The compromise reached did little to help France's military readiness in 1870. Examine the extent of and the possible purpose behind the political concessions that Napoleon III made during the 1860s and in 1870, immediately before his fall. When the war began in July 1870 there was an underlying controversy about the character of the Emperor's authority, which, on the surface, was concealed by a reassuring plebiscite that concealed the regional variations normally exposed in elections. The regime could not survive military defeat. By the end of the essay it should be evident that the regime was unable to survive in 1870 not simply because of military defeat – that, of course, is a very important factor when explaining the Emperor's departure – but also because of considerable disenchantment with the political system over which he presided.

2 'A showman and a sham dictator.' Examine this view of the Emperor Napoleon III.

3 'Napoleon III's foreign policy was a catalogue of disasters.' Discuss the truth of this statement.

Question 13

In what ways was the safety of the Third Republic threatened between 1879 and 1914?

Tackling the question

In order to answer this question it is worthwhile understanding how the Republic had been secured in the 1870s. There was much support for monarchists in the election for the National Assembly in February 1871. This was not so much an indication that the electorate preferred a monarchical form of government, but rather a sign that they desired peace with Prussia. Once peace was made and the Commune crushed, by-election results revealed a preference for republicans. Progressively, the monarchical majority diminished. In addition, France's remarkable economic recovery after 1871 and divisions among the monarchists increased public confidence in the Republic. Yet uncertainty remained. When the still monarchist-dominated Assembly granted a seven-year presidential tenure of office to MacMahon, a committed monarchist, it may have prolonged the Republic, but it had not guaranteed its permanence.

Nevertheless, the Constitution of 1875, which made an almost furtive reference to the Republic, established that the National Assembly recognised the Republic as the acceptable and continuing form of government. It was MacMahon's ill-judged attempt to manipulate the Constitution, by means of a provocative use of his presidential prerogative that threatened to weaken parliamentary government, which eventually undermined the credibility of the monarchical cause. Henceforth, presidential power would not be used to dissolve the Chamber, and the ministries, usually a coalition of political groups, would be fashioned by the majority in the Chamber. There had been a marked shift in the balance of forces in the Constitution, which thereafter enabled the legislature, not the executive, to be the decisive power in the state. How then could the Republic be threatened? This essay will explain how threats from the right and the left were countered during the period from 1879 to 1914. By the eve of the war, the repelling of the major dangers to the Republic had reinforced confidence in its durability.

Answer

France moved uncertainly towards establishing a republic after 1871. Despite the Constitution (1875) precluding a restoration of monarchy by constitutional means, republicanism was not yet secure. MacMahon's provocative use of his presidential prerogative could not prevent the electorate returning a republican

Guidance notes

Begin by explaining how parliamentary government had triumphed before the end of the 1870s. Then outline the threats to the Republic, from the right

---

and the left, before 1914 – Boulangism, the Panama scandal, divisions in French society prompted by the Dreyfus case and threats from the left after 1900.

majority (1877) and the Assembly being able to insist that a ministry should be representative of that majority. Thus, parliamentary government had triumphed. Thereafter, with the Presidency unable to oppose the legislature, any future challenge to the Republic from the right would be extra-constitutional and potentially revolutionary. Briefly, Boulangism threatened to destroy the Republic in the late 1880s. The convictions of anti-Dreyfusards had a pronouncedly anti-republican inclination. Nevertheless, the two crises were overcome because in neither case was an alternative to republicanism credibly fashioned. Nor, before 1914, was the revived hostility of the left towards the government translated into widespread support as firm measures were taken to restore public order. Thiers' claim that 'the Republic is the government which divides us least' seemed vindicated.

Why was the Republic, despite appearances, soundly based in these years? How was stability in government achieved despite frequent changes of ministry?

Frequent changes of ministry (1871–1914) might suggest that France was incorrigibly politically unstable. Unlike Britain, France did not develop the machinery for establishing party discipline, but preferred shifting alliances so that disagreements on policy could cause ministries to collapse and much manoeuvring to form another. Yet if ministries were fragile, continuity was secured by ministers being prepared to serve regularly in rapidly changing ministries. Moreover, whatever the temporary disarray at governmental level, organisations like the *Conseil d'État* ensured that there was minimal disruption. Finally, the Republic consistently enjoyed the support of most of the electorate and most of those who sat in the Assembly. Taken together, these factors gave the Republic stability despite the protracted dramas that occasionally seemed to threaten its existence.

What was the significance of the Boulanger crisis? Explain why he won much public support and why he represented a threat to the Republic. How was the threat that he posed overcome?

The appointment of General Boulanger, with seemingly impeccable republican credentials, as Minister of Defence suggested no danger to the Republic. Nevertheless, the capacity of this impressive soldier for self-advertisement encouraged many – including members of Déroulède's recently formed *Ligue des Patriotes* – to see him as destined to recover Alsace-Lorraine, humiliatingly forfeited in 1871. Boulanger responded to public adulation by winning a series of by-elections through advocating the dissolution of Parliament, revision of the Constitution and a return to plebiscitary government. He might have destroyed the Republic and restored Bonapartist-style authoritarian government unconstrained by the legislature if he had had the courage to effect a *coup d'état*, although his task would have been difficult now that Paris was no longer able to determine political developments throughout France. The threat evaporated as firm government persuaded him to flee France. His appeal to left and right – to socialists and monarchists alike – indicated that there were many who rejected the Republic, although he made little impression in rural France. Indeed, elections in 1889 revealed more than 60% supported the Republic. Thus, Boulangism – bereft of its leader – was more a focus of disenchantment with government than a movement able to provide an alternative form of government.

Yet the Republic could not afford to be complacent. The Panama scandal of the early 1890s, involving some political figures in financial irregularities and forcing Clemenceau to retire temporarily from public life, was enough to induce cynicism concerning the probity of politicians and to pose an insidious potential threat to the durability of parliamentary government. The low poll in the elections of 1893 would appear to be testimony of this.

Why did the Panama scandal represent an insidious threat to the Republic?

Nor did the Dreyfus Affair, especially after 1898, enhance the stability of the Republic. Efforts to accord justice to Dreyfus, a soldier manifestly wrongly convicted for espionage (1894), was dramatised by Zola's article, 'J'Accuse' (January 1898), published in Clemenceau's *L'Aurore*. France became divided between Dreyfusards, unprepared to tolerate injustice for reasons of state, and conservative elements – like the army, the Church and militants claiming a belief in order and discipline – who considered the matter as disruptive of stability and likely to discredit the army. That Dreyfus was a Jew aroused anti-Semitic sentiment. Not until 1906 did justice prevail. After 1899 successive republican governments, appreciating that the Republic was threatened and aided by radicals and socialists – the latter urged by Jaurès to cease campaigning against the 'bourgeois Republic' – secured measures circumscribing the army's power and influence, and, sustained by widespread anti-clericalism, separated Church and state (1905). Thereafter, much Church property was sequestrated. The protracted crisis had demonstrated that, while the affair was a catalyst of discontent, it produced no coherent alternative to republican government.

What were the issues raised by the Dreyfus Affair? What effect did the matter have upon the army and the Church? What was the impact of the Dreyfus Affair on the strength of the Republic?

The Republic seemed secure. Socialists, led by Jaurès, seemingly resolved to achieve their objectives by parliamentary methods, consolidated the Republic's newly found unity. However, Millerand's efforts to introduce conciliation and arbitration procedures in industrial relations made little headway. The Senate blocked the introduction of a system of progressive taxation. By 1906 the Congress of the *Confédération Générale du Travail* was disowning links with any political doctrine and advocating the

Now consider the threat from the left before 1914. Note that the syndicalist measure of a general strike was successfully countered by the republican government.

general strike for expropriating the capitalist classes and reconstructing society on syndicalist lines. Clemenceau, as Minister of the Interior, while sympathetic to the social and economic problems of trade unionists, deplored violence and used uncompromising measures to maintain order. Thus the *Bloc Républicain* gradually withered away after 1906 and collapsed by 1911.

Emphasise that the political maturity of the Republic had enabled it to overcome the crises that it had faced.

By 1914 the Republic had undermined the right's potential for discrediting republican government, although vestigially and incoherently anti-Semitism and vehement nationalism remained. Latterly, the challenge of the left was handled firmly and adroitly by the government, which had matured during the Dreyfus Affair and was enjoying electoral endorsement from most Frenchmen.

Related questions

1 What was the significance of Boulangism?

After 1877 the legislature, not the executive, was the decisive element in the French state, President MacMahon having been discredited by the provocative use of his prerogative. Thereafter, that ministries were usually brief and always at the mercy of political manoeuvrings threatened to bring politics into disrepute and endanger the Republic, especially in the 1880s when economic and social distress was widespread. The Boulanger crisis was the more serious because, with support from the right and left of the political spectrum, it presaged a return to authoritarian rule buttressed by plebiscite, thus threatening to end the parliamentary government that had been so recently secured. In the event, Boulanger, a symbol and focus for the discontented, lacked the will or the inclination to seize power. In the immediate aftermath of the crisis, the Republic seemed strengthened. However, anti-parliamentary nationalist sentiment resurfaced in the Dreyfus Affair after 1898, and the political instability, implicit in restricting presidential power in the late 1870s, remained. A first paragraph on these lines would show that you had grasped the implications of the question.

Now, in successive paragraphs, account in detail for Boulanger's rise to power and the reasons for his popularity; examine the potential implications for France of his popularity. Then explain how Boulanger was stopped. How, immediately, was the Republic strengthened by Boulanger's failure? But there were adverse effects of the crisis too. Nationalism hostile to parliament, imbibed by monarchists and right-wing republicans, kept alive revanchist sentiment. It showed itself in the anti-Semitism associated with the anti-Dreyfusard cause. The eventual defeat of the various elements hostile to Dreyfus revived anti-clericalism and led to measures that curbed the army and the Church. *Action Française*, a militantly nationalist newspaper, urged the idea of 'integral nationalism', violently attacked the Republic and exercised some influence in French politics until 1940. Nevertheless, it was nationally organised syndicalism rather than nationalism which, less than two decades after the Boulanger crisis, posed the more serious problems for the Republic.

2 Discuss the view that the crises that from time to time afflicted the Third Republic in France before 1914 were superficial rather than real threats to stability.

3 What was the significance of the Dreyfus Affair in the history of the Third Republic before 1914?

What were the main features of France's external policies between 1871 and 1904?

Tackling the question

After 1871 the official policy and the public mood in France gave a low priority to revanche for the loss of Alsace-Lorraine. Occasionally, thought of a compromise arrangement with Germany, perhaps involving Alasatian autonomy, was mooted, but little more. Even when anti-German sentiment revived after 1900, the rivalry focused on economic and colonial matters rather than on the restoration to France of the lost provinces. For two decades after 1871 Bismarck had succeeded in keeping France diplomatically isolated. A French rapprochement with Britain was precluded by their imperial rivalry. Bismarck's fear of a Franco-Russian alliance became a reality when, try as he might, he could not prevent the gradual disintegration of Russo-German relations at the end of the 1880s. The Franco-Russian alliance of 1894 signalled a rapid flow of French funds to Russia as the latter sought an expanded industrial economy. However, in the 1890s the alliance did not function as a serious anti-German front, partly because the Tsar did not wish to become involved in a revanchist crusade and partly because France was loath to support Russia's Balkan aspirations.

Colonial expansion boosted France's self-assurance and economic and military strength while avoiding immediate conflict with Germany, although it risked – doubtless to Bismarck's satisfaction – the prospect of engaging France in rivalries with other imperialist powers. Indeed, France's imperial policies led to clashes with Italy and Britain especially, but eventually the volatility and unpredictability of Wilhelmine Germany inclined France towards an entente with Britain in 1904, which also reflected a comparable British view about the danger emanating from Germany. Thus, by the end of the period under consideration, France had well and truly escaped from the discomfort of diplomatic isolation and had an alliance with Russia that had a sure foundation in economic and financial interest and an entente with Britain that soon became a tacit alliance.

Answer

Examine the scope of France's external policies between 1871 and 1904. What anxieties did France have in its period of

After 1871 France's external policies were dominated by the problem of Germany. Even when the immediate consequences of the defeat of 1871 had passed, the growing demographic and industrial imbalance between them had worrying implications for

France. Initially, France's ambitions were necessarily modest in a period of 'contemplation'. Its diplomatic isolation was in large part determined by Germany in these years. After Bismarck's fall (1890) the search for an ally, hitherto fruitless, culminated in the Franco-Russian alliance (1893–4). When that was reinforced by the Anglo-French *entente* (1904) France enjoyed some security against a powerful and, latterly, unpredictable German power. If France was unassertive in the context of Europe, it retained its freedom of action outside Europe and after 1880 became the second colonial power. Yet the gaining of 10 million square kilometres of colonial territory could not really compensate for the loss of Alsace-Lorraine.

diplomatic isolation between 1871 and 1894? How did France compensate in these years for its loss of Alsace-Lorraine?

France's defeat in 1871 obscured its underlying strength. As it was relatively self-sufficient economically, France did not need a large export trade. Nevertheless, its growing wealth under Napoleon III had made it a leading exporter of capital and entrepreneurial skills, thus producing a large income from foreign investments. French engineers and bankers had built many of Europe's railways, and the Suez Canal, opened in 1869, was the latest triumph before the débâcle of 1870–1. The same strengths prevailed after 1871. It was an asset to French foreign policy that the French money market remained adept at channelling the savings of small investors into overseas funds. Moreover, France had intellectual and cultural influence abroad and sent out many Catholic missionaries partly because of the persecution of religious orders at home. Indeed, missionary expansion often preceded or accompanied colonial acquisition.

What strengths did France have after 1871 which it was able to exercise abroad? Stress in particular its financial strength.

After 1871, having sought to reinforce the defences of its eastern frontier, France strove to find an ally. While Bismarck was in office – until 1890 – he was able to keep France diplomatically isolated, but the system of alliances he devised to achieve this was beginning to collapse by 1887. His Reinsurance Treaty (1887) with Russia violated the spirit, if not the letter, of the Austro-German alliance (1879). In any case it proved not to be durable, in part because of the protective policies of each power, whereby Germany imposed duties on imports of Russian grain and Russia protected its 'infant' industries as it industrialised. That eroded mutual confidence. By the late 1880s Russia had become increasingly dependent on French loans to finance its economic development so that a sure foundation for an alliance was being laid. The increasingly incautious conduct of German foreign policy after 1890 meant that the Franco-Russian alliance (1893–4), its secret terms directed against Germany and its allies, gave France a measure of security against potential German aggression.

Explain how France eventually emerged from its diplomatic isolation and that it was France's financial strength and flexibility that helped to make possible an alliance with Russia at a time when the Russian government sought investment from abroad in order to expand the industrial base of the Tsarist Empire.

What was France's attitude to the lost provinces in these years?

While German attitudes to France fluctuated – sometimes friendly, sometimes menacing – the Alsace-Lorraine issue precluded *détente*. The lost provinces were at the core of French patriotic feeling and the hope of regaining them was never renounced. Governments invariably obeyed Gambetta's injunction to 'think of it always, speak of it never', and relied on justice to put the matter right eventually. No plans existed to regain Alsace-Lorraine by diplomatic or military means, and the French avoided any overt military support for pro-French elements in the two provinces.

How did France cultivate its interests in the Mediterranean after 1871? Why did its relations with Italy and Britain deteriorate? But what interest did France share with Britain concerning the Mediterranean despite the Franco-Russian alliance?

After 1871 French interest in the Mediterranean focused on Algeria, with its highly developed trade with France, the need to protect which fell on the French navy. Algeria was a natural base for extending French control over Tunisia and Morocco. This resulted in unfriendly relations with Italy, especially after France's annexation of Tunis (1881), thus depriving France of a potential ally. Indeed, Italy joined the Triple Alliance (1882) and in the Mediterranean Agreements (1887) aligned itself with France's maritime rival, Britain. Anglo-French relations deteriorated after Britain established its control in Egypt (1882). France resentfully considered this as excluding French financial and cultural interests from Egypt. Nevertheless, France continued to co-operate with Britain in the general policy of sustaining the Ottoman Empire, and the Franco-Russian alliance did not lead France to support Russian claims to the Straits. Indeed, after 1890, the main cause of alarm in the area was the growing economic and political influence of Germany.

Consider the extent of the French Empire in the closing years of the nineteenth century. Why were Britain and France at odds with each other? What was the apparent effect of the Franco-Russian alliance on Britain?

Especially after 1880, France expanded its empire vastly, incurring, particularly, rivalry with Britain. Beyond the Mediterranean all its possessions in west and central Africa were linked into a huge, if not populous, territory and indirect rule was established in Indo-China. By 1885 Madagascar was virtually a protectorate. By 1900 France was undeniably a world power, with much of its expansion in territory not coveted by other powers. If there was no territorial clash with Germany before the Moroccan crisis (1905–6), in west Africa, the Sudan and Siam, France posed a direct threat to Britain. Indeed, in the late 1890s France seemed the main enemy rather than Germany, the alliance with Russia having strong anti-British overtones despite its anti-German terms. Yet if the Fashoda crisis (1898) demonstrated that colonial expansion could lead to conflict, France did not alarm Britain as a world trading power or by building a great battle fleet, as did Germany.

The Anglo-French *entente* (1904) liquidated their remaining colonial disputes – in response to their common apprehensions about a powerful, unpredictable Germany – and Britain's *entente* with Russia (1907) created the Triple Entente, centred on France. To have provided security for France through this alliance system, to have seized every opportunity that offered itself for overseas expansion and to have restored France to the first rank of world powers, virtually without risking war or disturbing the European balance of power, was a remarkable work of skill and resolve on the part of those who directed French policy.

What had France achieved by 1904? Why was an Anglo-French *entente* negotiated by 1904? Explain the nature of France's achievement by that year.

Related questions

1 How may it be explained that France almost went to war with Britain in 1898, but was prepared to conclude an *entente* with Britain in 1904?

In the immediate aftermath of the Franco-Russian alliance in 1894, the cornerstone of French security before 1914, France placed emphasis on colonial expansion and a conciliatory attitude towards Germany. Britain, at the same time, was embracing imperialism with unprecedented fervour. France's colonial expansion – second only to Britain's – had been encouraged by Bismarck after 1871 as a distraction from the vexed question of the lost provinces of Alsace-Lorraine. That expansion, to Bismarck's satisfaction, increased tensions between Britain and France, especially over Egypt, and was exacerbated by Britain's reconquest of the Sudan in 1898, an act that provoked the French to undertake a brief, potentially dangerous, military confrontation with Britain. After the Fashoda crisis there was a slow mending of relations, interrupted by the Anglo-Boer War (1899–1902). The improvement was inspired very much by their common fear of an unpredictable, powerful Germany threatening the security of both. In these circumstances, their colonial rivalry seemed arid and detrimental to their real interests.

After the introductory paragraph, explain in some detail the nature of the Anglo-French rivalry in Africa in the late nineteenth century; the significance of the Fashoda crisis of 1898; the factors that impeded and assisted the development of Anglo-French accord between 1898 and 1904; how and on what terms the Anglo-French *entente* was secured in 1904. The *entente* between France and Britain profoundly disturbed Bülow, the German Chancellor, even though he put a brave face on the matter. He was conscious that, despite Germany's confidence that the traditional enemies, Britain and France, would not find common ground, the *entente* marked the establishment of a new alignment of the powers, boding ill for Germany's future security in central Europe. Even so, he hoped, in vain as it transpired, that the Franco-Russian alliance might be endangered by it, as Britain was the ally of Japan, which was at war with Russia. To German chagrin and discomfort, the *entente* was sufficiently resilient to survive the ordeal of the first Moroccan crisis of 1905–6. In retrospect, the transformation in Anglo-French relations between 1898 and 1904 was the necessary foundation for the coalition of France, Russia and Britain which opposed the central powers in the crisis of 1914.

2   'Born in defeat, the Third Republic had by 1904 not only overcome internal opposition but regained for France the status of a major power.' How far do you agree with this statement?

3   Examine the reasons for colonial and imperial rivalries between 1884 and 1914.

Question 15

To what extent was the creation of the German Empire in 1871 Bismarck's achievement?

Tackling the question

In his memoirs Bismarck insisted that he always worked for the unification of Germany. Despite what has been called the 'peaceful dualism' between Austria and Prussia within the German Confederation before 1848, he may well not have given any priority to Prussian solidarity with Austria as early as 1850, immediately before he became his country's representative in the Frankfurt Diet. His distaste for Austria grew thereafter. By 1856 he was asserting that Austria and Prussia were both ploughing 'the same disputed acre' and that Germany was 'too small for us both', and he was foreseeing an Austro-Prussian war. Even before Bismarck became Prussian Chancellor in 1862, Austrian diplomatic fortunes were at a low ebb. Rapport between Austria and Russia, although not always easily sustained, had been a consistent feature of the European scene since 1815. That link had been broken as a result of the Crimean War. Worse was to follow for Austria. By 1860 Piedmont, assisted by Napoleon III, had virtually excluded Austria from the Italian peninsula. That Britain was an observer rather than a participant in European affairs after 1856, and as time past a discreet supporter of German unification as a bastion against the possibility of an expansionist France, was also grist to Bismarck's mill. During the 1860s there was no hostile coalition that might stand in his way. In any case, other factors assisted Bismarck in his aims, not least the industrial revolution in Germany, which had helped to give unity to the scattered provinces that had comprised Prussia since 1815. Moreover, the Zollverein, initiated by Prussia in the 1830s, had steadily increased the economic interdependence of Germany and at the same time excluded Austria from its benefits.

Just as it may be said that Hitler exploited circumstances as they arose in pursuit of his defined objectives, Bismarck too had a grand design that he advanced by improvisation as circumstances arose, thus showing himself to be a consummate opportunist. It cannot be denied that the creation of the German Empire required Bismarck's political skills if it were to be achieved. However, the factors that assisted his cause included there being no serious impediment to his fashioning policies in his quest for German unity, as there was little likelihood that other powers would be willing or able to intervene.

Answer

On the surface, German unification seems to be almost exclusively attributable to Bismarck's diplomatic skills. Three nicely

Consider why there should be a reluctance to attribute the

---

unification wholly to Bismarck's diplomatic skills.

calculated wars achieved a German Empire under Prussian auspices. Yet his success depended much on his being able to take advantage of Prussia's strength, acquired before he became Prussian Chancellor (1862). An incipient German nationalism in Napoleon's time grew gradually thereafter. Prussia's acquisition of Rhineland-Westphalia (1815) produced economic benefits as well as territorial influence right across Germany. The Zollverein – a customs union established in 1834 – paved the way for Prussia's economic ascendancy in Germany. Finally, Austria – Prussia's principal rival for control of Germany, weakened by diplomatic isolation, defeated ignominiously in Italy (1859) and economically vulnerable – was defensive and uncertain in 1862. Thus, Bismarck had a sure basis upon which to pursue his ambitions.

To what extent did nationalist sentiment in Germany assist Bismarck in achieving German unification?

The quest for unification necessarily required the presence of nationalist sentiment in Germany. Napoleon's short-lived Confederation of the Rhine provided a foretaste of a consolidated Germany. Thereafter, the role played by Germans in expelling Napoleon fostered an infant nationalism. That sentiment tended to be espoused by educated liberals, but after 1815, when Germany comprised 39 states, watched over by the autocratic powers of Austria and Prussia, there was little scope for it to flourish. Briefly, the uneasy co-operation between Prussia and Austria was ended in 1848 when the Frankfurt Assembly sought in vain the creation of a constitutional German state. Nevertheless, Bismarck was able to capitalise later on the aspiration for unity already established before 1862.

Now discuss the implications for Germany of the growing strength of the Prussian economy, helped as it was by the acquisition of the Rhineland in 1815. What was the importance of the Zollverein, established in 1834? What were the most rapidly expanding areas of Prussia's economy, which considerably strengthened Prussia before Bismarck became Prussian Chancellor in 1862?

Bismarck also benefited from the supremacy of the Prussian economy in Germany. After defeat by Napoleon, Prussia experienced the advantages of a radical overhaul of its financial and economic system. When Prussia gained the coal- and iron-producing areas of the Rhineland (1815), it became rich in raw materials. Above all, Prussia was able to extend its influence in Germany by means of the Zollverein (established in 1834), a customs union linking the smaller German states to Prussia. While membership of it did not mean overt political subordination to Prussia, withdrawal from it entailed economic and commercial disadvantages, so that states stayed within it. Scope for extending Prussia's influence was augmented by its capacity to negotiate trade treaties on the Zollverein's behalf. The Zollverein's trade increased rapidly, and credit was readily available either from German banks or abroad. Moreover, Prussia's economy expanded conspicuously in the 1850s with the development of an extensive railway network, flourishing coal and steel industries and the most highly developed chemical industry in the world. Thus, Bismarck had a sound economic foundation upon which to seek unification.

Meanwhile, Austria languished politically and economically. As a result of the Crimean War (1854–6), the Austro-Russian axis, a recurring feature after 1815, was broken. Austria's diplomatic isolation tempted France to support militarily successful efforts to oust the Austrians from Italy by 1860. Austria's military humiliation was accompanied by the increased restiveness of its Slav subjects, and its declining economy was excluded from the benefits of the Zollverein, denied to Austria by Prussia. Again, Bismarck could further his objectives secure in the knowledge that Austria was finding it increasingly difficult to assert itself in Germany.

Consider how Prussia was assisted by the political and economic weaknesses of Austria. How did the Crimean War damage Austria diplomatically? Note the internal tensions of a polyglot empire in a Europe where nationalism was a source of inspiration to many.

Yet in 1862 the institutions of the Confederation, restored at Austria's insistence in the Olmütz Punctuation (1850) after the short-lived effort to unite Germany under Prussian hegemony, were still in place. It was Bismarck's achievement that he undermined the status quo by a sustained and astute diplomacy calculated to undermine Austro-Prussian relations and justify war. The apparent Austro-Prussian co-operation over the revived Schleswig-Holstein question, causing war with Denmark, culminated in the Convention of Gastein (1865). This contained complex provisions on joint rights of sovereignty in the two duchies, which produced the tensions that Bismarck wanted as both sides took arbitrary steps leading to a diplomatic impasse. With France assuring Bismarck of its neutrality in an Austro-Prussian war and Italy an ally, Prussia comprehensively defeated Austria at Sadowa (1866). By excluding Austria from Germany and establishing the Prussian-dominated North German Confederation, Bismarck fundamentally changed the balance of power in Europe.

With the advantages outlined in earlier paragraphs explain how Bismarck was able to exercise his diplomatic skills to exclude Austria from Germany by 1866.

Napoleon III, at a serious disadvantage diplomatically *vis-à-vis* Prussia, nevertheless sought territory, ineptly and unsuccessfully, in order to acquire prestige – Luxembourg, part of the Palatinate and even Belgium. He concluded his incompetent handling of foreign affairs by overplaying his hand over the issue of the Hohenzollern candidacy for the Spanish throne (1870). Bismarck was able to exploit the news of France's insistence that the candidacy should never be renewed, contained in the Ems telegram, by editing it in terms insulting to France, thus obliging Napoleon to engage in a war for which France was not militarily prepared. France's humiliating defeat (1870–1) precipitated the

Further, demonstrate his accomplished exploitation of France's diplomatic blunders, which in 1870 culminated in war.

establishment of the German Empire, incorporating the hitherto reluctant south German states and – fatefully – Alsace-Lorraine.

Conclude by insisting that Bismarck's achievements need to be considered in the context of a Prussia which, even before 1862, was coming to dominate Germany, particularly in economic and commercial terms. That is not to say that Bismarck's political judgement was not crucial to the establishment of the German Empire.

It is not enough to accept the impression given in Bismarck's memoirs that German unification was almost exclusively attributable to his personal diplomacy. The Zollverein had already made most of Germany an economic unit. The industrialisation of Germany was gaining momentum. An efficient civil service was in place and, by 1862, a large and modern Prussian army was being created. Even the diplomatic setting was not mainly Bismarck's work. Russia was weakened by the Crimean War, Austria was isolated and weak, both politically and economically, and Britain, especially after Palmerston's death (1865), was loath to be involved in continental affairs. Nevertheless, Bismarck's judgement of what was politically possible rarely erred, so that he was able to capitalise on Prussia's advantages, which would have existed whoever had become Prussian Chancellor in 1862.

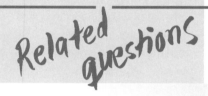

Related questions

1 'Diplomacy rather than force secured the unification of Germany in the years between 1861 and 1871.' How true is this judgement?

Unimpressed by abstract principles, Bismarck believed that the 'egotism' of states could be satisfied only by their fighting for whatever served their interests. The conviction that 'the great questions of our time' would not be resolved by 'speeches and majority resolutions', but through 'iron and blood' would appear to have been faithfully reflected in the three wars that Prussia fought before 1871 in order to achieve Bismarck's resolve to unite Germany. Each conflict was preceded by a ruthless diplomacy, calculated to break down at the moment that best suited Bismarck. Diplomacy was not, to Bismarck, an alternative to war in gaining his objectives. Ultimately, it was subordinate, despite its indispensability, to the use of arms. However, consider also developments affecting Prussia – economic, military and administrative – which crucially underpinned Bismarck's blending of diplomacy and war. The advantages that he inherited in 1862 were invaluable as he sought to achieve German unity under Prussia's auspices.

Now consider his relations with Austria after 1862. To what extent did Bismarck's willingness to assist Russia in thwarting the Polish revolt of 1863 adversely affect Austria? What were the diplomatic and military steps that led to Bismarck being able to conduct a victorious war against Austria by 1866? How then, after 1866, did Bismarck secure the co-operation of the south German states and so facilitate their acceptance of incorporation in a united Germany? How did Bismarck exploit France's ill-judged actions to precipitate a Franco-Prussian war in 1870? Bismarck had ensured France's diplomatic isolation by reinforcing Britain's ingrained suspicions of French territorial ambitions. Austria had no intention of going to war. Italy resented the French military occupation of Rome. Russia had no vital interest at stake and had been bought off by Bismarck acquiescing in the abrogation of the Black Sea clauses. Each of Bismarck's three wars in the 1860s had been short and decisive, the preparatory diplomacy serpentine and protracted, but essentially subordinate to the notion of resolution by war.

2   'Anyone who has looked into the glazed eyes of a soldier dying on the battlefield will think hard before starting war.' Why then, in spite of this claim, did Bismarck resort to war on three occasions between 1862 and 1870?

3   'In the period 1862–71, Bismarck exploited Austrian weakness and Prussian military strength to secure the creation of a German Empire.' How far do you agree with this verdict?

Question 16

'Bismarck sought security for the German Empire
in Europe in 1871. By 1890 Germany dominated Europe.'
How far is this a valid claim for Bismarck's foreign
policy between 1871 and 1890?

Tackling the question

In retrospect, the German Confederation, established in 1815, had been an element of stability in Europe. It served as a complex barrier to any restiveness that might shape expansionist policies by Russia or France. At the same time, the particularism of the many German states ensured that there would not be a sufficient degree of collective action by them which might threaten states neighbouring the Confederation. Thus, before the 1860s Germany may be seen as Europe's soft centre – 'a passive element, a shock absorber in the international system', as it has been described. The new German Empire was not such a boon. From the start, it was the most populous state in Europe, except for the Russian Empire. Its military power was unequalled and its economy the most enterprising on the European mainland. It was difficult to believe that this new political entity would desist from waging war in future, given that under Bismarck's leadership three wars had been engineered in the 1860s. For his part Bismarck was aware that Germany's centrality in Europe made it vulnerable to pressure from a coalition of powers, especially one that included France and Russia. Thus, he sought to remove this insecurity by avoiding war, so that Germany, a satiated state as he saw it, could digest its gains.

After 1871 his policy was one of peace, even though the capitals of Europe must, initially, have doubted that this would be his aim. He strove successfully for many years to keep France diplomatically isolated because he felt that a resentful France might seek an ally – most dangerously for Germany, Russia – to assist it to recover Alsace-Lorraine. Bismarck's assurances to his neighbours that he meant to pursue peaceful policies ensured that no coalition was formed against the new Germany. However, in his resolve to avoid war, the duplicitous means that he used – especially after 1879, when he began the construction of secret agreements – aroused suspicions of Germany's intentions. For twenty years peace was maintained, but after Bismarck's fall from power in 1890 the elaborate and tortuous diplomacy that he had fashioned collapsed and Germany's unpredictability – associated as it was with undoubted German strength, military, commercial and economic – gradually persuaded the powers to sink any differences they might have had in order to coalesce, for fear that otherwise they might be faced with the danger of German hegemonic power in Europe. The essay requires you to examine the nature of Bismarck's fears in 1871 and then to assess to what extent, if at all, he had been able to allay his anxieties by the time of his resignation in 1890. Does the notion of Germany's domination of Europe not need to be qualified?

Answer

The creation of the German Empire (1871) was a reaffirmation of the fundamental change in the balance of power in Europe that occurred in 1866. A dynamic, centrally placed entity existed that was capable of exerting a disquieting pressure on all its neighbours. Bismarck, the principal architect of this transformation, now convinced that Germany was a satiated state needing tranquillity in order to digest its gains, sought peace. For the moment most European states were prepared to acquiesce anxiously in the new dispensation, although France, bruised and isolated, nursed a longer-term resolve to restore to itself the lost provinces of Alsace-Lorraine. Before 1890 the apparent dominance of Bismarck's diplomacy in Europe ensured that his policy of peace prevailed, but despite his elaborate system of secret alliances, Germany did not acquire a sense of durable security. Provocative policies thereafter aggravated that vulnerability further.

> Make sure that your analysis embraces the whole of the period under discussion. To what extent was the peace and security sought by Bismarck for the new Germany achieved in the period 1871–90? To what extent may it be said that Bismarckian diplomacy was successful before 1890?

During the period 1871–90 Bismarck feared an encircling Franco-Russian alliance, which might precede a war designed to restore Alsace-Lorraine to France. Thus, Bismarck was anxious to avoid a rift between Austria-Hungary and Russia that could encourage Russia to seek an alliance with France. Initially, Austria and Russia were concerned to be conciliatory towards each other in the Balkans, as was demonstrated in the Convention of Schönbrunn (June 1873). Germany's accession to it (October 1873) created a Dreikaiserbund – a loose agreement which, at that stage, was potentially sufficient insurance against an eruption of Austro-Russian tension.

> What was the relevance of the Dreikaiserbund in keeping France isolated diplomatically?

The Near East crisis (1875–8) did not at first produce Austro-Russian friction. The Andrassy Note (December 1875) and the Berlin Memorandum (June 1876) reflected their joint concern about Turkish excesses in the Balkans. Russia's willingness to cede Bosnia-Herzegovina to Austria-Hungary as the price of the latter staying out of a Russo-Turkish war, which began in April 1877, augured well for their future co-operation. However, the Treaty of San Stefano (March 1878) angered Austria because it did not cede Bosnia-Herzegovina and established a 'big' Bulgaria. The additional hostility of Britain and France towards Russia ensured that Russia was obliged to accept revision of the treaty at the Congress of Berlin (June 1878). Austria occupied Bosnia-Herzegovina without annexing it, and the 'big' Bulgaria was trisected, much to Russia's dissatisfaction. With the Dreikaiserbund dead, Bismarck feared that an isolated Russia might turn to France.

> What effect did the Near East crisis of 1875–8 have upon the Dreikaiserbund? You will need to demonstrate some knowledge and understanding of the events and intricate diplomacy of this protracted crisis.

How did Bismarck seek to prepare the way for a restoration of the Dreikaiserbund after 1878? Stress that the Dual Alliance of 1879 was a means to recreating the Dreikaiserbund.

In order to counter the danger of this occurring, Bismarck negotiated the Dual Alliance (1879) with Austria – a defensive alliance against attack from Russia either assisted by another power (say, France) or alone. The alliance enabled him to exercise a restraining influence over Austria, which might help him to minimise Austro-Russian tension in the Balkans. Italy was drawn into the alignment in the Triple Alliance (1882), as it sought to escape isolation after its diplomatic rupture with France when it failed to secure Tunis (1881). Bismarck's real objective, however, was the revival of the Dreikaiserbund to give him a reliable basis for the restoration of Austro-Russian accord.

Why was the restored Driekaiserbund after 1881 flawed? What made it a fragile agreement? Why did its collapse come at a particularly difficult time for Bismarck in his relations with France?

A sufficiently mollified Russia was ready to acquiesce in the restoration of the Dreikaiserbund (1881), this time organised by Bismarck, who sought a durable stability in the Balkans. Despite his diplomatic ingenuity, his plans were flawed. While Austria-Hungary and Russia officially sanctioned that Bulgaria should be united if Russia so desired, and that Austria-Hungary should eventually annex Bosnia-Herzegovina, neither Austria-Hungary nor Russia accepted Bismarck's concept of spheres of influence in the Balkans. Moreover, the potential changes, undisclosed to other powers, would have breached the terms of the Treaty of Berlin (1878). When Prince Alexander of Bulgaria, hostile to Russia, promulgated Bulgaria's union with Eastern Roumelia and subsequently found himself at war with Serbia, Austria-Hungary's ally since 1881, the Dreikaiserbund was sorely tested. The fragile accord was eventually undermined by Russia's clumsy kidnapping of Alexander of Bulgaria in order to replace him with a Russian nominee. Bismarck was now faced with his recurring fear of an isolated Russia turning to France, at a time when the latter was gripped with revanchist feeling inspired by Boulanger.

In what sense may the Reinsurance Treaty (1887) be considered as evidence of Germany's insecurity? Why did the Reinsurance Treaty not bring the security that Bismarck sought?

The vulnerability of Bismarck's diplomatic arrangements was apparent when, without Austria-Hungary's knowledge, he approached Russia for the agreement – known as the Reinsurance Treaty (1877) – that committed Russia and Germany to refrain from supporting aggressive designs by France on Germany and by Austria-Hungary on Russia. He had felt obliged to violate the spirit of his 1879 agreement with Austria-Hungary. It was a desperate attempt to preclude a Franco-Russian alliance. Yet, the pan-Slav movement in Russia disapproved of it and Russo-German relations were threatened by resentment at each other's protectionist policies – that is, Germany's protective duties against imports of Russian grain and Russia's protection of its 'infant' industries as it industrialised. Further erosion of the agreement was implied by Russia's increasing dependence on French loans to finance its economic development. The basis for the Franco-Russian alliance was being laid.

At the end of the Bismarckian era (1890), materially Germany dominated mainland Europe. Its efficient industries promised a commercial ascendancy. Its well-equipped and disciplined army was considered to be second to none. It was becoming an imperial power, so that there was the prospect of enhanced influence beyond Europe. Despite this apparent strength, however, Germany harboured doubts about security. The Reinsurance Treaty was not renewed in 1890. It seems that Bismarck felt almost from its inception that it might not prove to be durable. His encouragement of the Mediterranean Agreements of 1887 – involving Italy, Britain and Austria-Hungary – reflected his fear of Russian aggrandisement in the Balkans. Twice, in 1887 and 1889, he sought unsuccessfully an alliance with Britain. His system of alliances, therefore, did not give Bismarck diplomatic control of Europe. Its contradictions foreshadowed its collapse. The legacy of his failure was a growing isolation for Germany, which ultimately produced the 'encirclement' that he feared and that was the basis for the general war of 1914.

What factors gave Germany domination in Europe in 1890? But in what ways did Germany remain insecure? Why had Bismarck's system of secret alliances not given Germany the safety that Bismarck sought? What were the consequences of Bismarck's failure in this respect?

Related questions

1   'The balance of power in Europe was seriously disturbed by the creation of the German Empire in 1871.' Assess the truth of this statement.

The creation of the German Confederation in 1815, although it failed to satisfy any German nationalistic sentiment, gave a measure of stability to central Europe, in that the 39 states comprising it could have been overrun or annexed only by an ambitious leader of Napoleonic brilliance and resolve – no such leader emerged after 1815. Moreover, the complex and cumbersome federal structure prevented the organisation of Germany into a single state that might have posed a threat to its neighbours. Contrast the fragmented Germany before 1866 with the united Germany after 1871. In terms of population, military capacity and commercial and industrial development, the new German Empire was the most powerful state in continental Europe. It was dynamic and capable of exerting pressure on its neighbours to an alarming degree. Moreover, Bismarck, on the evidence of Prussia's three wars since 1862, had gained an awesome reputation by stressing 'iron and blood' in his foreign policy. Would the new Germany embark on war for a fourth time?

This is the basis on which you may pose further questions. What were Bismarck's ambitions in Europe after 1871? What specific steps did Bismarck take in the 1870s to maintain European peace? Why did his complex diplomacy of secret alliances ultimately fail? What were the consequences of that failure? What were the consequences of the profound disturbance in the European balance of power in 1871 by the year 1914? In 1871 Europe's soft centre was replaced by a disturbingly powerful state, capable of menacing its neighbours and of being menaced by those same neighbours in combination. Once Bismarck, whose diplomacy sought to minimise tensions after 1871, was gone, the fear thereafter generated by Germany's provocative policies abroad showed how much Europe had benefited in terms of security by having the loose federation, centrally placed in Europe, after 1815.

2   'Bismarck's foreign policy was determined by his fear of a Franco-Russian alliance.' How far do you agree with this assessment?

3   To what extent was Bismarck's foreign policy after 1871 determined by fear of France?

Question 17

'Internal and external policies were
indissolubly linked in Wilhelmine Germany.'
To what extent is this verdict valid?

Tackling the question

Bismarck towered above his contemporaries. His diplomatic and political skills have impressed historians. In devising the Imperial Constitution, he had to consider the residual particularist sentiments of the German states and recognise that a unitary state was unacceptable to them. In D.G. Williamson's words, the Constitution involved 'real if fragile compromises between the Prussian Crown, the German states and the Liberal movement'. However, the Constitution also reflected Bismarck's distaste for popular participation in politics. Government, in his view, was a matter for rulers and officials, not the people. The Reichstag, to which government was not responsible, contained a plethora of political parties that were manipulated unscrupulously by Bismarck so that they, in turn, merely sought satisfaction for their sectional interests. By 1890, under Bismarck's auspices, the Reichstag remained politically immature and this was to be a damaging legacy of Bismarck's ascendancy.

According to Max Weber, 'he left behind a nation without any political will ... accustomed to submit to anything which was decided for it'. This had serious implications for German politics, since the rapidity of industrialisation was creating social and political tensions that could not be solved within the existing constitutional framework. Vested interests – the military and Junker élite and patriotic leagues, for example – were hostile to parliamentary government, which could alone in the long term hold out the hope of a break in Germany's political stalemate. Thus, it may be argued, Bismarck cannot escape considerable responsibility for retarding Germany's political growth and, by so doing, helping to generate the tensions and contradictions in German society that may have persuaded the German government to seek domestic political respite in forward policies abroad, which were potentially damaging to the peace of Europe.

Answer

Guidance notes

To the accompaniment of rapid industrialisation and demographic change, Germany experienced social tensions that appeared to threaten potentially revolutionary disruption during the Wilhelmine period after 1890. The Imperial Constitution (1871), which calculatedly avoided instituting responsible government,

Explain the scope of the question set. Show how the Imperial Constitution of 1871 had little compatibility with the political implications of rapid industrial and demographic change in Germany in the last quarter of the nineteenth century. What, may it be argued, were the consequences for Germany in its foreign policy?

Examine the consequences of Bismarck avoiding responsible government in the Imperial Constitution. What effect did this omission have upon the political parties in the Reichstag? Why, by the eve of general war in 1914, was there the threat that the legislative process in Germany might be disrupted?

Discuss the efforts made by the German government to secure a coalition of interests against the rising Social Democratic Party.

nevertheless permitted universal male suffrage for the election of members to the Reichstag, which, in its composition, ultimately gave socialists, anxious to redistribute economic wealth and promote social reform, a larger representation than any other political party (1912). Thus, increasingly the Reich government could not rely upon a stable, conservative-inclined majority. It may be argued that an assertive foreign and military policy was a manoeuvre designed to integrate politically anti-socialist interests, so that there might be parliamentary majorities for its legislative programmes. In the event, apprehension about Germany's intentions obliged Britain to abandon its 'isolation' and negotiate *ententes* with France (1904) and Russia (1907), in an effort to contain Germany's intimidating nationalistic energies in central Europe and to curb the anti-British implications of *Weltpolitik* – Germany's efforts to gain extensive, even prevailing, influence in Europe and beyond.

It was a feature of German politics that a government unaccountable to a representative assembly was obliged to handle a plethora of political parties, each inclined to press ruthlessly for its sectional interests, secure in the knowledge that the Reich Chancellor would need to allow concessions to ensure that legislation was endorsed by a majority in the Reichstag. Thus, political parties – like the Reich government itself – had little incentive to behave responsibly. Yet, after 1900 the right-wing groupings with the Zentrum in the Reichstag, hitherto the basis upon which the government secured majorities, were increasingly difficult for the Chancellor to contrive because by 1912, with 110 seats in an assembly of 397, the SPD was the largest party. In this circumstance, while the parties might agree with the Emperor that co-operation with the SPD was unacceptable, they failed to coalesce with the government to effect important legislation. A rupture of the legislative process threatened. Thus, it was tempting for the Reich government to rally people and parties with disparate, but anti-socialist, views behind causes that could be regarded as in the common national interest.

At the turn of the century, the Reich government's parliamentary majorities for legislative purposes were bought by promoting nationalist and armaments policies. While commercial and industrial interests accepted the Navy Laws of 1898 and 1900 as military support for ever more profitable penetration of overseas markets, agrarian interests were ready to acquiesce in the Navy Laws in return for higher protective tariffs against foreign competition. The government's intention was to secure the combined support of these interests against the SPD, the apparently revolutionary potential of which was considered by the government as the prime threat to political stability. Moreover, government policies calculated to enhance Germany's position internationally were served by the support of the same divergent, anti-socialist interests.

The wooing of these interests against the industrial workers was counter-productive, in that it alienated further the socialists and helped to promote, on the right, even more radically nationalist sentiment, keen to promote an arms race and military preparations. The exorbitant costs involved raised the thorny issue of the distribution of tax burdens. Central government was unable to raise direct taxation, but depended heavily on regressive indirect taxation on basic items of consumption, which was particularly burdensome to the mass of the people. Especially after 1902, when protective tariffs on grain and other agricultural produce were introduced, the SPD agitated vigorously against indirect taxes.

When in 1908 Bülow, the Reich Chancellor, tried to combine an increase in indirect taxation and a death duty – the latter to raise one-fifth of the 500 million marks required by government – the Conservatives combined with the Zentrum to oppose a direct levy on inherited wealth and insisted, with success, on reverting to the established policy of dependence on indirect taxation. Such a policy may well have contributed to the SPD's electoral success in 1912, after which the weakened Conservatives were unable to stop the passing of the Finance Bill (1913), which included the imposition of a wealth tax. For many anti-socialists the future for German society seemed bleak. Civil war, for them, could not be ruled out.

On the eve of general war in 1914, the Kaiser and his advisers were deeply anxious about the centrifugal forces within German society that could be unleashed and the menace implicit in the 'encirclement' of Germany arising from the *ententes*. Both seemed two sides of the same coin. There was evidence of a growing rift between the Reich and Prussia, the largest federal state. Germany's diplomatic isolation was qualified only by a firm alliance with the ramshackle, multinational Austro-Hungarian Empire. The Finance Bill (1913), which produced tensions over the distribution of tax burdens, was a response to deteriorating circumstances in the Balkans, as the Ottoman Empire collapsed, and the weakening position of the Dual Alliance *vis-à-vis* the Triple Entente. There was a fear – ultimately to prove an erroneous one – that Russia, which had initiated military reforms after the débâcle of 1904–5 against Japan, might by 1917 be unstoppable.

How did the fiscal structures enshrined in the Imperial Constitution have serious repercussions for the German government after 1900? How did this assist the Social Democratic Party to gain electoral support?

What were the consequences of Bülow's efforts to introduce a measure of direct taxation in 1908? What impact did this have upon the thinking of many conservative-minded people in Germany?

Consider the acute problems in Germany on the eve of war in 1914. The government seems to have been afflicted with deep worries concerning not only social tensions within Germany, but the implications of what it perceived to be 'encirclement' of Germany by unfriendly powers. Note the government's exaggerated fear of Russia's military strength and its worries about the combined power of France and Russia. How far may these anxieties have determined foreign policy decisions in 1914?

Indeed, French and Russian army bills were, on the eve of the war, outmatching Germany's efforts and inducing, in military circles, widespread despondency. Worries about the future military balance were stealthily being translated into a predisposition to wage preventive war.

Conclude by considering the potential link between the willingness of the German government to entertain involvement in war in 1914 and the social and political tensions within Germany.

The assassination of the Archduke Ferdinand and his wife (28 June 1914) seemed to German generals to afford an opportunity to counter, by war, the threats implied by 'encirclement'. Bethmann Hollweg, the Reich Chancellor, hoped unavailingly to limit the confrontation to one between Austria-Hungary and Serbia. However, by early July, the Kaiser, with the support of his generals, was seriously deepening the crisis by allowing Austria to deal with Serbia as it thought fit. His colonial and naval ambitions had long since withered, despite his encouragement of nationalist sentiment. Rising tensions at home were accompanied by a decline in the prestige and authority of the Hohenzollern monarchy. On the other hand, victory in war, based on the implementation of the Schlieffen Plan, was just conceivable. In that event, political and social tensions within Germany – long since much in evidence – might be checked.

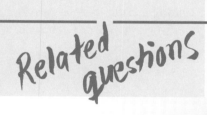

Related questions

1 What was the political, economic and social impact upon Germany of the outbreak of war in 1914?

In the July crisis of 1914 the German government, which had usually sought to restrain Austria-Hungary's provocative actions in the Balkans, gave Austria a blank cheque to deal with Serbia as it thought fit. Germany seemed to be prepared to run the risk of involving itself in a war that was unlikely to remain indigenous to the Balkans. Sustained by its Schlieffen Plan, into which was built surprise and rapid movement, it embarked on a European war that, with misguided confidence, it believed could be brief and decisive. But the war dragged on. It tested not only Germany's military strength, but also the robustness and flexibility of its economy, its administrative competence, its political stability and ultimately its social cohesion. These factors need to be considered in detail in the body of the essay.

Consider the extent to which the German people were willing to accept war in 1914, before showing how the generals, Hindenburg and Ludendorff, effected 'a silent revolution' that enabled them to manage an economy dedicated exclusively to war. Why was Bethmann Hollweg obliged to resign in 1917? What were the economic and social effects of concentrating most effort on meeting the demands of war? Consider the work of the War Raw Materials Office

(KRA), inspired by Rathenau. Why, by 1918, had the economy collapsed? Consider why and how financial problems weakened the war effort of the government. What was the effect of the Allied naval blockade on the German population? What was the nature of the discontents that manifested themselves? Explain the consequences of the sudden collapse of the German armies in 1918. Emphasise that the short-term effect of defeat was the collapse of the institution of monarchy. The myth that the German armies had not really been defeated in 1918 reinforced the popular belief that Germany's great power status could be recovered, and that the diktat of the Versailles Treaty was the consequence of a defeat engineered by the 'left' and weak politicians, and not by the army. While it seemed that there was scope for a new political and social order in 1919, that was to be nullified by the 'stab in the back' legend and the economic and social effects of the war.

2   'Bismarck failed to resolve Germany's domestic problems after 1871.' How far do you agree with this claim?

3   'A modern monarch, determined to lead Germany into a new era.' How far do you agree with this assessment of the Emperor Wilhelm II in the years before the onset of general war in 1914?

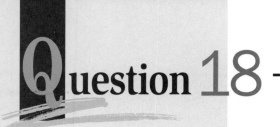
How far was there the likelihood of political revolution in Germany by 1914?

Tackling the question

As a result of rapid industrialisation and demographic change, Germany experienced social tensions which, by 1914, were perceived by some of those in whom power had been vested by the Emperor to threaten such political disruption that revolution might occur. The Imperial Constitution of 1871 had not established responsible government, although universal male suffrage had been granted for the elections of members to a Reichstag that had limited powers. With the passage of time, socialists were increasingly elected to the Reichstag, so that by 1912 they had a larger representation than any other political party. Thus, the Reich government could not rely on a stable conservative-minded majority in the Reichstag. Despite a rapid transformation from an agrarian to an industrial economy, German society remained rigidly stratified and was not experiencing much upward social mobility. Opportunities for economic betterment and social advance were limited in Wilhelmine Germany. Migrants to industrial centres, seeking a better life, found themselves working long hours in unhealthy conditions, enduring poor housing and an inadequate diet, their initial expectations disappointed. Any hope of socialists securing decisions that would modify or undermine established social, economic, cultural and political hierarchical patterns seemed remote. This essay will consider whether the discontents were so grave that political revolution was a distinct possibility by 1914.

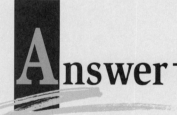

Answer

The quotation from Max Weber may help to establish the point that, despite political frustrations, most socialists in Germany remained non-revolutionary. Even so, how did those who wielded power in Germany regard those who were excluded from political influence? What effect may their anxieties have had upon the German government's attitude to the threat of war in 1914?

In 1917 Max Weber claimed that it was the legacy of Bismarck's political ascendancy before 1890 that Germany was 'a nation accustomed to submit ... to anything which was decided for it'. Despite a social and demographic transformation accompanying rapid industrialisation, the Kaiser's government – not responsible to a Reichstag elected by adult male suffrage – remained conservatively Junker dominated, out of kilter with a legislature where socialists (SPD) were the largest party by 1912. Although there was unrelenting governmental hostility towards them before 1914, the socialists remained moderate and non-revolutionary, reluctant to exploit a government lacking consistent central direction and led by a temperamental and notoriously indiscreet Emperor.

Nevertheless, such were the anxieties of the political and social élite in the Kaiser's entourage at the failure to crush the political opposition, that the possibility of victory in a patriotic war producing unity of purpose tempted the government to discourage a diplomatic resolution of Austro-Serb tensions, which were soon to precipitate a general conflict in late July 1914.

The basis for authoritarian government was established in the Imperial Constitution (1871), fashioned by Bismarck. Notwithstanding a Reichstag elected by manhood suffrage, there was no responsible government. Indeed, the Reichstag had few powers of initiative and no right of interpellation. Constantly threatened with dissolution, its political parties ruthlessly manipulated by Bismarck, the Reichstag desisted from opposing the authority of the state. Ostensibly, a federal system obtained, with individual states enjoying a considerable degree of autonomy, but the 45-member Bundesrat, the Federal Council, gave Prussia – with its restricted franchise ensuring Junker domination – 17 seats, sufficient to ensure that constitutional amendments were blocked. However, considerable powers were left to individual states, including the financial prerogative of collecting direct taxation – a privilege that caused acute financial difficulties in the Wilhelmine period, when increased rearmament had to be financed. After 1890 especially, the prevailing ultra-conservative influence of the Junkers in the army, the government and the bureaucracy was to become increasingly incompatible with the social and economic developments reflected in the composition of a Reichstag with restricted powers.

Now consider the constitutional basis for authoritarian government in Germany. What was the nature of the Imperial Constitution of 1871 and how did Bismarck manipulate it to his political advantage? What ultimately were the consequences of allowing the states alone to levy direct taxation?

Rapid industrialisation stimulated working-class consciousness and prompted the founding of the Social Democratic Party (SPD) in 1875. Its support burgeoned as Bismarck submitted the new party to twelve years of remorseless persecution (1878–90), but in the 1890 election it won 19.7% of the vote and 35 seats. Bismarck's introduction of social insurance legislation – Sickness Insurance Law (1883), an amended Accident Insurance Law (1884) and Old Age and Disability Insurance (1889) – seems to have weakened the militancy of the party during the Wilhelmine period. Nevertheless, support for socialism increased subsequently, providing evidence that such concessions were yielded because of the strength of the movement.

Examine the origins and development of the Social Democratic Party (SPD). Show how Bismarck attempted unsuccessfully to contain support for the SPD by the use of the carrot and the stick.

Apart from Caprivi's unsuccessful attempts to reconcile the classes in a period of global economic malaise (1890–4), the Kaiser did not disguise his hostility to the SPD. The Reichstag

How did the German government treat the socialists, subsequent to Bismarck's resignation in

1890? How did the Erfurt Programme not faithfully reflect the views of many socialists about the way change might be carried out? What evidence was there of rising living standards between 1895 and 1907? How did SPD candidates fare in the election of 1912?

refrained from endorsing his recurrent efforts to restrict the franchise, conscious that to do so would further diminish its influence. Intemperately, the Emperor repeatedly denounced socialists as 'enemies of the state'. Such provocation stirred little revolutionary fervour in the ranks of the SPD. Although the Erfurt Programme (1891) reiterated the party's commitment to Marxism, in practice the SPD remained reformist rather than revolutionary. Many of its influential adherents were trade unionists, who, in the Wilhelmine period, won concessions and practical gains from employers. Moreover, the working classes were docile, placated by generally slowly rising living standards. Average wages rose 37.5%, while living costs rose 22% in the period 1895–1907. However, conspicuous numerical support for SPD candidates – 4.25 million votes secured 110 seats in the Reichstag (1912) – was erroneously equated in some governmental circles with revolutionary menace.

Why did Germany experience acute financial problems? In large part because of the federal tax structure as defined in the Constitution of 1871. What political impact did the Tariff Law of 1902 have?

Additionally, Germany's financial problems exacerbated the government's problems. The federal tax structure, as defined in the Constitution (1871), restricted the government to dependence upon indirect taxes and to matricular contributions from the separate states. The Tariff Law (1902) – designed in part to promote a union of agrarian and industrial interests – did little to relieve Bülow's financial problems as Germany embarked upon an expensive forward foreign policy, requiring enhanced military and naval expenditure. Indeed, the regressive nature of the Tariff Law assisted the SPD to gain 25 seats in the 1903 election. Moreover, the opposition of the electorally significant SPD, the Zentrum and the Progressives after 1909 reinforced the inconsistency between the Reichstag's increasingly radical composition and the deep conservatism of imperial government.

Consider the factors that precluded opponents of the German government from exploiting its weaknesses.

Yet the opposition failed to exploit the government's shortcomings and restrict the Kaiser's powers under the Constitution. The Kaiser's irresponsible comments to the *Daily Telegraph* (1908) enraged many in the Reichstag and irretrievably weakened relations between the Emperor and his Chancellor, Bülow, but they did not lead to permanent constitutional change, which would have increased the Reichstag's power at the expense of the monarchical principle. Bismarck's legacy had been an immature legislature, pitilessly manipulated by him in the government's interest, untutored in methods of budgetary control and reduced to mere economic interest groups, which, after 1890, found it difficult to unite as a parliamentary body on crucial issues.

After 1912, despite the leftward shift in German politics as a result of its new accretion of electoral strength, the Reichstag remained loath to challenge the government. Indeed, having supported an unprecedentedly large peacetime military budget (October 1913) – even though the SPD had earlier consistently opposed military spending – it was unable subsequently to discipline the army over the Zabern affair (November 1913). Nevertheless, what tentative suggestions there were by 1913 for an advance towards collective ministerial responsibility in the federal government met with no positive response from the Kaiser's government. Such pressure inclined the government towards the notion of a patriotic war as a dubious response to the failure to silence opposition. Any notion of political revolution in 1914 was more in the minds of an anxious government and its Junker supporters, sustained by a precariously anachronistic Constitution, than in the subversive resolve of an opposition, including the SPD, representing the majority in the Reichstag. In the event, when war came (August 1914), the SPD, along with other political parties, readily endorsed war credits and subscribed to the *Burgfrieden*.

> Conclude by showing that, as war approached, the Reichstag failed to challenge the government effectively. So was the prospect of revolution more in the minds of those who wielded power than in the minds of those excluded from power? Give evidence to support your conclusions.

Related questions

1   What were the characteristics and the consequences of the political system established in Germany by the Imperial Constitution of 1871?

The centre of political gravity in the Imperial Constitution was not in the Reichstag, elected by universal male suffrage, but in the hands of the Emperor. The executive was not responsible to the Reichstag. The Emperor alone could nominate and dismiss the Reich Chancellor and other ministers. The Social Democratic Party, widely supported by the growing industrial proletariat, had become the major party in the Reichstag by 1912, but did not change the constitutional position. However, even authoritarian rulers often seek ways to legitimate their policies by gaining the support of most of their subjects. Germany's quasi-autocratic regime, equipped with a Reichstag the powers of which were limited, sought solutions to the empire's political contradictions outside of the existing political structure. Germany's assertive policies abroad, especially after 1900, may be evidence of this. The objective was to win patriotic support that transcended party loyalties. By making the points raised above, you will have shown your grasp of the scope of the question posed.

  Examine each of those points in detail, beginning in the second paragraph. Show how the Emperor's authority contrasted with the restricted powers of the Reichstag. In respect of the latter, show that you know the nature of the political parties within the Reichstag. Now show that you know of the characteristics of the Social Democratic Party – it was not narrowly political, but extended its involvement to sports, leisure, extra-mural education and other outlets for working-class energies. Is it appropriate to describe the imperial regime as illiberal? It may be argued that it was illiberal enough to generate social and political dissent, but sufficiently liberal not to seek to eradicate all opposition. What impact did ostensibly non-political activities have on German politics? Consider the roles of the patriotic leagues like the Pan-German League, the Navy League and the Defence League. They served as indicators of levels of social and ideological conflict in German society. In conclusion, it may be argued that the political, social and economic division in German society reflected similar divisions in French and British society. On the other hand, it may seem that Germany's internal tensions were more acute because of the rapidity of economic change in the empire and the absence of a developed parliamentary system. Thus, Germany's circumstances did little to encourage a spirit of compromise and moderation.

2   What problems faced Bismarck in Germany in the period 1871–90 and how successful was he in dealing with them?

3   'Autocratic, militaristic and seemingly strong. In reality Wilhelmine Germany suffered acutely from internal divisions and dissent.' How far do you agree with this judgement?

What were the consequences of the
Treaty of Berlin of 1878?

Tackling the question

After 1815 it may be held that for several decades the Concert of Europe preserved the status quo. By 1854, on the eve of the Crimean War, Europe territorially was very much as it had been in 1815. Yet all the time there was a deep-rooted anxiety that the Ottoman Empire might collapse and that its dissolution would dangerously aggravate existing rivalries among the powers in the Balkans. The disappearance of the Ottoman Empire would create a vast power vacuum where a variety of peoples speaking a variety of dialects – Bulgars, Greeks, Serbs, Macedonians and Albanians, to name some – were intensely jealous of each other. Yet the empire, against all expectations, was to survive throughout the nineteenth century, albeit reduced at different stages – in 1830 when Greece became independent, and in 1878 in the Treaty of Berlin when the *de facto* independence of certain parts of the empire was recognised as independent *de jure*. Its administration was always conspicuously incompetent and corrupt, but in a crisis it was able to survive because it usually found European powers prepared to support it. *In extremis* it seemed to be able to depend on the tenacity and brutality of its soldiers to rescue its authority when it was threatened.

There was a crisis in the 1850s when Russia decided to break with the consensus among the powers that, if humanly possible, the Ottoman Empire should be preserved. But with Russia's defeat in the Crimean War in 1856, the policy of maintaining the empire was reasserted, so that in the 1870s Austria-Hungary and Russia, with conflicting interests in the Balkans, were generally not prepared to push their rivalry to the point where war was the likely result. An agreement in 1877 enabled Russia to go to war with Turkey without Austrian interference, but when a victorious Russia imposed the Treaty of San Stefano in March 1878, its unacceptability to other powers provoked a serious diplomatic crisis that was ameliorated by the Treaty of Berlin of June 1878, the consequences of which are the subject of this essay. With the help of this agreement, the Ottoman Empire in the Balkans was able to survive, albeit precariously, into the twentieth century.

Answer

Guidance notes

The Treaty of Berlin (1878) may be considered as exemplifying the efficacy of congress diplomacy in defusing a major international crisis. In European terms, territorially it was an improvement on the earlier Treaty of San Stefano (March 1878), which was emphatically rejected by the powers as persuasive evidence

Show that, while the Treaty of Berlin may have suited the major powers – Russia excepted – it had serious shortcomings from the viewpoint of the peoples of the Balkans. Nevertheless, to what extent may it be said that the treaty helped to bring a durable stability to the region?

of Russia's long-established resolve to fill any political vacuum arising from the collapse of the Ottoman Empire in the Balkans. Locally, the treaty fashioned a grim heritage of unfulfilled territorial ambition, which might have been lessened had the Treaty of San Stefano proved durable. In its aftermath, Bismarck sought patiently, but ultimately unsuccessfully, to establish more than a tenuous diplomatic relationship with Russia, smarting from having to forfeit territory despite victory in war. By 1894 France was the beneficiary of his failure. That most of the treaty's terms were observed for more than 30 years owed much to the powers' preoccupation with extra-European interests for most of the period 1880–1905. Russia's defeat at Japan's hands (1904–5) preceded a resumption of its interest in the Balkans, with dire consequences for the stability of the region and, ultimately, European peace.

Explain why the Treaty of San Stefano of March 1878 was unsatisfactory to most of the major powers. Therefore, how did the Treaty of Berlin suit the major powers?

To the powers, the Treaty of San Stefano was unacceptable because the creation of the 'big' Bulgaria, stretching from the Danube to the Aegean, seemed to portend a vast extension of Russian influence in the Balkans. Moreover, Russia had reneged on its agreement in the Convention of Budapest (January 1877) to cede Bosnia-Herzegovina to Austria-Hungary. The trisection of Bulgaria checked Russia's alarming pretensions. Britain and Austria strengthened their positions as countervailing powers in the Near East, the former by gaining Cyprus in a separate convention and the latter by occupying and administering, but not annexing, Bosnia-Herzegovina. Germany, without territorial ambitions in the region, was relieved that the crisis had been resolved without an Austro-Russian war. France, although a rival of Britain in the eastern Mediterranean, shared Britain's anxieties at the potential danger of Russian penetration of that area. Thus, the settlement at Berlin suited the conveniences of the powers.

Explain why the Treaty of Berlin was unsatisfactory to the peoples of the Balkans. Give examples of how these small powers were displeased with the treaty.

Locally, however, the treaty left many problems unresolved. Certainly, Turkey had forfeited half of its European territory, but where its writ still ran, misrule – and therefore scope for discontent – would remain. Ethnographically, the 'big' Bulgaria was superior to the truncated Bulgaria authorised at Berlin. The return of Macedonia to the Turks was to create problems for the future. Serbia resented not acquiring Bosnia-Herzegovina. Romania was not satisfied with Dobruja as compensation for ceding Bessarabia to Russia. The failure to demarcate the Greek–Montenegrin frontier was long to be a source of tension. Moreover, the Greeks were disappointed at not receiving Crete. Indeed, no Balkan state was comfortably reconciled to the territorial arrangements made for it, so that, in essence, the treaty was fragile and contained the seeds for later Balkan conflicts. Nevertheless, the spontaneous union of autonomous eastern Roumelia and Bulgaria (1885), although evidence of the shortcomings of the 1878 treaty, proved to be the only territorial change before 1912–13. Despite Austria-Hungary's annexation of Bosnia-Herzegovina (1908) – a violation of the treaty – it did not change the reality of Austrian rule there.

The treaty had far-reaching consequences for the European states system. In 1878 Bismarck, host for the Congress, was blamed by Russia for the latter's diplomatic defeat. Moreover, Russo-German relations were soon to suffer because of a tariff 'war', which in 1887 weakened Bismarck's anxious efforts to buttress his alliance system with the Reinsurance Treaty. Arguably, such an agreement could scarcely be durable as it was contrary to the spirit, although not the letter, of the Austro-German Treaty (1879). Despite Bismarck's restoration of the Dreikaiserbund (1881), Russo-German relations were always precarious after 1878 – a factor that eventually worked to France's advantage when, after 1888, it gave valuable financial aid to Russia in order to advance Russia's economic development.

> What impact did the Treaty of Berlin have on Germany's relations with Russia?

The interests of the major powers – except Austria-Hungary – in pursuing competitive territorial expansion in Africa and Asia for two decades before 1905 distracted their attention from the Balkans and probably helped to make the Berlin settlement the more lasting. The Berlin Colonial Conference (1884–5) heralded the partitioning of most of Africa north of the Zambesi among the powers, and acquisitiveness in China threatened a 'scramble' that was thwarted only by the Boxer Rebellion (1900). Russia's quest for the 'warm water' port of Port Arthur (gained in 1898) and its efforts to extend its influence in Persia and Afghanistan, drew it away from a vigorous pursuit of its traditional objectives in the Balkans. In consequence, when Turkey defeated Greece (1897) there was no serious threat to the status quo in the region, as there might have been had the circumstances been as highly charged as they were during the 1870s.

> What impact did extra-European imperial expansion have upon the preservation of the status quo in the Balkans?

After its defeat at Japan's hands (1904–5), Russia began again to promote its interests in the Balkans. In the wake of the seizure of power by the Karageorgevic dynasty in Serbia (1903), Austro-Serb relations deteriorated. The consolidation of the alliance system occasioned by Britain's *ententes* with France (1904) and Russia (1907) increased the prospect of Austro-Russian misunderstanding. Following the Bosnian crisis (1908), Russia increasingly identified itself with the protection of Slav interests, thus diminishing Austro-Russian resolve to preserve the status quo. In

> What factors precipitated the collapse of the provisions of the Treaty of Berlin after 1905?

1912–13 the Balkan powers themselves ousted Turkey from the region, aided diplomatically – initially, but not ultimately – by the endeavours of the powers in the Treaty of London (1912). Nevertheless, remaining tensions in the Balkans contributed to the crisis after the assassinations at Sarajevo (28 June 1914), which precipitated European war (1914–18).

Related questions

1 How did a Balkan crisis in July 1914 precipitate a European war, when two earlier crises (in 1908–9 and 1912–13) did not?

After 1905, following years of uneasy Austro-Russian accord over the Balkans, there was a progressive decline in that relationship. This manifested itself in a series of crises, each more serious than the one preceding it, which culminated in general war in 1914. The traditional Austro-Russian rivalry in the region was aggravated not only by Austria-Hungary's precarious stability, which seemed directly threatened by an implacably hostile Serbia, but also by Russia's conviction that its status as a major power depended upon its ability to protect its established interests in south-east Europe. The crises of 1908–9 and 1912–13 were able to be resolved diplomatically – the latter barely so – but diplomatic solutions in the aftermath of the assassinations at Sarajevo on 28 June 1914 were not sought vigorously, while the powers took active steps to defend what they perceived to be their national interests. Austria-Hungary's decision to go to war with Serbia brought about a conflict that could not remain indigenous to the Balkans.

Examine the role of each of Germany, Russia and Austria-Hungary in the successive Balkan crises. Thus, for example, demonstrate that Russia could not risk war in 1908, did not need to do so in 1912 and 1913, and could hardly avoid war in July–August 1914. Before 1914, south-east Europe had survived two acute crises without war, but each of those crises had dramatically heightened European tensions. After the Bosnian crisis of 1908 and 1909, Russia could not afford to be worsted again in the Balkans. By 1914, conscious of the direly threatening centrifugal forces within its empire, Austria-Hungary felt an imperative need to crush Serbia. Germany too felt endangered – it entertained an exaggerated fear of Russia's potential militarily; it could not afford to abandon its sole reliable ally; internal social and political tensions may have tempted the Kaiser and his advisers to risk a war that might bind German people together in a common enterprise. Additionally, Serbia, assertive and volatile, appeared to be poised to administer the *coup de grâce* to Austria-Hungary. The earlier crises had exacerbated the tensions that in July 1914 dissolved into a war, when the major powers lost confidence in the efficacy of diplomacy as a means of protecting their national interests.

2 Examine the view that, above all else, it was Austria-Hungary's concern with the Balkans that led to the outbreak of war in Europe in 1914.

3 'At the Congress of Berlin (1878) the complex Eastern Question was handled successfully by negotiation.' How far do you agree with this claim?

Question 20

'The powder keg of European politics.'
Show how the plight of the Balkans contributed
to the outbreak of general war in 1914.

Tackling the question

There is a widely held view that Germany was mainly to blame for ensuring that the July crisis of 1914 led to a general war. In 1919 the victorious powers certainly believed so. After its defeat in 1918, Germany rejected the notion of exclusive responsibility with its Allies for bringing war about in 1914, as insisted upon in Article 231 of the Treaty of Versailles (1919). Rather, it argued, no single power could be held responsible – a sentiment endorsed from radically different standpoints by President Wilson and Lenin. Wilson blamed secret diplomacy and the acquisitiveness of the European powers before 1914, while Lenin regarded the conflict as an inevitable struggle between inherently aggressive capitalist powers. Although Lloyd George retrospectively claimed that Germany was not uniquely responsible – the powers had 'slithered over the brink' into it – Albertini's view in the early 1940s was that Germany pursued a high-risk policy that made it especially culpable. This latter view drew attention to Germany's policies before and during the war.

After Taylor's claim that 'the sole cause for the outbreak of war was the Schlieffen Plan', Fritz Fischer in 1961 sensationally asserted that Germany sought war and was possessed of expansionist aims – not dissimilar to Hitler's later – hoping to ameliorate internal social, economic and political tensions. That Germany could be held responsible – if any power could – for the outbreak of the First World War generated much indignation because it was at that time still a political issue. However, from an academic viewpoint, Fischer's contentions led to a considerable interest in the hitherto neglected history of the Wilhelmine Empire. Recently, Wehler has emphasised 'the primacy of domestic policies' in determining Germany's high-risk policy in 1914. Herwig has stressed the deep anxieties – even paranoia – of the ruling élite, who were nevertheless still 'dominated by a remarkable egotism'. He insists that the escape from Germany's political contradictions was, to the German government, only to be achieved by 'a mad bolt' – that is, the high-risk policy. Fischer, who has also analysed the decision making of the Russian government in 1914, demonstrates that 'mad bolt' policy when he argues persuasively that, to the Germans, the Tsar's mobilisation order was provocative beyond endurance only because by then Germany was resolved on waging war and was, for domestic reasons, merely awaiting a pretext for beginning it.

nswer

What factors increased dangers to European peace after 1890?

Within six weeks of the assassinations of Franz Ferdinand and his wife at Sarajevo (28 June 1914), the major powers were embroiled in a general war, the immediate steps to which seemingly following a pre-ordained path. While the potentially unsatisfactory terms of the Treaty of Berlin (1878), the partial collapse of Bismarck's system of alliances before 1890, and the gathering gloom in Anglo-German relations after 1890 are all elements in the background to war in 1914, more immediately, when Russia was forced to withdraw from the Far East (1905) and Britain made *ententes* with France (1904) and Russia (1907), most diplomatic disputes thereafter occurred in or near to Europe. It did not need the *ententes* to be transformed into alliances for the tenor of European relationships to change ominously. Equally important, after years of accord over the Balkans, there was a marked deterioration in Austro-Russian relations, which presaged the first major crisis in Europe since 1878. Moreover, the precarious stability of Austria-Hungary seemed directly threatened by an implacably hostile Serbia, whose vigorous nationalistic spirit simultaneously posed a potential danger to the Ottoman Empire, within which Slavs still yearned for their freedom.

Show how the Austro-Russian accord, which helped to minimise tensions in the Balkans, collapsed early in the first decade of the twentieth century. Note the increased militancy of Slav nationalism. Why did relations between Austria-Hungary and Russia become sour after the Bosnian crisis of 1908–9?

A prerequisite for minimising tensions in the Balkans was Austro-Russian accord. In May 1897 they had agreed to maintain the status quo there. In the wake of a Macedonian revolt, in the Murzsteg Punctuation (1903), Austria and Russia agreed jointly to supervise reforms in Macedonia, in effect imposed by them on the Sultan. Yet the violent termination of the pro-Austrian Obrenovic dynasty in Serbia (1903) was soon followed by Serb advocacy of the Yugoslav concept of uniting Serbs, Croats and Slovenes in a federal state – a notion prejudicial to Austria's security. The threat persuaded Austria's foreign minister, Aehrenthal, to precipitate the annexation by Austria of Bosnia-Herzegovina, occupied by it since 1878. In 1908 Izvolski, Russia's foreign minister, without consulting his government, agreed to this in return for Austria giving Russia diplomatic support for the opening of the Straits to Russian warships. After the annexation, Austria failed to give this support. This was a humiliation for Russia that undermined their recent co-operation.

Discuss the responses of all the powers to the tensions in the Balkans in the aftermath of the Bosnian crisis of 1908–9. How did Germany react to its failure to undermine the Anglo-French *entente* of 1904?

Tensions in the Balkans were exacerbated after 1908, especially between Austria and Serbia, each of which regarded the other as resolved on its destruction. Conscious of the danger from Austria, Serbia – convinced that only the break-up of Austria-Hungary could give it security – strengthened ties with Russia. Russia, for its part, became convinced that Austro-German co-operation during the crisis of 1908 boded ill for the future securing of its vital interests in the Balkans. Moreover, the lack-lustre response of Britain and France to Russia's Balkan policies encouraged Germany to exploit France's military intervention in Morocco (April 1911) as a breach of the Algeciras agreement (1906) and a Franco-German agreement (1909), in the hope of undermining the Anglo-French *entente*. That Germany failed in this reinforced its sense of being 'encircled' – a feeling already intensified by the Anglo-German naval race – and made Austro-German actions in the volatile Balkans even less predictable than hitherto.

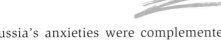

It was no comfort to any major power that Italy should by force wrest Tripolitania and Cyrenaica from Turkey (1911–12), because it exposed Turkey's military impotence even at the hands of a weak power. It encouraged the Balkan states to combine to oust Turkish power (1912). This they had achieved within months of their agreement. However, both Austria and Russia were alarmed: Austria because it could not accept an expanded Serbia with access to the Adriatic, and Russia because a pro-Austrian Bulgaria, possessing Constantinople, would be a threat to its security. If the co-operation of the powers in the Treaty of London (May 1913) diminished Austro-Russian anxieties, the Second Balkan War (June–August 1913), humiliating Bulgaria and further expanding Serbia, left a legacy of acute tensions internationally. Not only were influential elements in Austria resolved to crush Serbia, but, to Russia's alarm, Germany, by proffering military assistance to Turkey, seemed potentially to have the capacity to seize the Straits. Moreover, in September 1912, Poincaré of France had assured Russia that France would fulfil its obligations to Russia if, in a Balkan crisis, Russia found itself at war with the central powers.

> What were the seriously damaging effects of Italy's acquisition of Tripolitania and Cyrenaica – that is, Libya – in 1911 and 1912? Discuss its impact on the Balkan states. Explain the consequences of the Balkan wars of 1912 and 1913.

Russia's anxieties were complemented by Germany's fear that Russia, having reformed its armies after 1905, was potentially irresistible. In addition, it also worried that Serbia's burgeoning strength would, in the event of war, concentrate Austria's attentions southwards, thus depriving Germany of indispensable Austrian support on its eastern front, should there be war with Russia. This encouraged Germany to acquiesce in Austria's resolve to crush Serbia after the assassinations at Sarajevo. The Kaiser gambled that Russia would not intervene. That Serbia responded unacceptably to Austria's ultimatum of 23 July prompted an Austro-Serb war (28 July), which determined Russia, confident of French support, to defend Serbia, believing that otherwise its influence in the Balkans would be completely undermined. The concatenation of events thereafter activated Germany's Schlieffen Plan. Russia and Germany went to war (1 August). Almost

> How did Germany's anxieties contribute significantly to the tensions in the Balkans by 1914? How did Germany gamble in July 1914?

How did Austria's and Russia's intentions in 1914 contribute to the outbreak of a general war?

immediately, France was inevitably involved (3 August). Germany's prerequisite of defeating France before attacking Russia necessitated an invasion of Belgium, ostensibly Britain's justification for entering the conflict (4 August).

Europe was to pay a high price for the diminishing importance of extra-European colonial rivalry after 1907. Crises in the Balkans could be indigenous to that region only if the powers declined to intervene actively. That Austro-Russian intervention did not go beyond diplomatic efforts (1912–13) enabled Balkan tensions to be contained temporarily. After 28 June 1914 neither Austria nor Russia was willing to avoid its respective intention of destroying or protecting Serbia, so that a wider conflict, involving the major powers, almost inevitably arose from strife in a region which, after 1907, had become, in M.S. Anderson's phrase, 'the powder keg of European politics'.

Related questions

1 To what extent did militarism contribute to the outbreak of general war in 1914?

In 1914 the relationship between military planning and decision making in each combatant state was complex and determined not only by the position of the army and navy in society, but also by the extent to which civilian government exercised control. In addition, decisions were influenced by the character and implications of programmes for armaments, strategies and precise operational intentions. The degree to which each society was fashioned by militaristic values influenced a state's readiness to accept the prospect of conflict. All states in 1914 were preparing for war, even though they might not necessarily have been seeking it. Britain wished to avoid war, but took few steps to do so. France sought the recovery of Alsace-Lorraine, but was loath to start a conflict which, assisted by allies, might achieve that objective. Russia might have felt that failure to protect Serbia from Austro-Hungarian aggression would jeopardise its status as a great power, but, preoccupied with acute domestic problems, it was not seeking to be involved in conflict. Germany's internal tensions, together with its preoccupation with 'encirclement' and fears that France's and Russia's military strength was increasing to the disadvantage of the central powers, might have prompted it to entertain war before Russia became unstoppable.

A militaristic ethos is invariably accompanied by an arms race. This there certainly was in 1914. All powers were engaged in it. Retrospectively, Lord Grey of Falloden wrote that 'the moral is obvious; it is that great armaments lead inevitably to war'. We may contest this. After all, the Cold War, accompanied as it was by a terrifying competition in manufacturing highly technological weaponry, did not lead to the war that many half-suspected it would.

Arguably, in 1914 it was not the scale of armaments that caused war, but the nature of the rivalries between the powers, which was expressed in military preparedness. Of all the powers in 1914, Germany is often considered to have been imbued with a military spirit – there is a view that the Kaiser might have been more influenced by his military advisers than by members of his civilian government. The brutality of the implementation of the Schlieffen Plan gave that impression to contemporaries and was amply reflected in Asquith's declaration to the House of Commons in February 1915 that 'we shall never sheathe the sword, which we have not lightly drawn, until the military domination of Prussia is wholly and finally destroyed'.

2 Why were the affairs of the Balkans of increasing concern to Russia and Austria-Hungary before 1914?

3 'Germany should bear the responsibility for the outbreak of a general war in 1914.' How far do you agree with this assertion?

Question 21

'A disappointed liberal.'
How far is this a valid judgement on the reign of
Tsar Alexander II of Russia (1855–81)?

Tackling the question

Tsar Alexander II has been dubbed the 'Tsar liberator'. If to be a 'liberator' implies the granting of political freedom to his people, Alexander was not such. Like his predecessors – and, indeed, his successors – he was convinced that it was a precondition of his empire's coherence and well-being that there should be no sharing of political power. His declaration in March 1856 that 'it is much better that this [the emancipation of the peasants] come from above, than from below' underlined his determination to retain full control in his own hands. In truth, Alexander's early years in the service of his father suggest that he was unlikely to embrace notions of political freedom for his people. Since about 1840 he had taken part in civil and military affairs, accepting without demur the autocratic course set out by his father, Nicholas I. He presided over most of the secret committees on matters related to the peasantry and participated in seeking to ensure that the rigorous censorship before his accession was imposed.

However, defeat in the Crimean War alerted in him a perception that the domestic political course associated with his father was in a state of crisis. It was not the disposition of the new Tsar that was to lead to reform, but what he felt was an inescapable necessity for change, which, if neglected, could lead to the collapse of tsarist autocracy. The word glasnost – meaning 'thaw' – has been attributed to the year 1856. Censorship was relaxed and an impetus thereby given to constructive proposals and plans which gave the impression that large-scale transformations were impending. Yet even amidst the excitement of anticipated change, Alexander would never allow his unlimited and unaccountable authority to be impaired. He stubbornly and consistently rejected the need for and the possibility of a constitution for Russia. Autocracy was, in his view, irreplaceable. Thus the concept of his being a 'liberator' did not go beyond improving the circumstances and material lot of his people, but denied any sharing of political power with his subjects.

Answer

Explain how the word 'liberal' is inappropriate as a description of Tsar Alexander II or, indeed,

No Russian Tsar – not even Nicholas II at the end of his turbulent reign – was prepared to shed his autocratic powers. Thus, none could be described as 'liberal', for that would have required a sharing of power and guarantees of certain civil freedoms – of speech, the press, assembly and association. Alexander II was convinced that the preservation and well-being of his vast, polyglot empire demanded the maintenance, even the enhancement, of his autocracy. That autocracy was threatened by the débâcle of the Crimean War (1854–6), so that the abolition of serfdom in 1861 was prompted by the urgent need to avoid widespread, potentially uncontrollable social unrest and to resolve Russia's fundamental social problem. Reform of the legal system, local government and the army – all of which ameliorated the conditions experienced by Alexander's subjects – were inescapable corollaries of the decision to abolish serfdom. They were liberalising measures, but in no way did they qualify the Tsar's absolute authority. Long before the end of his reign, he lamented that the changes which he had instituted had not removed dissatisfaction with his regime and threats to his personal safety. Exhausted by his conscientious labours, Alexander ultimately accepted Loris-Melikov's proposals for reform in 1881, but again they did not make any inroads into his absolute authority.

of any Tsar of Russia. Stress that, whatever measures were undertaken, they fell short of making political concessions that would have impaired his absolute authority.

Nicholas I, Alexander II's father, had been painfully aware of the problem of serfdom, with its profound social and economic consequences for Russia, but the fear of political collapse had dissuaded him from doing more than mitigating the sufferings of the serfs. The disaster of the Crimean War threatened social disorder and soon convinced Alexander that the abolition of serfdom could not be long delayed. He insisted that it should be accomplished from above by royal decree, the product of positive royal action, rather than from below, the consequence of irresistible pressure from a rebellious peasantry. This was consistent with the beliefs of a man who did not embrace liberal tenets, and who, during his father's reign, had not deviated from the oppressive course set by him. The abolition of serfdom was a pragmatic decision and not inspired by the political disposition of the Tsar.

What factors determined the decision to emancipate the serfs?

The edict abolishing serfdom in 1861 was substantially the work of liberal-minded bureaucrats. It was a compromise laboriously worked out with the nobility, who lost one-third of their lands. The emancipated peasantry soon discovered that personal freedom was too often accompanied by possession of insufficient, sometimes infertile, land and that repayment of the government indemnity threatened burdensome debt. Furthermore, freed household serfs usually enjoyed no land in their new freedom. Thus, the ending of serfdom did not always mitigate at all the harsh conditions of peasant life. Indeed, the disenchantment contributed to the development of the unrest that made the last

Examine the nature of the Edict of Emancipation of 1861. What were the effects of the measure on the peasantry? What were the longer-term implications of the edict?

decade of Alexander's reign one of simmering discontent and violence.

Consider critically other reforms, corollaries of the 1861 edict, and emphasise that the measures taken did not constitute an erosion of the Tsar's political authority.

Other reforms were unavoidable in the wake of emancipation and, taken together, aligned Russia more closely than hitherto with western European practice. In this respect the new judicial structure (1864), while authorising that elected JPs should deal with petty cases and that regular courts should deal with more serious offences, still required that political offences should be tried in camera. Thus, those who challenged the autocracy could still expect little mercy. In the reform of local government in 1864, elected *zemstva*, operating at local and provincial levels, facilitated a measure of popular participation and some responsibility for welfare services – education, rural medical and veterinary services. However, such freedom was inhibited by government-appointed provincial governors and the requirement to carry out orders from various ministries concerning recruitment, the billeting of soldiers and transport. The Municipal Statute (1870) conceded local self-government for towns where elected town councils – *dumas* – were analogous in function and status to district *zemstva*. The provision of water and paving, the lighting of roads and the organisation of hospitals and schools may have helped to improve social conditions, but they did not amount to any erosion of the Tsar's ultimate authority (as, indeed, they were not intended to).

Discuss the potentially radical implications of relaxing press censorship and improving access to and the quality of education – including the implications of providing scope for improving basic literacy in the army.

If certain changes may have benefited the material lot of the people, the relaxation of censorship early in the reign inevitably stimulated criticism of the regime. If it was viewed as a necessary safety valve immediately after Alexander's accession, criticism of the government's constructive measures by the late 1860s led to restrictions that merely fanned discontent. Improvements in education, while essential if Russia was to modernise, carried with them the prospect of a more informed population that was potentially more critical of the absolutism that Alexander wished to reinforce. Increased access to secondary education, the modernisation of syllabuses and enhanced academic freedom in universities promised much, but early expectations were not fulfilled and student unrest contributed to the widespread unease by the late 1860s. The reorganisation of the army after the disaster of the Crimean War, besides extending conscription to all and removing barbaric punishments, made provision for basic education for recruits, thus increasing literacy and the capacity to criticise the regime. That Alexander II should renege on some of his educational reforms and tighten censorship once more did nothing to allay discontent.

During the reign, reforms affected almost every aspect of Russian life. Yet the social and economic transformation was uneven and incomplete. Alexander feared and resisted any suggestion of political concessions to his people. By 1865, anxious to ensure that his autocratic powers remained unimpaired, he adamantly rejected demands for a central *Zemstvo*. Thus, the traditional autocratic simplicity of Russia remained intact. It was this reality that stirred student unrest and the founding of revolutionary societies. By the 1870s terrorism grew apace. Organisations like 'People's Freedom' saw assassination as a prelude to revolution.

> Why did Alexander II's efforts at reform fail to placate his people?

Repeated attempts on his life and widespread dissatisfaction with his rule eventually persuaded Alexander to undertake further reform. The huge burden he had personally assumed in administering and governing his vast empire was weakening the practice as well as the theory of autocracy. Yet even Loris-Melikov's creation of preparatory governmental commissions, comprising invited public figures of appropriate competence who were able to draft Bills, did not compromise the Tsar's power to decide whether the commissions met, what they discussed and whether their draft Bills became law. Alexander would never grant a constitution. He remained convinced of the efficacy of tsarist autocracy. His personal disappointment was that whatever reforms he had initiated had done little to reconcile his people to his rule.

> Illustrate Alexander's inflexibility in defence of his autocracy by reference to the nature of the Loris-Melikov reforms at the end of his reign.

Related questions

1 'An unenlightened despot.' How far do you agree with this view of Tsar Nicholas I of Russia (1825–55)?

Even after 1906, the Tsar retained the title 'autocrat', although under pressure of events he had forfeited the adjective 'unlimited'. If Nicholas I was an 'unlimited autocrat', he did not preside over a despotism where neither law nor custom protected persons and property from completely arbitrary rule. Indeed, Nicholas I's Fundamental Law of 1832 proclaimed that 'positive laws emanated from autocratic power'. Thus, a standard existed whereby the legality of his Acts could be assessed. Nevertheless, the victims of his repression were hardly likely to draw a nice distinction between despotism and absolutism. If to be 'enlightened' means to perceive the scale of the problems facing one's country and to devise effective means for remedying those problems, it may be said of Nicholas that he was painfully aware of the former, but failed in respect of the latter to do more than invoke palliatives to meet his difficulties. Rather than an 'unenlightened despot', he may be described as a tormented, not unintelligent, autocrat, who was vainly seeking solutions to Russia's problems.

He was conscious of the grim plight of the peasantry, but did no more than tinker with the problem of serfdom by taking measures to ameliorate the conditions of the serfs. On the other hand, his odious system of internal security showed that those who were considered to be politically subversive could expect short shrift from the regime. The written word was especially suspect, although the repression did not prevent the flowering of a brilliant age for literature critical of the regime. Nicholas's rule was undoubtedly capricious and oppressive, but it cannot be compared to the appalling excesses of totalitarian regimes of the twentieth century. At the time, it compared unfavourably with what was known of law and politics in western Europe, where there was some sharing of political power. Nicholas I was supreme over institutions and laws, and was sustained by a Code of Laws that enshrined the unlimited authority of the autocratic ruler. In his relentlessly austere fashion and with his inflexible bent of mind, his rule failed to respond to necessary change, and with the Crimean War the social system over which he presided came to grief. Aware of Russia's acute problems, he opted for survival rather than for radical solutions that had unpredictable consequences for his autocracy.

2   'There was little to distinguish the plight of Russia at the end of his reign from what it had been at his accession.' How far is this a valid verdict on the reign of Tsar Alexander I of Russia (1801–25)?

3   'The Tsar Liberator.' How far may this title be appropriately applied to Tsar Alexander II of Russia?

Why was tsarism able to survive in 1905 but not in 1917?

Tackling the question

In his recent biography of Nicholas II, Dominic Lieven has demonstrated that in the Russian system of government before 1917 everything depended on the qualities of successive Tsars. If, like Nicholas II, the Tsar was weak and vacillating, even able advisers, like Witte and Stolypin, could find their plans and policies frustrated. Nicholas was always faithful to the domestic ideal of family life and seems to have regarded his conduct of affairs of state as an extension of his duties as a family man. Even in 1917, on the brink of abdication, he could write, 'I am responsible before God and Russia for everything that has happened and is happening', and that he had 'always been directed by the wish to preserve the Crown in the form in which he had inherited it from his father in order to hand it on in the same form to his son'. It was an outmoded vision, for Russia was experiencing unprecedented social change and fighting a modern technological mass war that required an executive authority for which his paternal approach to his duties was entirely inadequate.

It was not his *métier* to have to preside over a government where ministries were preoccupied with education, land tenure, communications and the advancement of industry and trade. In the civil service, aristocrats were being superseded by technical specialists and career bureaucrats, who were vastly increasing in number. This was not to Nicholas's liking. He was never able to cope with the monumental task of co-ordinating and leading the complex facets of modern government. There was no Imperial Chancellery or even a personal office where officials could brief him on draft policies. Instead, he became dependent on courtiers, who were easily able to poison his view of an able minister, like Witte or Stolypin. For respite from modern problems he looked to the army, the Church and the peasantry. He had enjoyed military life in his youth and his confidants were often soldiers. The Church and the peasantry were reassuring components of an older and simpler Russia. He relished journeying to provincial Russia to savour the devotion of his people. Thus he was incapable of comprehending the economic restructuring that was indissolubly linked to political change, or to survive an era of necessary transition that could not be smooth. Had he been more thoroughly prepared and possessed of better judgement and political flair than he was, it is still doubtful whether he could have coped with the awesome problems faced by his huge, heterogeneous, obsolete and unwieldy empire.

Answer

Use the introductory paragraph to contrast the situations in Russia in 1905 and 1917. Four parallel points are raised for each of 1905 and 1917, all of which will be analysed more fully in the body of the essay.

In 1905 a temporarily unnerved government overcame the threat posed by the concerted opposition of middle-class reformists, much of the peasantry and the small, but growing industrial proletariat, by making sufficient political concessions to divide its opponents and recover much of its threatened authority. In 1917, during a long and unsuccessful war, the pent-up frustration of workers and soldiers in Petrograd expressed itself in massive demonstrations that abruptly swept away tsarism. While in 1905 tsarism probably owed its survival initially to the adroit political manoeuvring of Witte, who had been assigned to find a solution by a reluctant Tsar, in 1917 a supine, incompetent government could display no such ingenuity. Despite the humiliations of the Russo-Japanese War (1904–5), the army remained firmly loyal to the Tsar and was instrumental in dispersing the incoherent, but protracted, resistance to the regime after 1905. In 1917 the support of the army was fast declining – an indispensable prop of the regime was wanting. Military defeat in 1905 had not directly impinged on the material circumstances of the masses. By 1917 food shortages, rising inflation, the growth of working-class militancy (despite the government's efforts to suppress political expression), acute war weariness and the manifest incompetence of the government precipitated tsarism's collapse.

Consider how the regime was saved in 1905. Show how the concessions that Witte obliged the Tsar to accept enabled a temporarily unnerved government to recover its authority by means of a policy of 'divide and rule'.

Although it may be argued that most strikes and demonstrations before 1905 were prompted by economic rather than political motives, in 1905 the Tsar was faced by a broadly based political revolt, its demands largely fashioned by liberals who were seeking reform rather than the destruction of tsarism. If the defeats in the war with Japan were 'the catalyst which transformed the complex pattern of social and political agitation into a direct attack on autocracy', in Acton's words, then the tragedy of 'Bloody Sunday' (January 1905) profoundly affected the political consciousness of all classes. A seemingly concerted resistance superseded hitherto disparate movements of protest. The regime was shaken, the more so because its proposed concession of a consultative *Duma*, which would not have been a concession of principle, was peremptorily declined (February 1905). In the event, Witte's pragmatism was sufficient to divide the opposition. The October Manifesto gave the middle classes, who were fearful of the undisciplined militancy that they had helped to unleash, scope for insisting that resistance was unnecessary. However, the principles enunciated in the Manifesto – a range of civil liberties, the promise of an elected legislative *Duma* – did not immediately allay public discontent. Indeed, unrest was exacerbated and the Tsar's regime remained fragile. Nevertheless, despite ominous rumblings of army mutinies, most soldiers remained sufficiently loyal to crush the resistance of the unpacified, to impose martial law in Poland and to deploy troops in the countryside to end the increasingly incoherent opposition. They removed the soviets and ended the guerrilla-like urban risings of December 1905.

In practice, the *Duma* Statute (February 1906) and the Fundamental Law (April 1906), which established an uneasy equilibrium between reform and reaction, represented a toehold for Nicholas II to reassert his resolve 'firmly and unflinchingly' to adhere to 'the principle of autocracy'. To this end the State Council was to be elevated to a second chamber – a conservative body, half appointed by the Tsar and designed to counterbalance any radical tendencies in the *Duma*. There was to be no responsible government. The Tsar retained an absolute right of veto. Article 87 permitted the Tsar to sanction laws when the *Duma* was prorogued or dissolved. The first and second *Dumas* (April–June 1906 and February–June 1907) – the first liberal dominated, the second more radical in composition – were peremptorily dismissed for resistance to the government, after which the franchise was manipulated to produce more malleable *Dumas* between 1907 and 1914. All this, combined with the use of martial law, fierce repression and widespread use of 'Stolypin's necktie', prompted a sense of betrayal among the workers, peasants and middle classes, which boded ill for tsarism should a deep crisis arise in the future. Nicholas had forfeited his people's trust and compounded his problems by reliance on talentless ministers after Stolypin's assassination in 1911. The social polarity, ingrained in Russian society, remained virtually undisturbed. As war approached, strikes multiplied and the *Okhrana* undermined the laws of association of 1906, which had conferred basic trade union rights. It is a matter of debate as to whether tsarism was riding for a certain fall by 1914.

Upon this flawed political foundation, Russia went to war in 1914. Despite energetic conservative agrarian reform initiated by Stolypin, and advances in education and provision of insurance for workers, the politically evolutionary path had not been followed. War would be disastrous if it were not rapidly victorious. Indeed, the war of attrition wore down Russian resolve inexorably and undermined any vestigial respect for Nicholas. Recurring military reverses led to increasing dissatisfaction with the government. Public organisations – like the War Industries Committee and the *zemstva* bodies – vastly more able to administer the war effort than the ministries, were officially snubbed as a threat to autocracy. Efforts through the Progressive Bloc in the Duma to obtain a government 'responsible to public opinion' failed. The Tsar's decision to take command at GHQ in 1915 not

Show how the breathing space achieved by the October Manifesto of 1905 was frittered away in the years before the outbreak of war in 1914. Thus, mistrust was sown and a sense of betrayal eroded the confidence of the Tsar's subjects.

What were the consequences of being involved in a war of attrition after 1914 which certainly did not go Russia's way? Consider all the political factors that diminished respect for the authority of the Tsar.

only removed a self-proclaimed autocrat from the centre of government, but conferred on Nicholas responsibility for military failure. In Petrograd, incompetent ministers presided, Rasputin's influence increased and the Tsar's absence magnified the unpopular Empress's authority.

Show how the growing misery of the people prompted the circumstances that led to the collapse of tsarism. Conclude by emphasising that the erosion of confidence in the Tsar's regime was a process that began almost immediately after the crisis of 1905.

Meanwhile, the people's plight worsened. Shortages, including that of food, intensified as communications broke down. The railway system could not cope with problems of distribution. The increasing concentration of workers in towns and large factories, working long hours in insanitary conditions, gave an impetus to political militancy, feared by the middle classes who had eventually recoiled from the violence of the masses in 1905. There was rampant inflation too. Tales of battlefield misery and desertion reached every village. 'Is this stupidity or treason?' cried Miliukov in the *Duma* in November 1916, fearing a political explosion. The demonstrations in Petrograd (February 1917), prompted by shortages, but also orchestrated in part by political militants, could not be contained by force because mutinous soldiers would not quell the disturbances. This was enough to end tsarism. In 1917 there could be no reliance on a loyal army to protect the Tsar. The sense of betrayal after 1905, combined with conspicuous political incompetence especially after 1914, was a recipe for tsarism's demise.

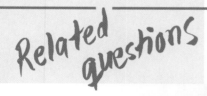

Related questions

1 Was tsarism doomed by 1914?

The cautious optimism generated by the Tsar's October Manifesto in 1905, which seemed to change Russia into a constitutional monarchy, rapidly declined as the government recovered its confidence and sought to minimise the impact of the concessions made. The newly created *Dumas* were soon elected on a restricted franchise. Nor was government responsible to the *Duma*. The Tsar was still styled 'autocrat', albeit without the adjective 'unlimited', after 1906. In reality there were still the gravest social impediments to Russia developing on liberal lines. In no other country in Europe were social tensions in the years before 1914 so marked as in Russia. Land problems remained unresolved. Humiliating conditions for workers in factories still prevailed. Widespread discontent was contained only by the coercive powers at the Tsar's disposal – the police, the Cossacks and, ultimately, the army. If by 1914 popular unrest, fuelled by the realisation that the heady aspirations of 1905 remained unfulfilled, jeopardised the regime's stability, the onset of general war brought military reverses, acute social and economic difficulties, and disastrous leadership that removed the last shreds of legitimacy.

That is not to say that there were no positive developments in Russia between 1905 and 1914. Certain ministries became subject to budgetary controls. The army was reformed after 1905. Primary education spread after 1908. Elected JPs were restored and the hated land captains forfeited their judicial role. Workers' insurance was introduced. However, reactionary influences in government still prevailed. The Tsar and his ministers and appointees to the State Council were not committed to reform. Land captains still had administrative capacities. There were restricted franchises for the *Dumas* and the district *zemstva*. There was no willingness by government to concede personal inviolability or religious toleration. Above all, there remained a social polarisation that continued insidiously to undermine the cohesion of society. By 1914 the future for tsarism looked bleak, with the Tsar's government enjoying less respect from its people than that of any other participant in the coming war.

2 'The ambiguous revolution.' How far is this a valid description of the events in Russia during 1905 and 1906?

3 'Witte and Stolypin came too late to save the tsarist regime.' How far do you agree with this verdict?

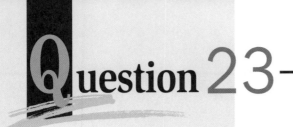

How fitting is it to describe the October Revolution in 1917 as 'Lenin's Revolution'?

Tackling the question

Now that communism in Russia has collapsed, scrutiny of Russian archives has produced a more critical view of Lenin than was once usually the case. The brutality of Stalin's regime was sometimes viewed as subverting the regime established by Lenin, whose premature death set the revolution on a path of which he would not have approved. Now there is an inclination to stress the continuity which, it is claimed, existed between the eras of Lenin and Stalin. The terrors of Stalin's times had their origins before 1924, it is averred. Until recent times, Lenin was seen as the instigator of a revolution which, whether it was liked or not, was a permanent feature of the international landscape. It proved not to be so. Indeed, its progressive degeneration over several decades was masked by censorship and propaganda eulogising the achievements of the Revolution of 1917. Lenin can now be seen as responsible for a 75-year aberration in Russian history, his application of Marxist principles fatally flawed even from the start. Inevitably this diminishes his reputation.

In addition, the selective use of Soviet archives has helped to portray him as one bent on the pursuit of power that was to be attained for its own sake. In its dogma and its pitiless application he seems to have shaped a Communist Party that reflected his own narrow character. For Lenin, the end justified the means and the loss of innocent lives was a small price to pay in pursuit of victory in the class struggle. It followed that he would not countenance the pleas of those, like Gorky, who wished to subject the *Cheka* to legal restraints. In 1922 he wrote, 'The more members of the reactionary bourgeoisie and clergy we manage to shoot the better.' Figes, author of *A People's Tragedy*, has estimated the total death toll between 1917 and 1921 as about 10 million. Certainly, most of the deaths were caused by famine and disease, although Figes believes that more died at the hands of the *Cheka* than in fighting the Whites. For national minorities, the revolutionary government was in effect colonialism. For the peasants, it was a restoration of a form of serfdom. For industrial workers, it represented more brutal exploitation than had been experienced in tsarist times. Thus, when Stalin eventually assumed Lenin's mantle, it is now often held that the former took over where the latter had left off. Since 1991 archival evidence has suggested that the Soviet system initiated by Lenin was worse than its severest critics previously suspected. At least his single-mindedness is a crucial facet of the question posed above.

Answer

The October Revolution would appear to be the product of the keen personal vision and implacable will of one man, Lenin. On his return to Russia in April 1917, he declared his uncompromising hostility to the Provisional Government. Even if one allows for the fluctuations in the Bolsheviks' fortunes during the summer of 1917, the power that Lenin sought was swiftly secured. Is there justification, therefore, in describing the October Revolution as Lenin's? Without denying the powerful influence that he brought to the events of 1917, it should not be assumed that the other Bolshevik leaders were without initiative or that the Bolshevik Party was lacking in vitality inside and outside of Petrograd. Moreover, the conditions for a seizure of power were favourable in 1917. The Provisional Government weakened its precarious authority by keeping Russia in the war, thus aggravating the existing miseries of the population, undermining the economy and increasing the disillusionment of a much battered army.

It may be argued that, when Lenin returned to Russia in April 1917, he transformed the political situation. Confident of his view of a revolutionary élite organised to seize power at the appropriate moment, he demanded, shrewdly but disingenuously, that all power should be vested in the soviets, perceiving that this appealed to the proletariat of Petrograd. He insisted that the war should be ended and all land nationalised. His strategy was accepted by the Bolshevik Party conference in April 1917. He was promptly 'occupying the ground towards which growing numbers of workers, soldiers and peasants were being drawn', in Acton's words. Yet it took time before the Bolsheviks were ready to seize power. The July Days were adjudged an inappropriate time, even though demonstrations showed that popular feeling was hostile to the government. Indeed, the Bolsheviks' inaction gave temporary confidence to the Provisional Government and forced Lenin into further exile. However, the government's revival was short lived. The war continued to go badly. The attempted rising by Kornilov in late August gave the Bolsheviks an opportunity to rally to the cause of defending Petrograd and to ensure that the taint of Kerensky's suspected initial collusion with Kornilov was exploited to his disadvantage. In September there was resistance within the party to Lenin's insistence that power should be seized – as late as October, Zinoviev and Kamenev still demurred. However, Kerensky's pre-emptive strike on the Bolsheviks removed choice and prompted the insurrection, inspired by Lenin, but in practice organised by Trotsky.

> The conventional view is to consider Lenin as central to the securing of the October Revolution. However, other factors should not be ignored – not only the contribution of other Bolshevik hierarchs and the activities of Bolshevik Party members and committees, but also, fundamentally, the conditions in Russia that made a revolution possible. However, that is not to represent Lenin's contribution as less than crucial.

> Consider the well-established perception of Lenin's indispensable contribution to the October Revolution.

Now discuss the calibre and contributions of other notable Bolsheviks, who, like Lenin, had returned from exile in 1917.

It does no justice to the other Bolshevik leaders or to the Bolshevik Party to give a monopoly of credit to Lenin for the October Revolution. Very active local Bolshevik committees and the astuteness of the Bolshevik leaders also had crucial parts to play. Trotsky was Lenin's intellectual equal, a consummate organiser and perhaps even more shrewd than Lenin in perceiving tactical opportunities. Kamenev was a dominant figure in the Petrograd Soviet, while Zinoviev was extremely capable at garnering popular support. Sverdlov was an all powerful figure in the Central Committee Secretariat. Like Lenin they all sought revolution and they were all talented at devising policies and organisation.

Show that there were times in 1917 when Lenin appeared to be endangering rather than advancing the chances of the Bolsheviks gaining power.

Indeed, they were not always well served by Lenin in 1917. In April they were justifiably alarmed at the precipitate way in which he demanded a seizure of power despite the Bolsheviks being a minority in the Petrograd Soviet. They felt that his undisguised relish for a European civil war, land nationalisation and the dictatorship of the proletariat could lose the party much support. The consequence of Lenin encouraging the street demonstrations in July was persecution of the party and Lenin's return to exile. Lenin might well have done mischief to the party's fortunes had the Central Committee acquiesced in his demand that power should be seized in September, when Kerensky would have still been strong enough to suppress the Bolsheviks.

How did the Bolshevik Party, through its innumerable local party committees, help to further the Bolshevik cause in 1917?

At this time the party as a whole did not lack vigour. In 1917 local committees of the party took decisions locally, despite the official requirement that they should always defer to central direction. Usually able to respond sensitively to local needs, many of the members were experienced and practical underground political workers not always impressed by the credentials of returned *émigrés*. By December 1917 they had recruited up to 300,000 members. Their role in bringing about revolution should not be underestimated.

Now consider the conditions in Russia in 1917, which suggest that the circumstances were tailor made for a dynamic revolutionary party to oust a beleaguered government.

However inspirational Lenin may have been – and not forgetting the indispensable support he had from immediate colleagues and local Bolshevik committees – the conditions for a seizure of power had to be fitting. The despair generated by the continuation of the war played into the hands of the Bolsheviks. There was little prospect of direct military intervention by Russia's allies to relieve its grim plight. Food shortages were aggravated by the peasants being loath to trade their produce when there were few consumer goods available, and by priority being given to the army's needs. Transport was disrupted, communications were dislocated.

In industry, shortages of raw materials reduced production and increased unemployment. Inflation outpaced wages. Many firms were forced to close down. The middle classes were anxious as the real value of their dividends fell. As the winter of 1917–18 approached, the unemployed, without financial relief, feared starvation. The Provisional Government could place no reliance on the police or the army to maintain public order in Petrograd and other towns, and in the country. Moreover, the Mensheviks and the Social Revolutionaries – both rivals of the Bolsheviks – were associated with the failures of the Provisional Government through coalescing with it in May 1917. Thus the Bolsheviks alone were untainted by governmental failure. Most army recruits were peasants who were already disenchanted with the government. Thus, conditions were ripe for assisting the Bolsheviks, who promised peace and food for the people, to gain power.

For most of the period between February and October 1917, Lenin was not in Russia. Yet Lenin's contribution to the seizure of power by the Bolsheviks should not be underestimated in consequence. The ultimate timing was largely his work. He, more than anybody, had the sense of urgency not possessed by most other Bolshevik leaders. Furthermore, it was Lenin who insisted that here should be no coalition with other parties. However, if Lenin and other Bolsheviks believed that their revolution was a prelude to the triumph of socialism worldwide, they were mistaken. With civil war and foreign intervention (1918–20) there was to be no relief from food shortages, but a lurch towards authoritarian rule that was to intensify the sufferings of millions of Russians.

Having considered all the factors that contributed to the Bolsheviks' political success in 1917, place Lenin's role in the context of events and developments, ensuring that Lenin's importance is not diminished to the point where he is no longer crucial in achieving the Bolshevik Revolution.

Related questions

1 Why were other political parties unable to mount an effective challenge to the Bolshevik Party between February and October 1917?

Although the October Revolution was in practice a *coup d'état* conspiratorially secured, it was also a faithful reflection of popular demands, at least in Petrograd and other major towns, articulated almost exclusively by Bolsheviks. Other groups – Liberals (Kadets), Social Revolutionaries and Mensheviks – sought to sustain the February Revolution by a complementary, but fragile, 'dual power', which was unable to prevent popular feeling becoming increasingly radicalised as they endorsed the continuation of the war and could not prevent an accompanying intensification of social and economic distress. The reluctant involvement of the Mensheviks and the Social Revolutionaries in the coalition beginning in May 1917 associated them indissolubly with a government becoming irretrievably discredited. The flexibility and ruthlessness of the Bolsheviks, led with iron resolve by Lenin, and their capacity to gauge the public mood enabled them to outmanoeuvre all other contending parties.

Nevertheless, there were disagreements among the Bolsheviks over policy, suggesting that they were not as disciplined or centrally controlled as Lenin would have wished. A considerable increase in membership, matching the Bolsheviks' identification with the people's needs, weakened Lenin's concept of a tightly knit party. Zinoviev and Kamenev, even in October, still did not believe the time was ripe for a seizure of power. It was Kerensky's pre-emptive strike against the Bolsheviks on 23 October that removed the latter's choice and prompted the insurrection, in practice organised by Trotsky. Growing support for the Bolsheviks in factory and soldiers' committees, local government and soviet elections and – supplementing this – for Left Social Revolutionaries, with whom the Bolsheviks were in temporary alliance, underlined their success in outmanoeuvring all other parties during the turbulence and confusion in Russia in 1917.

2 Why were there two revolutions in Russia in 1917?

3 Assess the contribution made by Lenin, from 1919 to 1924, to the creation of the Soviet state.

'A totalitarian state.'
Discuss the validity of this description as
applied to the Soviet Union under Stalin.

Tackling the question

The approach to this question is structurally identical to the similar question on Germany ruled by Hitler (Question 31). Indeed, the opening paragraph in each essay – a suggested definition of totalitarianism – may be the same in every detail. Stalin and Hitler are considered by many people to be the two most evil men of the twentieth century. Both turned the machinery of the state they controlled – the apparatus of the police, concentration camps and vast security organisations – against their victims. Hitler disposed of political dissenters, the mentally deficient, gypsies and all those whom he perceived to be racially worthless. Stalin's victims were those whom he conceived to be politically worthless peasants, members of the bourgeoisie, and all those within his own party and the state services who were – or were perceived to be – potentially or actually disloyal. Chechens, Volga Germans and Tartars were killed in huge numbers. Like Hitler, Stalin was still prepared to kill his own people even in the most direly difficult times of the war. Yet Western intellectuals travelling to the Soviet Union in the 1930s saw a 'new civilisation' that they had been primed to admire. Few recognised the tyranny that he had established, and many were even ready to believe the confessions of the victims of the purges and the so-called evidence produced at the show trials. Omnipresent fear is a component of a totalitarian state. The analysis will suggest that, like Hitler's Germany, Stalin's Soviet Union did not necessarily satisfy all the criteria of a totalitarian state, but there were sufficient characteristics of it to justify the application of the term to the Soviet Union under Stalin.

Answer

'Totalitarianism' implies all-embracing control by a political organisation that is equipped to scrutinise and pass judgement on every detailed aspect of a society that it holds in thrall. No vestige of opposition is tolerated. An insidiously penetrative police ensures conformity by intimidation and violence. An elaborate hierarchy of ideologically committed bureaucrats administers the state. Propaganda is calculated to muster unquestioning support for the regime. The education of the young, generously laced with indoc-

Guidance notes

Establish the criteria that may be associated with the term 'totalitarian state'.

trination, is geared to produce durable and unbending loyalty to the state. The economic system is likely to be highly centralised, efficiently monitored at the highest level and implemented decisively and productively in the regions according to established priorities. The whole system may be presided over by a charismatic leader, whose powerful, even hypnotic, oratory ensures that people's daily anxieties are transcended by a vision of a glorious future sustained by the prevailing ideology.

In that the definition is an abstraction, no state will necessarily match up entirely to the criteria established in the introductory paragraph. Show how, despite limits to the control that Stalin might exercise over his people, in practice totalitarianism as defined was established in the Soviet Union.

The 'totalitarian' state so described is an abstraction. Societies may only approach the 'ideal'. Under Stalin, within the Soviet Union conformity became commonplace as the sense of personal security was undermined. With the destruction of private enterprise, all became state employees. The overriding political and legal power of the state succeeded in virtually eclipsing the autonomous economic, social and cultural activities of the individual. Rigorous and comprehensive control seemed omnipresent. Stalin, dour and unostentatious – unlike Hitler – was no inspirational speaker, although this did not prevent the habitual extolling of his 'genius' and far-sightedness. However, he was not able to exercise absolute control over all facets of life – political, social and economic – in a state where traditional inefficiency, lack of a conspicuous work ethic and corruption were endemic. He could not decide all issues, although he could decide those that he chose to resolve. Perhaps it was decision making as a function of his choice, underpinned by terror, that enabled him to fashion a political system where opposition was intimidated and crushed. Arguably, this amounted to totalitarianism in practice.

Now examine the process by which Stalin established his awesome power over his people. What were the effects of the trial of the mining engineers at Shakty in the Donbass in 1928? How does the handling of the Ryutinists in 1932 show that Stalin was not able at that time to take his overriding authority for granted? How did he exploit the apparently mysterious circumstances surrounding the death of Kirov in 1934, so that his absolute authority could not be denied?

If, by the late 1930s, Stalin's authority was unchallenged, evidence suggests that this was not so before 1936. Certainly, the trial of the mining engineers of Shakty in Donbass (1928) succeeded in intimidating the industrial workforce and rendered precarious the existing managerial élite – 'the bourgeois experts' accepted by Lenin. In 1932 Ryutin, a Right Bolshevik, felt assured enough to publish a denunciation of Stalin, describing him as an 'evil genius', a political destroyer of the Revolution. Ryutin and his supporters were publicly tried and expelled from the party. No worse befell them, although their punishment prefaced the first major purge of the CPSU, by which about one-third of the total membership were expelled as Ryutinists. Thereafter, there were, in the party hierarchy, critics of the pace of industrialisation and collectivisation, and also of the measures taken to discipline party members. Among those with reservations about policy was Kirov, a popular figure in the party. His assassination (December 1934) seems to have been used by Stalin as a pretext for crushing potential embryonic resistance to his policies, and as a prelude to destroying his erstwhile allies and opponents. Some 55% of delegates to the Party Congress (1934) were executed by 1937, while 70% of delegates elected to the Central Committee (98 out of 139) met their deaths in the purges. By such means, Stalin's absolute authority was established.

Yet ensuring that state power penetrated to remote locations was formidably difficult. The secret police grew, but was susceptible to corruption, waste and inefficiency. The economy was not readily monitored. The movement of workers was not closely controlled until 1940. Money wages rose above the levels intended by the state because of competition for labour between different sectors of the economy. Forecasts of numbers within the industrial labour force made in 1929 were doubled in practice. Predicted production figures were above the massive industrial development that did occur. Thus, statistical information and the instruments of control available to central government were insufficiently sophisticated to meet the demands of totalitarian government as a theoretical concept. Central power was overwhelmingly powerful, but at the local level it was exercised crudely and erratically.

> What factors qualified the notion of the Soviet Union as a totalitarian state?

Nevertheless, Stalin's zealous custodianship of his powers and prerogatives, together with his odious personality – 'a singularly repulsive concoction of power, lust, megalomania, cynicism and suspicion' (Acton) – had the effect of weakening all political institutions and irreparably damaging their integrity, coherence and autonomy because they were always subject to the possibility of intervention and control by Stalin. Moreover, local political leaders – adherents of Stalin and benefiting from the weakness of local institutions – were able to establish their own local, surrogate tyrannies because central bodies were unable to exercise control over political organs at lower levels.

> Show how the way in which Stalin exercised his power caused institutional paralysis. With what effects?

Despite the menacing character of the regime, the aspirations of many were realised and there was scope for material and social benefits. There was a burgeoning bureaucracy and expanding party and police hierarchies. By 1939 white-collar workers numbered 11 million, 16% of the employed population. They included vast numbers of industrial managers, technical specialists and senior administrators, many of whom were of humble origin, but were beneficiaries of a higher education that would have been denied to their forebears. While they were as status

> Nevertheless, there were beneficiaries of the regime. Who were they? But stress that, despite their relative affluence, there was no real security for them.

ridden and privilege conscious as previous élites, the possibility of their becoming scapegoats for policies perceived to have failed was a constant anxiety. Yet the degree to which the regime was enthusiastically supported perhaps reflected a common apprehension that unity was a prerequisite for defending the Soviet Union against impending attack from the West.

Conclude by deciding whether, in the light of the evidence presented, you are justified in arguing that Stalin presided over a totalitarian state.

There were no autonomous sources of power or alternative focuses of loyalty in the Soviet Union under Stalin. Propaganda enabled a sustaining ideology to be consistently presented to the people. There was unimaginably brutal coercion of the peasants and relentless dragooning of industrial workers. The purges had, *inter alia*, ensured the unequivocal loyalty of the army, its new leaders indebted exclusively to Stalin for their promotions. New appointees knew that, if they caused trouble or failed to meet targets set, they were as susceptible to denunciation, dismissal, arrest and death as their hapless predecessors. In practice, Stalin's regime may be described as totalitarian.

Related questions

1 Discuss the view that Stalin already held the reins of power at the time of Lenin's death in 1924.

At the outset, establish the factors that in combination put Stalin in a strong position politically by 1924. Remember that, alone among the Bolshevik hierarchy, he had spent all his political life in the Soviet Union – there was no exile for him and the relative freedom that accompanied it. Lenin clearly admired the 'wonderful Georgian' and by 1912 he was a member of the Central Committee of the party. After 1917 Lenin bestowed on him wide-ranging administrative responsibilities which, while not intended to confer political ascendancy on Stalin, secured for him control of appointments to official positions. His grasp of the party apparatus became a crucial ingredient in enhancing Stalin's position politically after Lenin's death. His main rival, Trotsky, had no such power base. Lenin's failure to nominate a successor created a political vacuum that only the most ruthless – like Stalin – could fill. Aided by his advantages in administration, Stalin unostentatiously and skilfully exploited divisions over policy, discrediting and manipulating political foes and erstwhile allies alike, until by 1929 he had indisputably become the sole beneficiary of Lenin's legacy. Thus, Stalin's sure-footed intriguing after 1924 was derived in large part from his effective control of the party apparatus, secured before 1924.

With these points established initially, you can then explain in detail the crucial importance of Stalin's early appointments – including that of General Secretary – which gave him a head start over his rivals in 1924. In addition, what good luck did he have? An example might be the reluctance of the Central Committee to use Lenin's *Testament* against any individual in the hierarchy; moreover, the bonus of delivering the oration at Lenin's funeral suggested that he was well placed to succeed Lenin. What factors undermined the influence of Trotsky, so that after 1924 Stalin was able to portray him as an enemy of the Soviet Union? Note also that from his excellent political base he was able to undermine the Bolshevik leaders, whether they were dubbed Left or Right Communists. It may be concluded that his monopoly of power after 1928 was an affirmation or product of his control of the party apparatus achieved before 1924. Thereafter, fellow Bolshevik leaders were vulnerable to whatever pressures Stalin chose in order to undermine their political influence.

2   'At first sight, Trotsky might seem ideally placed to assume the mantle of Lenin.' Why, therefore, did Stalin eventually assume that mantle?

3   What was the basis of Stalin's power?

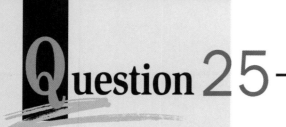
What, if any, were the achievements of Stalin within the Soviet Union, 1928–39?

Tackling the question

During much of the late 1920s, there was a vigorous debate among the Bolshevik leaders as to the efficacy of the New Economic Policy (NEP), which had been introduced by Lenin ostensibly as a temporary expedient to save the Revolution after the failure of War Communism in 1921. Around Bukharin were the so-called 'Rightists', who wished to allow the peasant to 'get rich' and to avoid a headlong rush into industrialisation. The 'Leftists', among whom were Trotsky and, after some hesitation, Zinoviev and Kamenev, were hostile to giving the peasantry any scope for holding the Revolution to ransom by withholding food supplies. They sought to force the pace of industrialisation, in part to enable the Soviet Union to defend itself against a potential attack from the West, and in part to eliminate private enterprise, which was alien to their ideological commitment to state control of all aspects of the economy.

Through much of this intense debate, Stalin was non-committal and inscrutable. For him political considerations were paramount and, with his control of the party apparatus in his role as General Secretary, he was able to exploit systematically the differences between the party leaders and outmanoeuvre them all, whether they were of a 'Leftist' or a 'Rightist' persuasion. Not until 1929 did he become explicit about his aims for the economy. Then it became clear that it was his intention to create for the Soviet Union, by a series of Five-Year Plans, a vast industrial base and, because he regarded the existing organisation of agriculture as a serious impediment to his economic strategy, to collectivise agriculture. The outcome was to make the Soviet Union a formidable industrial power, but it was at the cost of crippling long-term damage to agriculture and an immense sacrifice of lives. The brutality of the regime – millions died in the 1930s – and the longer-term unviability of the economy suggest that, apart from the scope that the rapid development of heavy industry gave the Soviet Union to resist Hitler after 1941, ultimately little was achieved. Indeed, the words 'if any' in the question set indicate that it is possible to argue that nothing of benefit to the Soviet Union may be attributed to Stalin's rule.

Answer

Consider the view that, despite the Soviet Union's achievements in the 1930s, the means used to

Although many historians are ready to concede that under Stalin's auspices the Soviet Union achieved a remarkable degree of industrialisation within a single decade, there is contention as to whether it was the appropriate path for the Soviet Union to tread and debate as to the means used. While, arguably, industrialisation served the Soviet Union's most immediate needs and enabled it to survive and eventually win a war at exorbitant costs against Germany, it failed in the long term to provide an economy susceptible to the demands of the consumer and industry alike. Moreover, the Terror, which progressively accompanied Stalin's political ascendancy, permanently muzzled dissent and sapped initiative. A society where all appointments required that individuals were agents of Stalin's implacable will meant that ill-conceived policies could change only according to the whim or calculation of the undisputed leader.

The New Economic Policy (NEP) of the 1920s, although initially it may have staved off the threat of the Bolshevik Revolution collapsing, did not produce the taxable wealth that Bukharin, in encouraging the peasants 'to enrich themselves', believed could be used to finance investment for promoting industrialisation. The peasants' fortunes revived modestly, but their methods remained inefficiently labour intensive. Their capacity to withhold food supplies in response to levels of industrial prices was construed by many orthodox Marxists as the peasants threatening to hold to ransom the proletariat for whom the Revolution of 1917 was carried through. By 1928 Stalin was resolved to effect a process of rapid industrialisation, which would be accompanied by a ruthless collectivisation of agriculture. He intended to mechanise agriculture, so that labour released from farming could be provided for industry. He deemed industrial production crucial if the Soviet Union – potentially the victim, as he saw it, of predatory powers that were uncompromisingly hostile to Bolshevism – was to survive.

Yet it was in heavy goods production, much of it located in areas beyond the fullest extent of Hitler's invasion after 1941, that Stalin's principal investment occurred, at a time when depressed Western economies were experiencing a decline in their established staple industries – iron and steel, shipbuilding and coal production. By the late 1930s, an incipient recovery in those economies, which was to be interrupted by war, was in the form of structural change that promoted light engineering and advanced technology, which was responsive to a consumer demand bolstered by government stimuli. In contrast, Stalin virtually ignored consumer demand and concentrated upon conspicuous expansion of coal, steel, oil and electricity production. By the third Five-Year Plan, coal production had increased from 35 million to 150 million tons annually, steel from 3 million to 18 million tons,

accomplish them were, in the longer term, damaging to Soviet interests.

Why did Stalin decide to end the New Economic Policy (NEP), despite its initial value in saving the Revolution in the early 1920s? Note that, while there were plausible economic reasons for ending it, Stalin also had political reasons for doing so.

Now consider how Stalin endeavoured to industrialise the Soviet Union in the 1930s. Assess the nature of the policy in the light of developments that were taking place in other advanced economies at the same time. Quote statistics to show how the Soviet Union's industrial capacity was markedly expanded. How would Stalin have been able to justify giving little emphasis to the production of consumer goods?

oil from 12 million to 26 million tons and electricity from 18 million to 90 million kW (1927–40). Only collective needs were to be satisfied. Moreover, such a policy could be justified in terms of Marxist theory, in that it was an emphatic rejection of the capitalist ethic's corrupt dependence on discredited consumerism.

What long-term disservice did Stalin do to the economy of the Soviet Union?

Despite such notable progress, the nature of the Soviet Union's industrial development precluded it from making up lost ground in pursuit of the advanced nations – the principal objective of Stalin's economic revolution. Once embarked upon, it continued to be followed long after the short-term benefit of assisting the Soviet Union to overcome German invasion (June 1941). Unresponsive to demand in the longer term, it ensured over-production of undemanded goods and under-production of goods in demand, thus causing recurrent shortages.

Examine the damage that the policy of collectivising agriculture caused to the Soviet Union.

Food scarcity was the consequence of a ruthless process of collectivisation, designed to provide the Soviet Union with the capital accumulation needed to promote industry. The most prosperous farmers – kulaks – pilloried for alleged profiteering and exploitation of poor peasants, were deported and often killed. Moreover, the confiscation of grain attending the change – 60% of peasant farmers were collectivised by 1930, 98% by 1941 – provoked peasant resistance. The new *kolkhoz* was regarded by peasants as a 'second serfdom'. In the early 1930s, peasants were victims of an avoidable famine as declining food supplies were deliberately diverted to the industrial towns. Peasants defied the regime by passive resistance, the age-old weapon of the weak, and in their passivity further subverted often misguided political interference. Quite apart from Stalin's malevolence towards the peasantry, whatever was progressive about collectivisation – the increased mechanisation, for example – assisted in achieving no more by 1939 than a recovery of agricultural productivity to levels recorded in 1913. Collective farms stifled all initiative and prompted the long-term stagnation of the rural Soviet Union. Soviet agriculture was never able to supply the country's needs.

What were the damaging social consequences of Stalin's ruthless policies?

The searing consequences of the Soviet Union's 'revolution from above' and the dubious benefits conferred by it would suggest a meagre return for the monumental suffering of the Soviet people. The sought-for economic transformation, limited in its gains, while sustained by a measure of popular support, calculatedly diminished the private sphere of a citizen's life, politicising social relations and signalling unambiguously that none could be neutral in building socialism. Whatever the permanent damage to the

Soviet Union's agriculture and the heavily qualified benefits of industrial change, Stalin's policies cowed the population and enfeebled any inclination to question or oppose.

Stalin's methods did not allow the Soviet Union to catch up with the West industrially. It is sometimes argued that, despite the almost exclusive emphasis upon heavy industry so that the Soviet Union could make war in defence of the homeland, in 1941 the Soviet Union was not ready for war and that other factors – *inter alia*, the Soviet Union's climatic extremes and Hitler's burdens elsewhere – contributed indispensably to the Soviet Union's ultimate military success. Some historians have argued that the hectic pace of industrialisation in the 1930s could not have been achieved in any case had there not been a sound basis for growth. Stone has claimed that the expertise and industrial structure existing before 1928 were prerequisites for whatever degree of success may be attributed to the Five-Year Plans. Shapiro has contended that a continuation of the rate of expansion achieved by the Soviet Union by 1914 would have secured no less by 1941 than Stalin's brutal methods. No later attempts to modify the economic straitjacket of Stalin's economic strategy met with success. Stalin's achievements appear to have been very limited, and to have had an immense social cost.

> Now is the time to conclude your analysis of the efficacy of Stalin's policies. Apart from the short-term benefits of industrial development, which equipped the Soviet Union to withstand the awful rigours of German invasion in 1941, many historians feel that little was achieved at huge social cost. Give some indication of the specific views of historians in the final paragraph.

Related questions

1 'His determination and his ruthless control of and indifference to the plight of his people secured his power whatever policies he pursued.' How appropriate is this verdict on Stalin in the period 1928–41?

The enormity of Stalin's campaigns of terror is no longer disputed. In his youth he acquired the discipline and resolution needed to survive as an active revolutionary. The various offices that he held after October 1917 equipped him uniquely to control appointments and ensure shrewd placing of those loyal to him. By 1929, having skilfully outmanoeuvred all his main political rivals, he ruthlessly implemented the collectivisation of agriculture and the reshaping of the industrial infrastructure, undeterred by the huge cost in lives. If he suspected a potential challenge to his political ascendancy, he did not shrink from purging his erstwhile political allies and many others in positions of authority. The evidence of his political career suggests that he coveted undisputed power and that orthodox Marxist policies were largely means to that end.

All of these points will need to be amplified in the body of the essay. Look in detail at the contribution of Stalin's early political experiences to the ultimate enhancement of his authority.

Consider the purpose of the Terror in effecting economic change after 1928. Note the slowly growing awareness of political leaders in the Soviet Union that Stalin was prepared to extend the Terror beyond that needed to further economic change. What was the significance of the purges of the late 1930s? If the social and economic aspects of Stalinism emerged at the beginning of the 1930s, the political face of it was manifest later in the decade. The 'revolution from above' did not necessarily predetermine the institution of the purges. Arguably, the personal dictatorship and the use of terror destroyed the party created by Lenin. Before 1924 every stage of his life equipped Stalin with skills and opportunities that later assisted him to establish his awesome power. You may well conclude that by 1941 his capacity for arbitrary and unpredictable interventions, and the pliant acquiescence of office-holders in his policies, ensured that influential dissent was more or less permanently muzzled.

2 'It is appropriate to conclude that up to 1945 Stalin was successful.' To what extent do you regard this claim as valid?

3 In what respects did the Soviet Union of 1929 differ from the tsarist Russia of 1900?

'Full of sound and fury signifying nothing.' How far is this a just verdict on Mussolini's foreign policy between 1922 and 1943?

Tackling the question

It is said that a journalist witnessing Mussolini's soldiers goose-stepping observed that it was like listening to Wagner on the flute. Under Mussolini's leadership, Italy's pretensions in its foreign policy proved to be out of step with its performance. All was to end in disaster for Mussolini, in full-scale war his armies becoming easy victims for the weakest of opponents. 'To make Italy great, respected and feared', and to trumpet the virtue of Italians proving themselves in war so that Italy could achieve great power status, was vainglory on Mussolini's part. There has been debate among historians as to whether Mussolini's foreign policy was essentially an improvised response to the domestic problems of a state in which securing his absolute authority internally was an overriding priority, or whether there were aims that Mussolini pursued consistently, either aggressively or with a studied restraint. The latter view has gained ground of late.

The areas where Mussolini showed most interest – the Mediterranean, the Balkans and Africa – were where Italian foreign policy had long been focused, but in pursuit of its interests it had always been handicapped by economic and military weakness. After 1918 Italians felt that they had been ill rewarded in the peace settlements, their irredentist aims remained unsatisfied, even though Austria-Hungary had collapsed, and their hopes for some of the mandated territories had been dashed. It seemed that the victorious powers shared Bismarck's view that Italy had a big appetite but no teeth. Mussolini was to exploit public disenchantment with 'the mutilated peace'. Nevertheless, in his earliest manifesto in 1919 his aspirations in foreign policy scarcely figured. Indeed, in it he denounced imperialism and urged that irredentism should be pursued by negotiation and not by force. This was soon to change. As the Facist Party grew in strength, it attracted militant nationalists whose hawkish views on Italy's quest for expansion Mussolini soon amply reflected. The Corfu incident of 1923 demonstrated that Mussolini was quick to strut across the international stage, flexing Italy's military muscle. Aggressive acts punctuated by occasional diplomatic moderation – as a guarantor with Britain of the permanence of Germany's western frontiers in the Locarno agreements (1925) and when healing the rift between the Italian state and the Papacy in 1929 – and the ability to convey an impression that Italy in his hands was militarily and potentially a sturdy ally, enabled him for a time to be taken seriously by Britain and France on the one hand and Nazi Germany on the other. However, despite his rhetoric to the contrary, Mussolini seems to have become painfully aware that Italy would be punching above its weight if it became involved in a major war. That fear was substantiated once it did so.

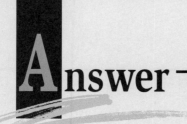

Answer

Why did Mussolini fail abjectly to achieve his extravagant aims in foreign policy? Emphasise Mussolini's style in his foreign policy.

Mussolini always insisted that war was the ultimate criterion by which a nation and its leader should be judged. From the outset, in 1922, he sought to make the Mediterranean *mare nostrum* and establish Italy's overriding influence in the Balkans. Moreover, he insisted that inherently superior Italians had a civilising mission that justified imperial acquisition. His extravagant ambitions were never realised. An appearance of parade ground efficiency and Mussolini's high-flown rhetoric for a long time concealed the reality of the inefficiency and incompetence of his armed forces. Until 1940 he avoided being put to any serious test. Before that, he craftily improvised his diplomacy, engineered conspiracies and engaged in minor, squalid conflicts without other powers' faith in his value as a potential ally being undeniably impaired. Mussolini was a swaggerer and a bully, given to intimidating posturing. Italy's ignominious military collapse after 1940, however modestly capable the opposition, proved that he was 'full of sound and fury signifying nothing'.

What was the significance of Mussolini's actions in the Corfu crisis of 1923?

Once in power, Mussolini almost immediately displayed an ugly nationalism in the Corfu crisis (1923). Despite his outrageous conduct against Greece, using force when Italy's *amour propre* had been minimally offended, he triumphed. It was ominous for the future of the League of Nations that Mussolini had learned that there was a reluctance to resist even blatant aggression in order to promote collective security – a concept that he regarded with contempt.

How did Mussolini fashion his foreign policy during the period of the 'Locarno spirit' between 1925 and 1929?

Before 1930 Mussolini, aggressive by inclination, improvised his policies, especially after 1924, in an atmosphere of apparent tranquillity in Europe that was encapsulated in the 'Locarno spirit'. Conspiratorially, he aggravated tensions by secret arms sales and encouragement to irredentist movements. Separatists were assisted in Yugoslavia. He helped Germany breach the arms restrictions imposed on it (1919). He pursued his ambitions in the Balkans, pivotal to which was the gaining of political and economic control of Albania, which was largely achieved by 1926. In Libya, however, a little publicised ten-year war against a handful of rebels, ending in 1932, exposed the shortcomings of his armies and demonstrated the innate brutality of his regime. Yet superficially he gained respectability by being a guarantor of the Locarno Pacts (1925) and negotiating the Lateran Treaties (1929).

How did Mussolini respond to the repercussions of the Wall Street Crash of 1929?

The repercussions of the Wall Street Crash (1929) destroyed the fragile 'Locarno spirit' and encouraged political extremism, especially in Germany. Japan too embarked on a period of imperial expansion when it absorbed Manchuria (1931–2). The belligerence of Germany and Japan, sustained by undoubted military strength, was in accord with Mussolini's temperament and ambitions, if not, despite appearances to the contrary, with his ability to achieve his objectives by force.

It was with a mixture of apprehension and admiration that Britain and France, fearful of Hitler's potential menace, sought Mussolini's friendship. Mussolini's apparent readiness to use force to prevent a Nazi coup in Austria (1934) impressed them. The outcome was their joining Mussolini at Stresa (April 1935) to co-ordinate policy against Hitler, who had embarked on rearming in violation of the Versailles Treaty (1919). That Mussolini might, indefensibly, attack Ethiopia was discreetly ignored. When the attack occurred (October 1935), although the League condemned Italy's action, the fact that sanctions were not rigorously imposed and oil was excluded from the embargo on sales to Italy revealed a reluctance to alienate Mussolini. The still-born Hoare–Laval Pact (December 1935) was further evidence of a desperate resolve to appease him. Such weakness earned Mussolini's contempt and drew him, against his better judgement, into close association with Germany.

> What were the consequences of Mussolini's temporary association with Britain and France in 1935? How did the Stresa Front come about and why did it so soon collapse? Why did its collapse draw Mussolini towards alignment with Hitler?

The key year in cementing ties with Germany was 1936. Mussolini's involvement in the Spanish Civil War (1936–9) was undistinguished and earned little gratitude from Franco. Nevertheless, not only was he associated with a manifestly strong power in the Rome–Berlin Axis (November 1936), but by November 1937 the anti-Comintern Pact had made Italy part of an irresistibly formidable political and military combination, without an obvious weak link if Mussolini's trumpeting of Italy's military strength was taken at its face value.

> What was the significance for Mussolini of the year 1936?

It was plain to see that Mussolini was impotent and submissive towards Hitler when he had the galling experience of having to accept the *Anschluss* (March 1938), having claimed that he had successfully resisted it (1934). If he earned, temporarily, the gratitude of millions for his part in convening the Munich Conference (September 1938), he knew that conflict, avoided on that occasion, would have exposed Italy's military weakness.

> How was Mussolini's weakness displayed by 1938?

By 1939 no power, not even Britain, was convinced of Italy's military reliability. Hitler, in a calculated slight, did not forewarn him of his invasion of Czechoslovakia (March 1939). Mussolini's

> How did Mussolini react to the developing crisis in 1939?

ill-organised invasion of Albania (April 1939) was to a degree prompted by the fear that Hitler might penetrate the Balkans – an area that he saw as Italy's sphere of influence. He was unpleasantly surprised by the guarantees that Britain and France gave in Eastern Europe. He feared the approach of general war. Hitler, aware of his weakness, did not consult him about his plans for invading Poland.

How did the war after 1940 expose Italy's military weakness?

After September 1939, Mussolini was torn between a desire to be involved and the reality of knowing Italy's impotence. It was only when Hitler was winning decisively in the west (June 1940) that Mussolini precipitately declared war on Germany's side. The consequences were disastrous. The Greeks defeated his armies after October 1940. His armies in North Africa were no match for Britain's. Ethiopia fell to Britain almost without resistance on Italy's part. Malta, on Italy's doorstep, remained in British hands. After the Axis collapsed in North Africa (late 1942), the invasions of Sicily (July 1943) and the Italian mainland (September 1943) were the culmination of a process by which Mussolini's incessant propaganda about Italy's military prowess was proved to be entirely unfounded. He was like 'a poor player that struts and frets his hour upon the stage, and then is no more'.

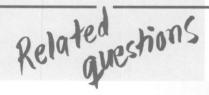

Related questions

1 How strongly would you argue that Mussolini's foreign policy in the 1930s was a direct consequence of difficulties in his domestic policies?

It may be argued that Mussolini's flamboyant rhetoric, trumpeting his resolve to make Italy 'great, respected and feared', unavoidably sublimated itself in acts of aggression, irrespective of economic difficulties in Italy and the social and political tensions arising from them. On the other hand, Mack Smith and Mussolini's contemporary, Salvamini, have insisted that Mussolini resorted to ill-thought-out and sometimes desperate expedients in foreign policy, in order to mitigate the impact of public disenchantment with his failing domestic policies. If revisionism was a strategic imperative in his foreign policy, he often improvised in his tactics. By the late 1930s he came privately to realise that Italy was militarily weak. By that time he conducted his foreign policy weakly and irresolutely, the stakes being much higher than hitherto.

After the introduction to the essay, it is necessary to show that Mussolini's economic policies were essentially militaristic and that autarkic policies reduced standards of living among his people. It may be significant that Mussolini's propaganda, justifying his impending invasion of

Abyssinia in October 1935, gave prominence to the scope for Italians to enjoy economic benefits if they were prepared to emigrate to East Africa. Italians were suffering because export-orientated industries, like textiles, were contracting and deflationary policies were sapping industrial workers' bargaining powers. It was a society burdened by unemployment and declining real wages. Italy's generous welfare provision may have been intended to counter any threat to public order. By the late 1930s Italy faced bankruptcy and, despite vast expense on armaments, did not possess an efficient military machine. Such problems were likely to influence Mussolini's foreign policy as war approached.

It may also be argued that, irrespective of domestic considerations and as if persuaded by the efficacy of his own propaganda, Mussolini was determined to cut a dash on the international stage and secure great power status for Italy – perhaps he believed briefly in 1936 that mere association with Hitler conferred international importance on Italy. To all appearances the Anti-Comintern Pact of 1937, with Italy a signatory, constituted the most formidable military combination in the world. On the other hand, it may have been that Mussolini, conscious of Italy's military and economic weakness, cultivated close ties with Germany because he could not afford to be associated with powers as apparently prevaricating as Britain and France. Yet by the late 1930s he was just as irresolute as they were. Italy's unimpressive performance in the Spanish Civil War probably persuaded Mussolini that it was ill prepared for war. Does this explain his mediatory efforts at the time of the Munich Conference in 1938? In 1939 he feared the approach of war. Hitler, aware of Italy's weakness, failed to consult him about his plans for invading Poland. The Italian economy had failed to produce the wherewithal needed to wage modern warfare. Italy's inept participation in the war after June 1940 provided ample evidence that this was so.

2 'I want to make Italy great, respected and feared.' How successful was Mussolini in achieving these aims between 1922 and 1943?

3 'There was an underlying consistency in Mussolini's foreign policy.' How far do you agree with this verdict?

How successful was the corporate state in solving Italy's economic and social problems in the period 1929–39?

Tackling the question

Like Hitler, Mussolini knew little about economics. At the time he came to power in 1922, he had no coherent economic policy to offer the Italian people. There was little evidence of advanced planning. Initially, his main concern was to consolidate his power. It was his good fortune that the degree of economic well-being enjoyed by Italy before 1925, while Mussolini was finding his political feet, coincided with a European postwar boom. At this time Italy was pursuing a liberal economic policy, masterminded by his treasury minister, de Stefani, which involved very limited public expenditure, stable prices and little intervention in industry by government. In a time of general economic expansion, *laissez-faire* policies helped company profits to swell. However, after 1926 there was serious inflation, an adverse balance of payments and a depreciating lira, to which the government's response was to apply protectionist measures that thereafter became a constant feature of the fascist economy.

Mussolini's principal aim was to make himself all-powerful, so that he could transform Italian society. His foreign policy was ambitious – no less than making Italy 'great, respected and feared'. This would have been an unprecedented state of affairs had Mussolini achieved it. In the event, he failed lamentably. He sought a major role in European affairs, an empire in Africa and Italian predominance in the Mediterranean and the Balkans. In order to achieve these grandiose objectives, he needed an economy that would sustain a powerful military machine. This meant autarkic policies and constraints upon export-orientated consumer goods industries. In pursuit of this, the problems that he had inherited from his predecessors – a country divided between north and south, rural deprivation and industrial under-development – were not seriously tackled. The corporate state, ostensibly to signal a productive partnership between capital and labour, was not the rational alternative to capitalism and state control of the economy that it purported to be. In the end, there were few who could claim to have been beneficiaries of Mussolini's rule.

Answer

Explain the concept of the corporate state before you examine concisely its

In seeking to establish a corporate state, Mussolini ostensibly intended to reorganise state institutions so that capital, represented by the employers, and labour would be integrated into mandatory, functional units called corporations, which were recognised by the state. It appeared to be a means whereby each specific grouping, or corporation, would enjoy a measure of self-government and have a capacity to participate with other corporations in the formulation of policy affecting the whole of society. In practice, the corporations were controlled by the fascist government existing outside the corporate system. Fascist officials were foisted on the workers' side within the corporate structure. Contrariwise, the position of employers, who could defend their interests within the corporations and deal directly with government through surviving autonomous bodies, like Confindustria, was strengthened. Thus, behind the façade of a proclaimed consensus between employers and employed, workers' economic and social interests were largely disdainfully neglected.

The proud boast made in 1929 by the Ministry of Corporations, set up in 1926, that it had removed class conflict in industry was a distortion of the truth. Indeed, from its inception, the fascist movement was resolved upon the disciplining of labour, whose trade union militancy it had endeavoured to crush even before 1922. Mussolini's initial response to working-class discontent was the formation of fascist unions – 'syndicates' – but, as in 1925, they were quite capable of organising damaging strikes themselves. Socialist and Catholic unions may have been undermined, but the uneasy rapport between Confindustria, the industrialists' confederation, and the fascist syndicates' confederation dismayed Mussolini, who was anxious to win the confidence of the employers. Thus, he authorised the fragmentation of the Confederation of Fascist Syndicates into six workers' confederations of syndicates alongside six corresponding employers' confederations. It was a blow to syndicalism. It had been undermined by the 'corporatist' ideology.

'Mixed' corporations – 22 of them were set up in 1934 – claimed to invest representatives of workers and employers with powers to fix wage rises, settle disputes, deploy labour, regulate apprenticeships, advise on economic matters and 'encourage improvements in production'. In truth, this was no more than propaganda, but effective for all that. It promised workers 'self-management' and 'managerial authority', innovation and protection of established interests, free enterprise and state monopoly. Some foreigners were impressed by Mussolini's 'third way' – an apparently rational alternative to capitalism and Bolshevism, especially attractive in an acute and confusing Depression. 'Italy', Salvamini claimed, 'had become the Mecca of political scientists, economists and sociologists', impressed by the organisation and the working of

shortcomings. What appeared to be the overriding purpose of setting up corporations? What was the real purpose in setting them up? What contrasting effects did corporations have upon workers and employers?

Now examine in some detail the undermining of workers' power by the 'corporatist' ideology. How, in the 1920, had fascist unions – 'syndicates' – failed to serve Mussolini's purposes? What steps did Mussolini take to undermine the Confederation of Fascist Syndicates and to what effect?

Explain what Mussolini claimed was the purpose of 'mixed' corporations. Show that this was propaganda, but that it was sufficient to persuade some foreigners that Mussolini had found 'a third way' of managing an economy between capitalism, which seemed to be failing, and Bolshevist state control. What was the reality in regard to corporations?

the corporate state. In practice, it was an elaborate façade behind which corruption and exploitation flourished.

Now examine Mussolini's encouragement to big business. Why was Mussolini's out-manoeuvring of the most radical elements in the fascist movement comforting to Confindustria, the employers' confederation? What was the purpose of the workers' book of 1935? How did Confindustria benefit from the falling value of the lira during the 1930s?

From the early 1920s onwards, industrialists were suspicious of radical elements within the fascist movement that were imbued with revolutionary syndicalist ideas. By 1925 Mussolini had rendered them innocuous, so that thereafter industrialists could the more readily identify with the regime. Confindustria could take comfort from the regime's clear intention to control labour, but not industry, and its sanctioning of private initiative, backed by the state, as the only effective way of securing maximum production. State control of workers was enhanced by the introduction of the work book (the *libretto*) in 1935, which controlled the movement of workers and registered their political activities. The inflated value of the lira (90 lira to the pound from 1934) delighted Confindustria as it destroyed weaker companies, increased the trend towards monopoly, lowered import prices and assisted in reducing wages. The onset of the Depression intensified these tendencies.

How was the growth of monopolies in Italy assisted by state intervention?

The growth of monopolies was assisted by state intervention. The creation of IRI (*Instituto di Reconstruzione Industriale*) was designed – as a kind of super bank – to regulate and secure credit, so that industry would have the necessary capital, which Italy's leading banks were no longer able to provide fully. This was doing the bidding of the monopolies. The economy was not modernised. There were no fundamental changes in the economic structure, no major technical innovations. The corporations helped big business. Autarkic policies were mainly fashioned to protect Italian industry from external competition.

Consider the impact on workers of state intervention in the interest of private enterprise. Show how workers' living standards fell. What was Mussolini's attitude to the deteriorating circumstances of most workers?

The considerable degree of state intervention in the interest of private enterprise was paralleled by severe constraints being imposed upon workers, whose independent unions were abolished in the 1920s and whose right to strike was denied. Employers gained from the absence of official regulations in respect of their employees, and the workers were burdened by government-approved employers' regulations and, especially in the Depression, inhibited by the fear of unemployment. The promotion of heavy industries – steel, armaments and shipbuilding, for example – capable of making heavy profits, was at the expense of export industries. After the late 1920s, workers' living standards fell. The eight-hour day was abandoned. Real wages fell by about 11% (1925–38). Unemployment rose substantially, probably to 2 million by 1933. Mussolini was not especially concerned by this deterioration, persuaded that Italians were in any case inured to hardship and that there was little prospect anywhere, let alone in Italy, of raising living standards.

Similarly, the peasantry were ill served by Mussolini, who did nothing to deal with long-standing rural poverty, which was now aggravated by declining emigration to the USA, or to improve farming techniques. In desperation, destitute peasants gravitated to towns in search of work and created shanty towns on the periphery of industrial areas. The north–south divide remained intact. Mussolini's preoccupation with the 'battle for grain' caused a decline in the production of citrus fruits, wine and olive oil – hitherto profitable exports. Land reclamation projects laudably improved health, but were limited in extent. Indeed, landlords were the beneficiaries of Mussolini's rule, their large estates preserved by Mussolini dropping proposed legislation in 1922 that might have led to their fragmentation.

> What adverse impact did Mussolini's economic policies have upon the peasantry? Give examples of the sufferings of the peasantry. What were the effects of Mussolini's preoccupation with increasing grain production? How important were land reclamation projects? Who, in the countryside, were beneficiaries of Mussolini's economic policies?

Even though the harshness of Italian life may have been mitigated by seemingly generous welfare provision – family allowances (1934), holiday pay, accident and sickness insurance – such panaceas could do no more than defuse working-class discontent. Industrialists and landowners had kept their independence in an economy where, in practice, the corporate state never materialised. There was no real consensus of any kind between workers and employers, as was initially disingenuously proposed. By 1940 there were intolerable economic and social tensions that, with ignominious defeat in war, the regime could not contain. Thus, the corporate state, in Cassel's words, was 'a true child of Mussolini: the great poseur brought forth an organism which was a travesty of what it purported to be'.

> Emphasise the bogus nature of the corporate state.

Related questions

1 Who, if anyone, benefited from fascism in Mussolini's Italy?

You may well decide that there were few beneficiaries from Mussolini's rule. An early task will be to explain what Mussolini's fascism was. There can be no lengthy explanation, but stress its anti-democratic character, Mussolini's cult of personality leading to the creation of the infallible and omniscient Il Duce, and the fraudulence of the corporate state. Who then were the beneficiaries of this kind of regime? Industrialists and landowners, perhaps (their gains are explained in the answer to Question 26); servicemen benefiting from the government's willingness to invest in rearmament, although many senior officers must have been aware that, despite Mussolini's expansionist policies and his extravagant rhetoric, they remained technologically ill equipped for facing a general war; those elements of the middle classes absorbed into the burgeoning bureaucracy of the fascist state; intellectuals and journalists who were prepared to serve the regime. But arguably even these were 'losers' once Italy became involved in the general war in 1940 and Italy suffered humiliating defeat.

Who more clearly did not benefit from the regime? The industrial working classes and the peasantry, whose problems are analysed in the answer to Question 27; those members of the middle classes who ran small businesses involved in the production of consumer goods, who were adversely affected by the autarkic policies, which damaged exports and prompted a trend towards monopoly that was beneficial mainly to industrialists; the Roman Church, which, despite the Lateran Pact of 1929, experienced a deterioration in its relationship with the state in the 1930s. In the end, during the war years, shortages of all kinds, the inefficiency of the government and the comprehensive nature of the military defeats suffered steadily by Italy eroded the confidence of all sections of Italian society.

2   What factors assisted the growth of fascism in Italy?

3   How far did fascism carry through a revolution in Italy?

> 'Germany's inherent strength was not seriously
> impaired by the Treaty of Versailles of 1919.'
> How far is this judgement valid?

Tackling the question

There is no consensus among historians about the fairness of the Treaty of Versailles of 1919. At the time J.M. Keynes, the economist, argued that the settlement 'by overstepping the limits of the possible, has in practice settled nothing'. The historian W.H. Dawson wrote that non-German populations were unreasonably favoured in the settlement, so that German frontiers 'are literally bleeding. From them oozes the life blood, physical, spiritual and material of large populations'. Certainly, Germans of all political persuasions considered the treaty to be an astonishingly harsh diktat, humiliating in its implications and its intentions. Reservations about the efficacy of the treaty, especially outside France, enabled successive German governments during the Weimar period to succeed in virtually restoring Germany's sovereignty by 1932, even if the territorial changes in the settlement had not been altered or restrictions on Germany's military capacity reduced.

The abject collapse of the Weimar Republic suggested to many who had reservations about the treaty that it had done nothing to assist a moderate regime to survive in its desperate struggle with the destructive phenomenon of Nazism. More recently, historians have tended to seek to redress the balance in respect of the harshness of the treaty. In his *Origins of the Second World War* (1961), A.J.P. Taylor considered that it was too lenient. Others have defended the treaty by insisting that France suffered more acutely than Germany from the impact of the war, and therefore justifiably claimed compensation and security. In view of what German hegemonic power in Europe would have meant had Germany won the war, it is sometimes said, the settlement was remarkably moderate. Indeed, there is a case for arguing that, despite German perceptions of the treaty being largely hostile, German strength was in a sense enhanced by the settlement. How could that have been? It is this view that the question set seeks to assess.

Answer

Guidance notes

The defeated Germans overwhelmingly regarded the Treaty of Versailles (1919) as an unacceptable diktat. Its terms were the product of hard-won compromises among the victorious powers, which were preoccupied with inhibiting a Germany that was potentially the most powerful state on mainland Europe. Insistent domestic pressures, clashing personalities and

Consider the circumstances in which the treaty was formulated. Even though there is the view that the treaty was disastrously damaging to Germany's political stability in the 1920s, in what senses may it be argued that fundamentally Germany was not seriously weakened by it?

differing conceptions of national interest made negotiations, even without German participation, contentious, even bitter. Other factors added urgency to their deliberations. There was serious political disorder in Central, Eastern and South-East Europe. Bolshevism seemed poised for an irresistible extension westwards. In retrospect, historians have often seen the treaty as having contributed to the exacerbation of corrosive tensions in German political life that later worked to Hitler's advantage. Nevertheless, despite the treaty's harsh rigour, with its industries undamaged, Germany retained the capacity for economic recovery. Moreover, with the fragmentation of the major empires by 1918, there was the scope for a restored Germany enjoying a movement in the balance of power in Europe much to its advantage.

Yet it is appropriate to emphasise the rigour of the treaty that so antagonised most Germans in 1919. Highlight the terms most resented by them.

Undeniably, the terms imposed on Germany appeared harsh. To most Germans, they were incompatible with the principles enshrined in Wilson's Fourteen Points (January 1918). In effect, Germany was demilitarised – forbidden to possess, *inter alia*, tanks, military aircraft and submarines. Conscription was abolished and its army restricted to 100,000 men, just sufficient to protect its frontiers. It lost all of its colonies. Article 231 obliged Germany to accept – with its Allies – full responsibility for initiating war, a view passionately contested by Germans. By 1921 reparations had been fixed at the vast sum of £6,600 million – a crippling financial burden. Moreover, Germany's frontiers were reshaped and it was obliged to yield one-eighth of its territory and 6 million of its people. Much resented was the enforced submission of ethnic Germans to Polish rule in land transferred, mostly without plebiscite, to the newly independent Poland. Germany's economic problems were aggravated by the immediate payment of reparations in kind to France, Poland and Britain. All of this seemed at odds with the conciliatory criteria mooted in Wilson's Fourteen Points, which Germany had belatedly accepted as a basis for peace, having emphatically rejected them on their initial publication.

Why did France seek a punitive peace? Why was the settlement not entirely satisfactory to France?

The substance of the treaty reflected France's anxieties about its long-term security. It was deeply conscious of Germany's capacity for reasserting itself unless restricted by rigorous, rigidly enforced terms. There was no longer scope for a Franco-Russian alliance to inhibit German external policies. France's quest for a punitive peace was urged on by a sense of inferiority, prompted by a numerically inferior manpower and a sluggish birth rate, and the memory of being twice invaded in 50 years. Failure to persuade the Allies that France should absorb land west of the Rhine and the Saar – exclusively German land – resulted in the compromise of a demilitarised Rhineland, France's enjoyment of the profits of the Saar's industries for 15 years and the promise, subsequently unfulfilled, that the USA and Britain would guarantee France's eastern frontier with Germany.

With hard bargaining needed to fashion compromises, and the fear that any renegotiation would imperil Allied unity, it was hardly surprising that German sentiment was ignored. In any case, Germany's actions near the end of the war – for example, the imposition of the Treaty of Brest-Litovsk (March 1918) upon Russia, which sanctioned vast German territorial acquisitions in Eastern Europe – helped to eclipse any notion of accommodating German sensitivities. Germany's denial that it alone was responsible for the war made little impression on the victors, who were unconcerned with the more remote causes of the conflict, but preoccupied with the suffering that Germany's part in the events of 1914 had precipitated. Thus, Germans nursed a lasting resentment at the treaty, encouraged not merely by the perceived severity of its terms, but by the injustice that they believed informed it.

Why were the powers indifferent to German views on a peace settlement? Consider German treatment of Russia in 1918, for example, as indicative of how brutally Germany might have acted had it won the war.

Nevertheless, Germany was far from ruined by the treaty. It may be argued that, by reducing the army to 100,000 volunteers, Germany was assured of a disciplined, well-motivated army that ultimately proved to be an excellent foundation for Hitler's vastly increased force after 1935. Its undamaged industries facilitated a rapid economic recovery after 1925, when it no longer gave the Allies 'most favoured nation' status. As early as 1921, Germany's steel production was triple that of France. In economic terms, the loss of its empire relieved Germany of a future financial liability. Moreover, in Eastern and Central Europe, new, inexperienced and untested small states came to replace the collapsed Habsburg and Tsarist Empires, thus relatively strengthening Germany in the region. It was no effective substitute for a Franco-Russian alliance that France established a network of alliances with Poland (1921), Czechoslovakia (1924), Romania (1926) and Yugoslavia (1927), none of which was a match for Germany. They would be at the mercy of a revived Germany with a restored military capacity. Moreover, the Treaty of Rapallo (1922), bringing together Germany and the Soviet Union to their mutual benefit, augmented French discomfort. In the aftermath of the war, Germany, far from being weakened geopolitically, had been strengthened.

Now consider the evidence that Germany was not fundamentally weakened by the treaty. Note the underlying strength of the German economy. May it not be argued that Germany's geopolitical position after 1919 was stronger than it had been in 1914?

Germany's relative strength was enhanced in other ways. Britain, increasingly uneasy about the settlement, sought Germany's recovery as an indispensable ingredient in a prosperous Europe.

In what other ways was Germany's relative strength enhanced after 1919?

After its disastrous, counter-productive intervention in the Ruhr in order to seize reparations, France, itself subject to economic pressures, was obliged to accept a more relaxed view of Germany, involving a rescheduling and a revision of reparations payments in the Dawes Plan (1924) and the Young Plan (1929). Despite appearances, Germany remained unconciliated, with Stresemann clearly indicating that Germany's ultimate objective was the restoration of German lands in the east and even the incorporation of the Sudetenland and Austria, neither formerly part of Germany. Consistent with 'the spirit of Locarno', surveillance of Germany's armaments was waived and by 1930 the last contingents of British and French troops left the Rhineland. Germany's economic recovery after 1925 had been accompanied by growing nationalism – a harbinger of Hitler's ruthless expansionism. When France and Britain conceded that Germany had a right to equality in armaments (1932), there was little left to obstruct a confident reassertion of German power in Europe.

Related questions

1 To what extent was Hitler's foreign policy governed by his determination to destroy the Treaty of Versailles of 1919?

Before 1933, despite Hitler's forthright condemnation of the Treaty of Versailles, it might have been surmised that, with the responsibilities of power, he would be satisfied with piecemeal amendment to its terms, as his predecessors had been. However, a more radical notion was contained in *Mein Kampf* and his *Secret Book* (1928) – the latter unpublished in his lifetime. In both books he stressed Germany's need to struggle for living space and not merely improve its existing frontiers. He insisted that races inevitably oppose each other and that the strong legitimately secured territory at the expense of the weak. A unifying concept of race, he argued, embraced by 'pure' Germans, was a springboard for a policy that would secure a new economic order for an expanded Reich, independent of the materially dominating and morally degenerating commerce among nations. Thus, the introduction should suggest that something more than the destruction of the Treaty of Versailles and the restoration of Germany's frontier was Hitler's intention.

How had German governments in the 1920s and the German people responded to the Versailles settlement? Why was Hitler not to be satisfied with a mere restoration of Germany's 1914 frontiers? How did Hitler lay the foundations for achieving his ultimate goals in foreign policy during the period 1933–5? By ceasing to allow Germany to be a member of the League of Nations and leaving the Disarmament Conference (1933); rearmament was a prerequisite for his future objectives. Why was Hitler able to reoccupy the demilitarised Rhineland in March 1936? What were the consequences of the presentation of his aims in foreign policy in November 1937, contained in the Hossbach Memorandum? They were *Anschluss* (March 1938) followed by the acquisition by Germany of the Sudetenland from Czechoslovakia – a concession that was a modification of the Treaty of St Germain, not the Treaty of Versailles. What was the significance of Hitler's actions in 1939, culminating in the Russo-German Pact of 23 August 1939? Note that as early as August 1939 – despite the agreement with the Soviet Union – Hitler was claiming that 'everything I undertake is directed against Russia'. Thus, the dismantling of the Treaty of Versailles was, to Hitler, an inescapable preliminary to an entirely new dispensation, stretching from Germany to the Urals. This was an expansionist policy that far exceeded in scale the mere reversal of the diktat of Versailles, but which was implicit in the racist credo explicitly stated in *Mein Kampf*.

2   Why did the Treaty of Versailles of 1919 prove not to be durable?

3   'The Treaty of Versailles of 1919 was too lenient.' What truth, if any, is there in this assertion?

'Fortunate to survive so many enemies for so long.'
How far is this verdict on the Weimar Republic valid
for the period 1919–24?

Tackling the question

There are historians who have accepted the deterministic view that the Weimar Republic was doomed from the start. They claim that anti-democratic forces of the left and right were present from the beginning and that, as the world economic crisis deepened after 1929, they strengthened their hold on the German electorate. It has also been argued that Ebert had little alternative in the knee-jerk reaction to the crisis at the end of the war but had to come to terms with the traditional élite if Bolshevism was to be contained. On the other hand, other researchers believe that those who were seeking a solution based on the model of the October Revolution in Russia were of little importance, that Ebert had greater freedom for manoeuvre than he imagined and therefore that he wasted the opportunity of giving the Republic a surer foundation at the outset when he enjoyed a decisive electoral advantage. Whatever the scale of the problems faced by the Republic before 1924, it survived. This is more than can be said for Italy, where democracy entirely collapsed in the face of fascism. In contrast, the Weimar Republic proved able to resist successfully the threat from the right and to survive in 1923 an unprecedented hyperinflation accompanied by a serious political crisis.

By 1924, with a new currency and calmer political conditions than before, it seemed at last to be set fair for the future. There seemed scope for consolidating democracy. However, much focus has recently been directed at the middle years (1924–9) in response to Borchardt's argument that, despite the appearance of economic recovery, there were serious weaknesses in the German economy, with workers receiving higher wages – determined by compulsory arbitration – than was justified by levels of productivity. For a time, he argues, a bitter distributional conflict between capital and labour was masked by inflation and capital imports. Thus, when the economic crisis beginning in 1929 came, the Republic speedily became ungovernable. This approach, therefore, looks to the period of relative prosperity for the many political ills of the early 1930s – the related essay deals with the issues raised by Borchardt's thesis.

Answer

Establish that the Weimar Republic survived during the period 1919–24 despite hostility to it within Germany and external

From 1919 to 1924 the Weimar Republic, beset by acute economic and social problems, was continually threatened by fierce, yet incoherent, political hostility from left and right, opposed to parliamentary democracy. Moreover, it was subject to sustained pressure from outside, especially from France, where the conservative-nationalist Poincaré insisted on precise application of the peace terms and was ready to weaken Germany further, unconvinced that France had gained full security at Versailles (1919). Despite almost continuous tribulation, the Republic had survived, albeit precariously, by 1924. To its dubious advantage, it had enjoyed, since November 1918, the commitment of the army, despite its ideological hostility, to the protection of the Republic (Ebert–Groener Pact). The army proved brutally effective in dealing with the rebellious radical left. Yet the disruption accompanying the hyperinflation of 1923 might have done for the Republic had not Stresemann acted promptly to introduce a new currency, the Rentenmark (November 1923). Moreover, the powers – even France – recognised the irresistible need to modify the reparations settlement. Even so, the political hostility to the Republic had merely been temporarily thwarted.

pressures. Note the importance of the army's agreed commitment to supporting the Republic after 1918. How was the Republic able to survive the hyperinflation of 1923?

The majority Social Democrats came to power because of the paralysis of will of the monarchical system to maintain order, following the frank admission of imminent defeat in the war (October 1918). This facilitated the creation of a democratic, pluralist political system buttressed by compromises, such as the Stinnes–Legien agreement between employers and the trade unions (November 1918), intended to minimise social tensions that might lead to revolution. Yet frequent and destructive pressure from the radical left and right – both essentially anti-parliamentarian – invited political instability, even though neither had the necessary organisation and cohesion to overthrow the Republic.

Now discuss the consequences of the establishment of a democratic, pluralistic political system in Germany after 1918.

Ebert's view of the revolution of 1918 as the moderate democratisation of the German state, involving rejection of radical political change, prompted the founding of the KPD and the precipitation of the so-called Spartacist 'rising'. It was inspired by a minority within the KPD who vainly sought a Bolshevik-style revolution in Germany. The radical left – the USPD and the KPD – thereafter, in their frustrations, often threatened insurrection. Grave disorder in Bavaria (1919), the activities of workers' self-defence units in Saxony and Thuringia and the 'Red Army' in the Ruhr (1920) were brutally repressed by *Freikorps* and regular troops. The military's co-operation in repeatedly crushing the radical left, adverse judicial decisions and the failure to participate in the demonstrations, organised by trade unions, that foiled the Kapp Putsch (March 1920) emphasised the left's ineffectiveness and its failure to win mass support.

How was the threat from the left contained?

How was the more serious threat from the right contained? Identify the rightist elements in postwar Germany,

More serious for the Republic was rightist opposition. There was an influential body of opinion among the judiciary and the civil servants, for example, who were previously servants of Wilhelmine Germany, that was able to threaten the new Republic by its professional judgements and actions. More overtly, there was the boorish opposition of *Freikorps* and paramilitary groups. Additionally, there were *Volkisch* groups, originating in prewar times, anti-Semitic in character and unhealthily preoccupied with the purity of the German race. These elements were fragmented and represented a potentially explosive mixture of discontent. In practice, attempted rightist putsches failed ignominiously. The Kapp Putsch (March 1920) was stopped by a general strike in Berlin called by the trade unions and joined by workers nation-wide. Hitler's ill-organised attempted putsch in Munich (November 1923) was put down by a conspicuously right-wing Bavarian government. Initially, the sole political party for nation-alists was the DNVP, but it was held together only by its negative posturing towards the Republic and was internally divided over the efficacy of participation in government (1924–8).

By 1924 the Republic's radical critics of the left and the right had manifestly failed, at least for the present, despite the utter chaos threatening in the period of hyperinflation (1923). The period of open civil war and putschist activity had ended.

Now discuss the role of the army in this period. What was its attitude to the Republic? Explain how the army was only ostensibly 'non-political'. Should it be viewed as a threat to or a defender of the Republic?

Of the autonomous elements within Germany, the Reichswehr, imbued with fervent nationalism, might have threatened the infant Republic had not the army been party to the deliberate engineering of existing political forces in 1918 to establish it. The Ebert–Groener Pact (November 1918) promised the army's help to maintain order. Thereafter, the army tolerated the Republic in its own interest, since civil war would have threatened the army's unity as much as the state's. Although the army was ostensibly 'non-political', von Seeckt – the chief of the Army Command – and other senior commanders were involved in political decisions in the Ministry of Defence without being answerable to the Reichstag. Crucially, while the *Reichswehr* leaders' sympathies were with the right in politics, they were dismayed by the rightist putsches that might have divided the army. Von Seeckt displayed dubious loyalty during the Kapp Putsch and in November 1923, in order not to be obliged to intervene in Bavaria, he warned Bavarian leaders – Kahr and Lossow – not to co-operate with nationalist extremists. Thus, the army preferred the role of defender rather than subverter of the state, in uneasy co-operation with a democratically elected Republic for which it had scant sympathy.

During the monumental disruption of 1923, with Germany's currency valueless, the Republic might have collapsed utterly. Despite the painful measures taken by Stresemann during his short-lived Chancellorship (late 1923) to halt passive resistance in the Ruhr and to introduce a new currency, the Rentenmark – achieved by implementing Article 48, at this point a vital tool of the state's defenders – such measures might well have been insufficient had not the powers, France included, realised that the problem of reparations had to be tackled. The Dawes Plan (1924) – evidence of America's resolve to re-establish economic peace in Europe – by establishing the principle that Germany's reparation payments should be compatible with its ability to pay, inaugurated a period of relative political, social and economic stability for Germany (1924–9). It may be persuasively argued that foreign intervention in 1924 facilitated the Republic's escape from a not inconceivable anarchy.

How was the Republic saved in 1923 and 1924?

By 1924 the Republic had weathered its postwar crisis, but it was a moot point whether the stabilisation of 1924 would lead to the consolidation of the democratic parliamentary system. The ambivalent political attitudes of the army did not inspire confidence. The perceived humiliation of the Treaty of Versailles and the hardship and ruin accompanying hyperinflation were generally blamed on the 'November Republic', for which, in 1924, there was declining electoral support. The grievances remained, although muted, in the phase of relative stability (1924–9), only to emerge with a new and deadly potency during the Depression after 1929.

In what sense may it be claimed that, even with the period from 1924 to 1929 appearing to be one of relative prosperity, the Republic was still insecure. How important were economic factors in undermining the Weimar Republic in the years before 1933?

Related questions

1 How important were economic factors in undermining the Weimar Republic in the years before 1933?

While economic factors have to be the principal concern of this essay, it is important that other factors should not be neglected. Early on there were threats of insurrection from the left and the right that were successfully resisted. In terms of political sentiment, the army may have been out of kilter with a democratic republic, but it did commit itself to the task of protecting the Republic. Disparate interest groups, inside and outside the Reichstag, often fervently nationalistic and anti-Semitic in character, pressed their dubious claims on beleaguered governments. Yet, after the economic and financial collapse accompanying the

Ruhr crisis of 1923, Germany, equipped with a new currency and reduced reparations payments as a result of the Dawes Plan of 1924, gave every appearance of enjoying an economic recovery.

However, even during the period of relative prosperity in the latter part of the 1920s, the economy was not without its problems. The German economic historian Borchardt has argued that excessive wage increases, encouraged by compulsory arbitration agreements, were not matched by comparable increases in productivity. The economy's competitiveness was weakened in consequence. Pressure on profits reduced the capacity of German industry outside the conglomerates to invest. High taxation was required for expensive social welfare policies. Under-investment caused high rates of unemployment even before the Depression began in 1929. Thus, Borchardt claims, there was a bitter distributional conflict between capital and labour, masked initially by inflation and capital imports. The compulsory arbitration schemes made wage settlements political issues, with employers and employees seeking political support within the Reichstag and through extra-parliamentary organisations. It is Borchardt's contention that, by the time the Depression began, the Republic was already ungovernable. The unavoidable deflationary policies that, for example, Brüning pursued were politically disastrous, and the social distress facilitated Hitler's rise to power. Under the impact of worldwide depression after 1929, the parliamentary system proved to be unviable and progressively the public exhibited at the polls a readiness to sacrifice liberties associated with the Republic for the smack of firm government.

2 Why did the Weimar Republic fail?

3 Why was Hitler able to recover from the disaster of the Munich Putsch in 1923 and become Germany's political leader by 1933?

'The collapse of the Weimar Republic was
inevitable, but the triumph of Nazism was not.'
To what extent is this judgement valid?

Tackling the question

While it may be argued by many historians that the infant Weimar Republic faced an abundance of problems, there are differences among them about the severity of those difficulties. Richard Bessel believes that the Republic was probably doomed from the start. Certainly, it inherited acute financial problems amounting to bankruptcy. There were communists and, more seriously, influential elements on the right who rejected the new state from the outset. Even in the period of apparent prosperity, agriculture was heavily in debt. Certain industries – coal, iron and steel were examples – were concerned about profitability and rationalisation, and even before 1929 were already producing structural unemployment. Government expenditure was exceptionally high and would be exposed as excessive once there was a grave economic crisis, as there was after 1929. Then the government's remedial deflationary policies threatened to destroy a Republic that was already declining in popularity in any case.

As the problems increased after 1929, the German voter turned to political parties that regarded parliamentary government with distaste. The Nazis were the principal beneficiaries of this. They gained considerable support from all those who were not previously mobilised by the communists, the moderate socialists and the trade unions. But was the support for the Nazis sufficient to ensure that they came to power? Kolb believes that Schleicher might have established a military government, but it is doubtful whether a highly developed and politicised society such as Germany in the early 1930s would have tolerated such a government for long, even though by 1933 the *Reichswehr* was well prepared for dealing with potential unrest. In the event, no Schleicher-led military regime materialised. A recent book by Henry Ashby Turner, Hitler's *Thirty Days to Power*, endorses Bullock's view that in the end Hitler was 'jobbed into office by a backstairs intrigue', which required an elaborate plot to deceive the octogenarian President Hindenburg.

Answer

Guidance notes

A multiplicity of difficulties besetting an infant democracy have traditionally explained the collapse of the Weimar Republic: the government's inescapable, but humiliating, acceptance of the diktat of the Versailles settlement (1919); a flawed constitution;

Examine the scope of the question. Show how the Republic survived the early difficulties that threatened to bring about its collapse, only to be overtaken by the dire effects of the Wall Street Crash of 1929. But was Hitler's rise to power an inevitable accompaniment to the Republic's collapse?

the debilitating absence of a democratic consensus; menacing threats from both the radical left and the radical right; acute inflation, culminating in hyperinflation, early on and deep depression latterly. Yet the Republic survived its earlier woes only for them to be dwarfed subsequently by the politically disintegrative effects of the world economic crisis. Although by early 1933 the NSDAP, led by Hitler, enjoyed no absolute majority in the Reichstag, the unlikelihood of other political parties co-operating effectively to keep him out of office meant that, despite Hindenburg's personal distaste for Hitler, his acceptance of the latter's participation in government could not be ruled out. In the absence of a Schleicher-led military regime, covert manoeuvrings ultimately persuaded a reluctant Hindenburg that, were Hitler to be appointed Chancellor, it would be possible constitutionally to inhibit his exercise of power.

Consider the adverse effects of the Versailles settlement on the Weimar Republic.

The Weimar Republic was born in circumstances of defeat and national humiliation. The sacrifice of much of Germany's peripheral land, sometimes without plebiscite – especially the Polish lands – was considered incompatible with the principle of self-determination enunciated in Wilson's Fourteen Points. Article 231, obliging Germany to shoulder full responsibility for the war, was deeply resented. Ultimately, reparations of £6,600 million, designed to keep Germany permanently weak, added to the burden of the democratic politicians who had signed the treaty, for it fuelled nationalist sentiment and nourished the myth of Germany having been 'stabbed in the back'. The persistent rhetoric of the right – the NSDAP especially – insidiously eroded support for the Republic.

To what extent did the Weimar Constitution weaken the Republic, if at all? Was it not the character of the political parties in the Reichstag that seriously weakened the Republic, rather than the number of them?

The nature of the Constitution, allowing the President to rule by emergency decree (Article 48), and the introduction of absolute proportional representation are often held to have weakened the Republic. While Ebert may have exercised presidential power in order to protect the democracy of the Republic, Hindenburg – unsympathetic to democratic procedures – used it habitually to sustain the government after 1930 when it no longer commanded a dependable parliamentary majority. Indeed, it was the nature of the parties, selfishly pursuing their sectional interests, rather than the mere multiplicity of them which potentially irreparably damaged the Republic. Although there were coalitions with varying degrees of success between 1924 and 1928, some political parties rejected the democratic system. The nationalists (DNVP) and the NSDAP favoured authoritarian government, as did the KPD – the communists – in their quest for proletarian revolution. Only the Zentrum – until Brüning, its leader, embraced semi-authoritarian government when he was Chancellor (1930–2) – the DPP and the SPD upheld democratic processes. These virtually ceased when Hindenburg exercised his presidential powers under Article 48 to enable Brüning's government to continue without dependence on parliamentary support.

Recurrent economic and financial problems contributed nothing to the Republic's stability. Even after the hyperinflationary traumas of 1923, economic recovery (1924–8) was dangerously dependent on foreign loans and was therefore susceptible to fluctuations on international money markets and the confidence of overseas investors. Moreover, by the late 1920s, despite some prosperity, high government expenditure on welfare and the infrastructure – amounting to 26% of GNP – high wage settlements, arising from compulsory arbitration, and under-investment prompted by pressure on profits meant that the economy was becoming increasingly uncompetitive. As early as February 1929, 3 million people were unemployed. The distributional conflict between capital and labour was corrosively infiltrating political life well before the dire effects of world depression were experienced.

> What impact did economic and financial problems have upon the Republic's chances of survival?

By the early 1930s the Republic's collapse was almost certain. Scarcely less certain was Hitler's rise to power. Before January 1933 the NSDAP's most conspicuous electoral success was in July 1932 when it won 37.3% of votes cast. This was notable under a system of absolute proportional representation and persuasive evidence that the NSDAP had sufficient support to justify its acceptance at least as a component of any government. A remote possibility was a military regime led by Schleicher, but he could not have counted on the support of the *Reichswehr* officer corps and there were lower and middle ranking officers who had Nazi sympathies. In any case, in such a politicised society as Germany had become, it seems unlikely that a military government would have been tolerated for long. In the event, despite Hindenburg's initial resistance to Hitler becoming Chancellor, ultimately it was backstairs intrigue – engineered by von Papen, Oscar Hindenburg (the President's son) and Meissner (Hindenburg's Chief of Staff) – which enabled Hitler, obdurately insistent that he should become Chancellor, despite declining electoral support as evidenced in the election of November 1932, to secure power.

> How did Hitler come to power?

Nevertheless, there were regional variations in electoral support for the NSDAP. It was much stronger in Protestant than in Catholic areas, in rural than in urban districts, and in small and medium-sized towns than in conurbations. White-collar workers, 20% of

> Where did the Nazis succeed in winning considerable electoral support and where did they fail to dominate electorally?

the labour force, were inclined to support the NSDAP. Recent research by Jürgen Falter suggests that one in four workers voted for the Nazis in July 1932, indicating that Hitler enjoyed merely considerable minority support in industrial towns. Yet it cannot be claimed that the manual unemployed turned to Hitler in large numbers. Where there were established ideologies or organisational loyalties – as in SPD and KPD strongholds – the NSDAP's electoral inroads were limited. Thus, Nazi success in Protestant rural Germany and among the middle classes occurred where existing political loyalties were weak.

What factors combined to enable Hitler to assume power by January 1933?

The NSDAP's electoral setback in November 1932, when its share of the vote fell from 37.3% to 33.1%, scarcely weakened its claim to a place in government. In his brief tenure of the Chancellorship (December 1932 – January 1933), Schleicher sought in vain to persuade a nervous Hindenburg to ban the NSDAP and the KPD. Thereafter, von Papen – now hostile to Schleicher for having orchestrated his removal for the Chancellorship in December 1932 – with the help of members of Hindenburg's entourage, succeeded in convincing the President that Hitler, hedged in by what they wrongly believed to be effective constitutional constraints, should become Chancellor. Such conservative elements shared some of Hitler's political preoccupations – nationalist fervour, virulent anti-communism and antipathy towards the democratic politics enshrined in the Constitution. Moreover, Hitler was benefiting from arid divisions between the SPD and the KPD, both at leadership level, where the latter regarded the former as a prop of capitalism, deflecting workers from the revolutionary path, and at grass-roots level, where mass long-term unemployment was causing social and economic fragmentation.

Assess the validity of the quotation in the question set.

By early 1933 the relative electoral strength of the NSDAP made it likely that, unless a military regime were established, Hitler would soon participate in government. An anxious Hindenburg was prevailed upon by von Papen to accept that Hitler could be controlled by a conservative coalition with broad parliamentary support. It seemed a plausible alternative to the unacceptability of short-lived, ineffective governments that had obtained since Brüning's fall in 1932. 'Jobbed into office by a backstairs intrigue' was Bullock's verdict. That this fateful decision was taken by a handful of men in January 1933 seems to endorse Henry Ashby Turner's view that 'impersonal forces make things possible, people make things happen'.

1 How valid is it to argue that by 1934 Hitler had established a dictatorship in Germany by entirely legal methods?

By 1932 the parliamentary strength of the Nazi Party would have justified its participation in government and not inconceivably the Chancellorship being bestowed on Hitler, its leader. Indeed, he insisted tenaciously that he would accept nothing less than the role of Chancellor. When this was conceded to him in January 1933, it could be argued that a legal path to office had been trodden by Hitler, in that the Nazi Party had, with other parties, competed in the constitutionally established electoral process. However, there was always an accompaniment of orchestrated intimidation and violence involved in the Nazis' garnering of votes, which qualifies claims that they proceeded entirely by legal means. The penchant for generating fear was displayed with much enhanced intensity and ruthlessness once the Chancellorship was in Hitler's hands, in order to remove political opponents and to ensure that, ostensibly legally, the Weimar Constitution was changed – that is, in practice, dissolved. Establish early in the essay that, in the aftermath of the failure of the Munich Putsch in 1923, Hitler decided to gain support legally through the ballot box, even though his unwavering objective was to destroy the parliamentary procedures of the Republic. Explain the methods – from intimidating uniformed processions by torchlight to overt physical violence – that were used to create an ethos of fear and intimidation. It was Hindenburg's and von Papen's misconception that they believed in 1933 that Hitler, as Chancellor, would be obliged to depend on the constitutional powers vested in the President.

Examine the illegal methods used by the Nazi Party to win the election of 5 March 1933, albeit with less than 44% of the electorate voting for it. What were the immediate consequences of the Reichstag Fire of 27 February 1933? How was arrest, violence and intimidation used to secure the two-thirds majority required for the passage of the Enabling Act, which gave Hitler power to rule without recourse to the Reichstag for four years? Did Hindenburg's signature, applied to the Decree for the Protection of People and State, not give a fig leaf of legality to the arrest of political opponents? Hitler's dictatorship was endorsed by the Reichstag as a result of a manipulation of the Weimar Constitution itself. Legally, there was no formal dissolution of the Weimar Republic, but the democratic spirit that informed the creators of it had evaporated. Thereafter, he was able to create a one-party state. Finally, examine how Hitler destroyed the SA in the 'Night of the Long Knives' (30 June 1934). There was no pretence of legality in removing a movement that he was persuaded represented a threat to his authority. It should be stressed that Hitler's undisputed power was gained by the use of a carapace of legality. Accompanying his achievement of absolute power was a patent criminality that was evident before and after he assumed power in January 1933.

2 'Doomed from the start.' How far is this a justified verdict on the Weimar Republic?

3 Why was the Weimar Republic unable to resist the rise of Nazism?

Question 31

'A totalitarian state.'
Discuss the validity of this description as applied to Hitler's rule in Germany.

Tackling the question

'Totalitarian' is a technical term, so before we can decide whether it should be applied to Hitler's Germany it has to be defined. It is a term that may be ascribed exclusively to twentieth-century regimes because in earlier centuries rulers did not have the means – modern communications, for example – that would have enabled them to exercise a very high degree of control over their peoples. Indeed, there are dictatorships in the world today, often in developing countries, where much is still primitive and governments are inefficient, brutal and unable to act with any consistency or clear purpose. In the twentieth century it is Hitler's rule in Germany and Stalin's in the Soviet Union that seem, to those historians who are ready to accept the term, to be fittingly described as totalitarian. Even so, despite the awesome power that both of them wielded, they may not fulfil all the criteria that a theoretical definition of the term would seem to demand. However, in practice you may conclude that, as long as a regime measures up to those aspects of totalitarianism that are most important in ensuring that the people governed are forced into subjection and fearful of the consequences of dissent, it may be described as 'totalitarian'. It was Mussolini who, in a speech in January 1925, inaugurating his fascist regime as a novel political system within the framework of the monarchical state, used the term 'totalitarian' to describe the character of his own government. In practice, he was much less able than Hitler or Stalin to sustain such a regime.

Answer

Begin by defining the term 'totalitarian'. List factors that together qualify a regime to be described as 'totalitarian'. You do not need to mention Hitler's Germany until the end of the paragraph, when you state what your task will be.

'Totalitarianism' implies all-embracing control by a political organisation that is equipped to scrutinise and pass judgement on every detailed aspect of a society that it holds in thrall. No vestige of opposition is tolerated. An insidiously penetrative police ensures conformity by intimidation and violence. An elaborate hierarchy of ideologically committed bureaucrats administers the state. Propaganda is calculated to muster unquestioning support for the regime. The education of the young, generously laced with indoctrination, is geared to produce durable and unbending loyalty to the state. The economic system is likely to be highly centralised, efficiently monitored at the highest level and implemented decisively and productively in the regions according to established priorities. The whole system may be presided over by a charismatic leader, whose powerful, even hypnotic, oratory ensures that people's daily anxieties are transcended by a vision of a glorious future sustained by the prevailing ideology.

The 'totalitarian' state so described is an abstraction. Societies may only approach the 'ideal'. While the term is not as readily accepted now as it was in the 1950s, especially now that the most durable example of it – the Soviet Union – has collapsed, some of the defined characteristics of it were clearly present in Nazi Germany. The brutal power wielded by the SS was awesome and emphatically discouraged manifestations of political dissent. The promotion of a single ideology by means of ubiquitous propaganda in an atmosphere of intimidation, orchestrated by a repressive police system and administered by an extensive party apparatus, must have blunted any wish to express an individual judgement. Moreover, there was the ingredient of a dynamic leader, the Führer – the fount of political power – in whom was vested, it was claimed, the will of the people. Yet if these characteristics of the Nazi state suggest 'totalitarianism', the Nazi Party did not in practice possess the degree of organisation and unity of purpose associated with the Bolsheviks. Nor was there the centralised control of the economy that might be expected in a one-party state where the ideology was intended to transform society.

> Now apply the defined term to Hitler's rule. Identify concisely those characteristics of the regime that match the criteria that you have established in the introductory paragraph. However, point out the factors that seem to conflict with aspects of totalitarianism that you have described.

Germany became a one-party state (July 1933), other parties having been dissolved or having dissolved themselves. Nevertheless, this did not presage the installation of an efficient governmental system. The relationship between the structure and role of the party and the machinery of the German state was never clarified. Indeed, the Nazi Party was geared to the seizure of power rather than to its practice, so that it was a source of contention within the party, which contained in the SA many genuine social revolutionaries, that Hitler retained the services of many bureaucrats who had underpinned the Weimar governments. The party's incapacity for undertaking the task of government was prompted by a disunity arising from the formation of a multiplicity of specialist organisations before 1933, with a view to broadening the base of Nazi support throughout Germany. Thus, the party had become fragmented and lacked a unified structure. However, after the mid-1930s, Bormann, assisted by Hess, created a Department for Internal Affairs, so that the party structure could be disciplined, and a Department for Affairs of State that sought to establish party supremacy over the state.

> You may consider an aspect of Hitler's one-party state – the difficult relationship between the structure and role of the Nazi Party and the governing of Germany – which shows that Nazi Germany was not always ruthlessly efficient.

By 1939 the party was more suitably qualified for the business of government, although internal divisions were never to be entirely eradicated.

Show how Hitler's singular personality was not well suited to watching over, guiding in detail and monitoring the way Germany was governed. What impact did this characteristic of his rule have?

Certainly, Hitler would seem to possess all the characteristics of a totalitarian ruler – personal charisma, a ruthless will, a capacity for generating unqualified admiration and fear. On the face of it, he possessed undisputed authority. He believed that his power would secure his passionately held objectives. Of course, as in the Soviet Union, no leader could control all aspects of policy. Both Hitler and Stalin depended upon subordinates for its implementation. Hitler's personality militated against his absorbing himself in the minutiae of policy. He abhorred committee work. He had no interest in the mechanisms that co-ordinated policies. Confusion in government was the result. Some historians consider that policies emerged from pressure of circumstances and that Hitler was reluctant to take decisions and often prevaricated, his preoccupation being his personal prestige and ascendancy.

Now focus on the German economy. Hitler demanded economic policies that would eventually enable Germany to wage war. Given this objective, he seems to have neglected to ensure that the means to achieve it were efficient.

Nor did Hitler have sufficient interest in or knowledge of economics to control the Nazi economy. Autarkic policies, deficit financing and gearing the economy to meet the demands of war were its main characteristics. However, there was no consistent or coherent plan for achieving political and military objectives through the operation of the economy. Initially, he depended on established expertise, but Schacht's influence as Minister of Economics (1934–7) diminished when he insisted that reducing arms expenditure was necessary if Germany was to escape acute balance of payments problems and the difficulties associated with a large budget deficit. Thereafter, Nazi influence over the economy – reflected in the Four-Year Plan controlled by Goering – increased substantially, but the quest for self-sufficiency did not enable Germany to possess an economy geared for protracted war.

Draw your conclusions, remembering that not all of the theoretical criteria need to be satisfied for a regime to be described as 'totalitarian'. That there should be no autonomous sources of power within the state is a crucial factor to consider. Even though Mussolini could speak of 'the fierce totalitarian will' of fascism, he was always

By 1936 it was principally the emerging power of the SS – almost a state within the state – which, in its capacity to intimidate and terrorise, created an ethos of all-pervasive subordination of the people to the state and its leader. Autonomous sources of power were silenced. The SS was the instrument used to destroy the SA, perceived by Hitler as a dire threat to his authority. The army, with its long established associations with political influence, was rendered innocuous as a political threat by an oath of loyalty to be taken by all soldiers. Politically reliable Nazis – like Keitel and Brauchitsch – presided over an army that was, in any case, encouraged to be loyal by the emphasis on rearmament. There is no evidence of any major domestic development being contrary to Hitler's wishes. His pursuit of continental conquest and racial supremacy provoked no measurable resistance. The guiding principle of unquestioning obedience to the Führer's will – despite confusion, misjudgement and inefficiency in the implementation of policy – was always sustained by incessant propaganda and fear. Thus, the term 'totalitarianism' does not seem to be an inappropriate description of the Nazi state.

vulnerable to the pressures of autonomous elements within the state, as Related Question 1 will demonstrate.

Related questions

1 What is meant by the term 'totalitarian state'? Illustrate your answer with reference to Italy ruled by Mussolini and Germany ruled by Hitler.

Describe the 'totalitarian state' in the way already demonstrated in the first paragraph of the answer to Question 31. It is a matter of judgement as to whether the degree of control exercised by a particular state qualifies it for the description. It may be argued that Mussolini and Hitler aspired to create such states, but that the latter was more successful than the former in achieving his objective. Mussolini, who fostered the cult of Il Duce, infallible and supremely wise, saw that an all-pervasive propaganda and the indoctrination of the young were indispensable elements in establishing a dynamic, disciplined society. Why then may it be argued that he failed to create a totalitarian state? No sustaining ideology was consistently presented to the people. There remained autonomous groups within the state with the potential to disrupt the unswerving loyalty demanded by a totalitarian ruler – the monarchy, the Roman Catholic Church and the army. The army was never totally loyal to him. Ultimately, it was the monarchy that proscribed the Fascist Party and appointed General Badoglio as Mussolini's replacement.

The factors that may determine a view that Hitler's Germany was a totalitarian state have been discussed in the answer to Question 31. While Mussolini's abject failures in war after 1940 paved the way for autonomous groups to plot his overthrow, even though Hitler's war effort was being gradually worn down by the coalition formed against him, within Germany, until his suicide in the bunker, his leadership had not been effectively challenged. There was no dependable springboard from which dissenting elements could conspire against him, notwithstanding the July Plot of 1944. This may be seen as confirmation of the totalitarian nature of the regime. In contrast, Mussolini's regime was merely authoritarian, fitfully intimidating and often vacuously posturing.

2 To what extent did the Nazi regime in Germany bring about a social revolution?

3 How far did Mussolini achieve a revolution in Italy?

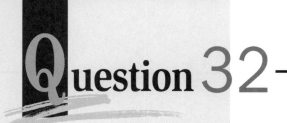
How much 'grand design' and how much
'opportunism' were evident in Hitler's foreign
policy from 1933 to 1939?

Tackling the question

Many views have been expressed about the nature of Hitler's foreign policy. Until the 1960s it was widely held that Hitler pursued long-term aims that he may have devised as early as the 1920s. H. Trevor Roper wrote of his 'known unchanging aims'. A.J.P. Taylor and F.H. Hinsley disagreed – the former explicitly and the latter by implication – in that they considered his foreign policy to be characterised by opportunism. Almost simultaneously with the publication of Taylor's *The Origins of the Second World War* in 1961, Franz Fischer drew attention to the issue of 'continuity' in German foreign policy in the twentieth century. That, in the First World War, he argues, Germany pursued expansionist aims calls into question the originality of Hitler's aims in the Second World War. A further refinement of interpretation has been Jackl's insistence that his racial ideology played a crucial role in the formation of his foreign policy, thus reinforcing the approach of Trevor Roper and Bullock that he always had a clear set of objectives. Hillgruber and Hildebrand have gone further by proposing that he was resolved on world domination, for which *Lebensraum* in Eastern Europe was an indispensable preliminary. There is a further view that sees Nazi foreign policy as a consequence of the pressures of the domestic economy. T.W. Mason stresses the economic crisis of 1938–9, which prompted a 'flight towards' war in 1939, in order to escape from the confusion arising from the absence of clear direction in most aspects of the Nazis' internal policies.

Answer

Explain the various explanations
there are of Hitler's foreign policy.

The judgement of the Nuremburg trials (1946) endorsed the widely held view outside Germany in the 1940s that Hitler had caused and planned war. Yet since 1946 other interpretations have arisen. Some historians consider it to have been a German war in which Hitler expressed the nationalism, militarism, relish for the use of force and adulation of the state that is deeply rooted, as Bullock has insisted, in German history. Alternatively, it may be regarded as an ideological conflict or merely as a war familiar in that it was concerned with material interests and the domination of Europe. If the war was not premeditated and planned, did it come about as an effect of Hitler's improvisations and opportunism? While there may be various interpretations on the matter, there is a prevailing view that Germany's resolve to expand was bound to be resisted eventually, and that up to a certain point there was an anguished acquiescence in German expansion, but that beyond that point it could be opposed only by means of a major conflict.

A.J.P. Taylor, in his *Origins of the Second World War*, considered that Hitler conducted his own foreign policy by improvisation. Contrariwise, there is the view that Hitler was obsessed by a 'grand design' – a notion articulated by Churchill at the time of *Anschluss* (March 1938) as 'a programme of aggression, nicely calculated and timed, unfolding stage by stage'. Shirer concurred in *The Rise and Fall of the Third Reich*, stating that Hitler had a blueprint for aggression. Neither 'grand design' nor 'opportunism' suffices as an exclusive explanation. It is widely held that Hitler's foreign policy cannot be considered to be mere opportunism. That is not to say that Hitler's actions were always precisely timed. A compromise verdict has emerged – that Hitler had a scheme of foreign policy, fuelled by his ideology, within which there was scope for taking advantage of opportunities attending circumstances and events. The basic scheme, in the view of Hillgruber and Hildebrand, was to restore Germany as a European power, secure *Lebensraum*, achieve racial objectives in respect of Jews and Slavs, and establish a new order in Europe before challenging the USA for world supremacy.

> Consider that neither of the two extreme approaches to Hitler's foreign policy – those of a 'grand design' and of 'opportunism' – can be exclusively acceptable. What is the alternative compromise?

While the German historian Golo Mann refers to Hitler as a 'demon', thus emphasizing his singularity and isolation, so that his foreign policy may be seen as the fruit of his own particular ideology and personal psychology, other historians have placed him in the context of German history. Fischer has stressed the continuity between Germany's objectives in the two world wars. There are undoubted similarities. In 1914 Bethmann Hollweg envisaged a *Mitteleuropa* under Germany's overriding control and influence. In September 1914 pan-Germans were calling for the annexation of the Baltic provinces and most of the Soviet Union and Poland, with territories formally annexed being cleared of their inhabitants and resettled with Germans. The Treaty of Brest-Litovsk (March 1918) betrayed the full extent of German war aims, with every intention of never relinquishing provinces containing even a few ethnic Germans. There were close, direct links between Hitler's notion of race and *Lebensraum* and those promoted earlier

> Consider the view that Hitler pursued with unprecedented urgency components of his foreign policy that he had inherited from his predecessors.

by the Pan-German League. It may be argued that Hitler's contribution to this line of argument was a new, unremitting urgency and a uniquely ferocious preoccupation with race that envisaged the elimination of all Jews and the reduction of Slavs to a servile state.

How important were economic factors in determining Hitler's foreign policy?

Thus, Hitler plainly inherited much that was already to be found in German history. However, elements of continuity are insufficient for explaining the character of his foreign policy. For those who put emphasis on economic aims as motives for German expansion, it is difficult to detach Hitler's personality and policy from any economic motivation because Hitler considered himself the master, not the servant, of economic forces. At most, economic pressure for expansion can only supplement, not replace, the impetus of ideological considerations.

Using detail from events in Hitler's foreign policy, show how neither of the approaches cited in the question set are acceptable exclusively.

Extreme views – unrestrained opportunism or the meticulous implementation of a premeditated programme – seem equally unlikely. Hitler did intend to dominate Europe and conquer the Soviet Union, but the process by which this was to be achieved was subject to hesitation and improvisation. The progressive demolition of the Treaty of Versailles as a prelude to expansion well beyond Germany's 1914 frontiers was calculated, but dependent in its timing upon events and circumstances. Thus, the timing of Hitler's intended reoccupation of the demilitarised Rhineland (March 1936) was largely determined by Anglo-French attention being focused on Mussolini's invasion of Abyssinia and the weakness of the League of Nations in responding to it. His political instincts overrode the understandable reservations of the military High Command about Germany's preparedness for such action. Similarly, Hitler took advantage of the outbreak of the Spanish Civil War (July 1936) by intervening on Franco's side to ensure the sustaining and intensification of a conflict that would distract attention from Central Europe.

Show how Hitler's determination to absorb Austria and Czechoslovakia was determined by circumstances and events.

The Hossbach Memorandum (November 1937), despite controversy surrounding it, at least made clear that Hitler intended to absorb Austria and Czechoslovakia. The timing of *Anschluss* (March 1938), however, was a clumsily improvised response to Schuschnigg's intention to organise a national referendum to decide Austria's future status. Pre-empting this precipitated a hurried, ill-organised invasion, legitimated disingenuously by Seyss-Inquart's 'invitation' to Hitler to intervene. If Hitler had now made 'an unalterable decision to smash Czechoslovakia', it may be argued that Chamberlain's diplomatic interventions (September

1938) were sufficient to persuade Hitler to desist from a military invasion in favour of a negotiated settlement that not only demonstrated Anglo-French resolve to avoid war seemingly at any cost, but undermined the economic and political viability of the Czech state, thus making its collapse – secured by Hitler (March 1939) – almost inevitable.

Nothing might have seemed more improbable than a pact between Germany and Hitler's avowed enemy, the communist Soviet Union (23 August 1939). It suited both parties for the time being, but it was prompted on Hitler's side by the possibility that Britain and France would honour their commitment to Poland and face him with the prospect of a war on two fronts, unless he could guarantee the Soviet Union's neutrality. Yet this in no way modified his ultimate and overriding intention of conquering the Soviet Union in the pursuit of *Lebensraum* and his racial policy. The Anglo-French declaration of war (3 September 1939), however, despite having grave consequences for those Allies, prefaced a war of attrition that Germany was not able to sustain indefinitely. Thus, Hitler's vision of Europe submitting to his implacable will was promoted – and ultimately undermined – by the exploitation of circumstances and events as they arose.

> Conclude by giving an explanation of the Nazi–Soviet Pact of August 1939, considered in the light of a 'grand design' and the pressing need to improvise.

Related questions

1 'Hitler was not entirely responsible for the outbreak of major conflict in 1939.' How valid is this view?

There is a consensus among historians that, although Hitler took advantage of opportunities attending circumstances and events, his foreign policy, fuelled by ideology, involved territorial expansion that at some time would have to be resisted. Initially, powers appeased him, allowing him to dismantle the terms of the Treaty of Versailles without offering resistance that went beyond verbal condemnation. Indeed, at the Munich Conference in September 1938 his acquisition of the Sudetenland was an unedifying and impotent response to Hitler's earlier threat to seize it by force. Britain's and France's appeasement of him ended abruptly when Hitler invaded the reduced Czechoslovakia of the Munich agreement in March 1939. Arguably, the policy of seeking to accommodate Germany's demands – pragmatically embraced also by the Soviet Union in August 1939, when Stalin sought to buy peace by accepting the dismemberment of Poland – contributed, as sins of omission, to bringing about a war that might conceivably have been avoided had steps been taken earlier, before Germany was strong enough to countenance going to war. Yet appeasement did not mean peace at any price, so conflict was certain at some time, A belated triple alliance did not materialise in 1939 as the will for making it did not exist. Ultimately, Britain and France, eventually undeterred by the implications of the Nazi–Soviet Pact, declared war, and by so doing involved Germany in a war of attrition for which its autarkic policies had not fully prepared it.

2 To what extent was the German economy geared to the waging of war by 1939?

3 Why did Hitler's Germany suffer such a catastrophic defeat in the Second World War?

Why was there not more open opposition to Hitler's Reich within Germany during the period 1933–45?

Tackling the question

It has been estimated that there were 250,000 political prisoners in Germany before 1939, and that 50,000 left Germany, many of whom had contributed significantly to German academic, economic and professional life. One historian has considered that Hitler's political victory in 1933 was that of one kind of German over another – in that sense there was a 'civil war' in Germany. The NSDAP, dubbed as 'politicians of catastrophe' in 1928, came to power five years later. Aided by an army of informers, the political left was almost immediately destroyed. The support for Hitler was consolidated by the jobs that the new regime created for the people. Hitler's supporters often originated from the governing classes: senior civil servants – often from the Foreign Office – army officers, some clerics and members of the judiciary, all of whom had been alienated by the Weimar Republic. However, although they may have sided with Hitler initially and shared some, but not all, of his political preoccupations, many gradually became opponents, at first seeing themselves as a 'loyal opposition' – a British concept, incomprehensible to and angrily rejected by Hitler. They were not natural opponents, but rather reluctant opposition. Ultimately, some of them were involved in the bomb plot of July 1944.

Historians differ about the motives of the resisters. Was it to salvage something after the disaster of Stalingrad? Were they conservative authoritarians? Their courage has not been disputed. Many of them met horrifying deaths. By 1941 nobody fighting the Axis powers wanted to know about 'good' Germans. In any case, with the need to keep the Soviet Union on the Allied side, any discussion with German opponents of the regime might be interpreted by the Soviets as seeking a separate peace – for his part, Stalin did not feel under any such restraint. In vain did Bishop Bell of Chichester, who knew Bonhoeffer, argue for acceptance of the good faith of many German resisters. Echoing the verdict on Becket, Eden described Bell as 'this pestilential priest'. The division of opinion on the German opposition persists. While some consider them to have been sincere and that what they did was important, others insist that they had performed vital services for the Nazis before they became opponents, and that their moral objections became real opposition only when they themselves were in danger.

Answer

Guidance notes

No regime, however harsh, will govern wholly unopposed. Authoritarian regimes inevitably force the opposition under-

What factors militated against successful opposition to the

Nazi regime in Germany between 1933 and 1945?

ground. Under Nazi rule, the regime sought total control of the people's lives and used a variety of techniques to achieve it. Perhaps inevitably, underground resistance became residual, never crystallising into a dangerous conspiracy organised to overthrow the regime. Only elements of the army before the war – such as, fleetingly, in 1938 – might have had the capacity to oust Hitler. During the war, the most active source of resistance was within the military intelligence service, but it proved unable to muster sufficient support for a coup. External support would have been crucial, but neither before 1939 nor during the war, when 'total victory' became the Allies' stipulated aim, could emissaries representing resistance have been offered assurances about the treatment of Germany after Hitler's elimination. Any plot against Hitler – as in July 1944 – was likely to be a suicidal gesture against an intolerable regime.

What machinery of repression did the Nazis use in order to control their own people?

Nazi efforts to exercise total control over the German people's lives boded ill for resistance to the regime. The apparatus of repression – police brutality, murder and torture, supplemented by insistent and vigorous propaganda, indoctrination of the young and a hierarchical organisation of political and social structures – reinforced a mood of at least outward conformity by the population.

Consider the scale and impact of resistance within Germany.

Yet there was resistance. Initially, opposition practised during the Weimar Republic continued to function, but it was gradually suppressed by the secret police. Communists were made ineffective as organised opponents, although individuals attempted heroic acts of defiance. In April 1939, according to Gestapo records, over 160,000 people were held in 'protective custody' for political reasons, 27,000 of them under indictment. Between 1933 and 1945 about 3 million Germans were held in concentration camps or prisons for political reasons. Thousands were executed or murdered, or died from torture. The numbers demonstrate the potential for popular resistance and also what happened to resisters. Many Catholic and Lutheran clergy organised clandestine networks, aided people in flight from the authorities and spoke out courageously against racial persecution. These activities were merely irritants to the regime, most of the population acquiescing in or supporting the regime, influenced by propaganda, nationalism or police terror.

What evidence was there of hostility in the army to Hitler's regime before 1939?

Briefly, resistance might have emerged in the army when Hitler removed Blomberg and Fritsch (1938). Some officers saw the dismissals as an attack on the army's integrity and were also alarmed at the threat of European war. Beck, Chief of the General Staff, and Canaris of the Military Counter-Intelligence Agency intended a coup, but did not have the vital support of Brauchitsch. When Beck resigned (August 1938), his successor, Halder, continued to plan to oust Hitler if Germany was driven into war, but the impetus for such a move was entirely lost by the Munich Agreement (September 1938). It was not until well after the war had begun that military opposition showed any signs of regrouping.

After 1939 the military intelligence service was the main source of potential resistance. Halder's resolve faltered once war began, for he felt that a coup would violate tradition and alienate the prevailing public mood in Germany. Also, he believed that the young officer corps was unreliable. It was not until after disaster at Stalingrad that further coup attempts were considered (1943). Briefly, led by von Treschcow, a potential conspiracy developed at the Army Group Centre, at Smolensk in the Soviet Union. Key military figures in Belgium and France prepared for an uprising. Groups of civil servants, politicians and officers – Goerdeler, the former mayor of Leipzig, Beck, von Hassel, a diplomat, among others – established a working relationship with the Kreisau Circle, led by von Moltke, which endeavoured to prepare for events after Hitler's death. While sociologically all categories and levels of the population, and politically the whole spectrum from left to right, were represented in the resistance, representation was numerically insignificant. Fear and propaganda geared to sustaining enthusiasm for war generally encouraged support for the government.

> What resistance was there from civilians and the military during the war years?

It would be a mistake to build up the German opposition and make it appear to be what it was not – a democratic alternative to Nazism. Survivors were not influential after 1945. Their movement was a reaction on the part of the governing classes, for the most part, who had discovered to their utter dismay that Hitler was no better than the Bolsheviks. Their sentiments reflected a broad basis of moral protest and a narrow one of professional disgust. However, those who resisted Hitler could derive no comfort from the Allies. An Anglo-Soviet agreement (July 1941) precluded negotiations and the conclusion of an armistice or treaty of peace 'except by mutual agreement'. Confirmation of this was contained in the Washington Pact (January 1942), which specified unconditional surrender of Germany as a war aim. Thus, emissaries sent by the resistance could expect no cessation of military advance or aerial bombardment while they attempted a coup. Moreover, before the Normandy landings

> What motivated wartime resisters and why were the Allies so indifferent to their resistance?

(1944) any unconditional surrender, such as the Allies demanded, meant in effect occupation of Germany by Soviet armies – a grim prospect for those leading conspirators, often politically conservative, who hoped for a non-communist government when Hitler's dictatorship ended.

What inspired resistance to Hitler inside Germany as the war moved, seemingly irresistibly, towards Germany's defeat?

Nevertheless, conspirators acted despite receiving no support or encouragement from the Allies, unlike other anti-Nazi resistance movements. In 1943 and 1944 assassination attempts were launched in the conviction that it was imperative to demonstrate that there were honourable Germans resolved to end the bloody conflict, even if Germany's territorial integrity and independence could not be saved. At least it would provide evidence that the Nazi ideology had not wholly permeated German society. It was in this spirit that the abortive conspiracy of 20 July 1944 was planned. While there were many courageous enough to volunteer to assassinate Hitler, few of them had the necessary access to him to achieve it. Stauffenburg's ill-fated attempt to kill Hitler at Rastenburg in East Prussia failed and, coupled with the three-hour delay involved in his returning to Berlin to lead the coup, meant that there was insufficient impetus for success. Hitler's retribution was characteristically brutal. Yet, for the conspirators, the practical purpose of the coup was not pre-eminently important. Self-sacrificially, the conspirators of 20 July 1944 came to symbolise the thousands who had resisted valiantly, but unsuccessfully, against an evil regime.

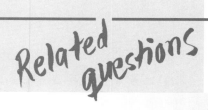

Related questions

1 'A state within a state.' How far is this judgement on the SS justified?

Research has suggested that the German state under Hitler was never an orderly, hierarchical organisation and that Hitler did not rule by means of explicit instructions to his subordinate authorities. Rather, they were left to compete to carry out what each believed to be Hitler's wishes. It is sometimes held that the institution that competed most successfully was the SS, which Buchheim has called 'the real and essential instrument of the Führer authority'. Some historians believe that it was so active and ruthless that it could always get the better of individuals or institutions rivalling it. This had led to the notion that, if it was the special representative of the Führer's wishes, it was set fair to become 'a state within a state'. Himmler, as Reichsführer SS after 1929 and head of the Gestapo after 1934, was in a position to centralise and Nazify the state's police services. By 1939 the party and state police organisation was unified in a single authority. Certainly ordinary people suspected that the secret police had countless informers watching and assessing even the most private aspects of life. There was a ubiquitous fear of contravening some rule or other.

It was only in the war years that Nazism assumed its terrible potential. As Germany expanded, Himmler sought to set up his organisation in Eastern Europe, but came up against the opposition of the Governor General of Poland, Hans Frank. It was clearly a contest to be responsible for the construction of a racial empire. Although Frank was eventually obliged to give way, it suggests that the notion of an SS state should not be overestimated. Despite its undoubted brutality, it could be disrupted by the determined efforts of competing government officials. Moreover, especially after 1943, as people became disillusioned about the course that the war was taking, the Gestapo – the secret state police – experienced declining co-operation from the people. Thus, the SS, despite the odious power that it could wield, was not omnipotent. The term 'state within a state', suggesting a capacity for independent action that other institutions in the state did not enjoy, may be considered an exaggerated view of the powers of the SS.

2   How far did Hitler rule with the consent of the German people?

3   'Most of the German people supported most of Hitler's policies most of the time.' To what extent do you agree with this viewpoint?

'The struggle between fascism and communism was incidental to the outcome of the civil war in Spain.' How far is this claim justified?

Tackling the question

Unless one has predetermined attitudes towards the matter, there can be no clear-cut explanation for the causes of the Spanish Civil War. Relative stress given to different events and stages can be no more than value judgements. Once the conflict was begun and despite foreign intervention, it was essentially a fratricidal struggle among the Spanish. There were many unresolved problems in Spain in the 1930s – *inter alia*, the pressing need for agrarian reform; the question of the identity of the historic regions of Spain; the secular jurisdiction of the Roman Catholic Church in a society seeking to modernise itself; the need to ensure that the army was under effective civilian control. It is not possible to ignore the international aspect of the crisis because in the 1930s Europe – itself on the brink of general war – was racked by political divisions that reinforced the divisions in Spanish society. However, it would be an oversimplification to regard the political polarisation in Spain as reflected in well-defined differences over ideology. Each side in the conflict had no obvious doctrinal unity. Indeed, intra-republican disputes constituted what has been described as 'the civil war within the civil war'. The nationalist coalition was the more coherent because Franco was able to persuade the Carlists, the Falange – the one patently fascist element in the coalition – the old Catholic Party and the monarchist generals to sink their differences, at least until the end of the conflict. The essay seeks to examine the reality behind the propaganda adopted by both sides that the conflict faithfully reflected the ideological divide apparent throughout Europe in the 1930s.

Answer

Explain how the notion of a struggle between fascism and communism in Spain between 1936 and 1939 is an over-simplification of what the crisis was about. Emphasise that there was a lack of ideological unity on both sides of the conflict.

In order to harness foreign support, the propaganda of both sides in the Spanish Civil War insisted that the conflict was a microcosm of the ideological rivalry dividing Europe in the 1930s. While the Spanish nationalists projected themselves as defenders of European civilisation against a godless communist conspiracy, the left, riven by differences over theory and practice, held that the conflict was part of a wider struggle between democracy and fascism. In essence, however, there were three main axes of conflict in Spain – the rights of landowner over peasant, Castilian centralism over regional identity, and authority over individual liberty. These axes also formed the structure of the intra-republican disputes, 'the civil war within the civil war', that gave the war its triangular aspect. This suggests that it was essentially a Spanish civil war, founded in Spain's social, economic and political history. Undeniably, its outcome depended much on international diplomacy that reflected an ideological divide in Europe. Nevertheless, there was no precise doctrinal delineation between the two sides in Spain – only the Falange, by 1937 neutralised within Franco's nationalist coalition, was unequivocally a fascist organisation, using the radical-nationalist ideas of the Italian model. For its part, the left represented a range of political sentiment from Trotskyists to democrats who were sympathetic to representative government on the Western European model.

An important element in the outcome of the struggle was the degree to which both sides were able to sink their differences and prosecute the war as one. Franco was more successful in this respect. The Falange, impressed by the notion of Mussolini's classless, corporatist system, and the Carlists, resolved on a monarchical restoration, were obliged to accept Franco's claim (April 1937) that he embodied 'the national will to unity as Generalissimo and Chief of State', able to control directly important appointments in the government, the party and the army. Such a rigid, authoritarian achievement was less easily achieved among republicans. Not only were there moderate republicans sympathetic to Western European democratic systems, but the radical left was divided. While the CNT (anarchist syndicalists) and Trotskyists sought immediate revolution through collectivisation and workers' militias, the Spanish Communist Party, influenced by Moscow, insisted that revolutionary change should be postponed until Franco had been defeated. Such divisions weakened the prospect of common resolve in prosecuting the war.

> Stress the importance of unity within the nationalist camp, achieved by Franco, in determining the outcome of the conflict. Contrast Franco's success in this respect with the greater difficulties in the republican movement in reconciling different elements so that the war could be waged with a common resolve.

An additional factor, blurring still further any crude distinction between 'fascist' and 'communist' within Spain, was the pragmatism that persuaded Catalans and Basques to give their support to the Republic. The principle of regional autonomy had been legitimised in the republican constitution, the Statute of Autonomy for Catalonia, endorsed by the Cortes (September 1932). Basque autonomy was more tardily achieved – not until October 1936. The nationalists plainly intended to reimpose a unitary state. Nevertheless, in May 1937, prompted by Stalinist communist insistence, bloodily effected, Catalonia ceased to be autonomous

> Examine closely the scope of dissension within the republican camp.

What was the impact of the ideological conflict in Europe upon the course and the outcome of the civil war? How was Franco better served by Hitler's aid than the republicans were by Stalin's aid?

within republican Spain. Thus, communist influence upon the Republican Government as much favoured the unitary state as did the nationalists.

The outcome of the conflict depended very much on the degree to which the burgeoning ideological conflict in Europe was translated into direct action by the contending powers in the Spanish conflict. Much depended on the way in which the two sides to the conflict, given internal political and military considerations, were able to utilise foreign aid. The policy of Britain and France to be non-interventionist obliged the republicans to depend on the Soviet Union, whose aid was determined by the interests of the Soviet Union and was accompanied by crippling financial exactions – most of the Republic's gold and silver reserves. Indeed, Soviet aid was probably designed to prolong resistance in the hope that a protracted conflict might be subsumed in a general European war against fascism. Hitler, on the other hand, when nationalist rebellion had apparently stalled (July 1936), responded positively to Franco's pleas for help and provided transport to ensure that the Spanish Moroccan army crossed the Straits to Spain. Thereafter, German and Italian help for Franco sought his victory and was often timely in its arrival and on easy financial conditions.

Now consider the relative performances of the nationalists and the republicans in the conflict.

It was advantageous to the nationalists' cause that their superior military structure and organisation enabled outside help to be effectively exploited. Thirty thousand officers were trained in 28 military academies, and militias, subject to strict military discipline, were subordinated to central control (December 1936). Even so, Franco would not be hurried militarily. Strategically, he was cautious and unimaginative. It was not until mid-1937 that he abandoned his costly 'obsession' with Madrid in favour of an important northern campaign that led to the almost immediate acquisition of the northern industrial areas of the Basque and the Asturias. His limited, plodding progress could often exasperate Hitler. The republican army, for its part, lacked coherence because of autonomous militia, elected officers and differences over strategy that encouraged insubordination. To an extent, the incoherence of the republicans' military effort was aggravated by Stalin's insistence that refraining from revolutionary objectives was a condition of his aid – arms, aircraft and tanks, military and political advisers – when popular enthusiasm for radical change at the outset, with workers seizing arms, had been an essential ingredient in stalling the attempted coup (July 1936).

Thus, there was no clearly defined conflict within Spain between communists and fascists, although the nationalists, under Franco's leadership, were able to subordinate vested right-wing interests to his will. Yet the ideological struggle between communism and fascism outside Spain was reflected in the aid received by the participants in the struggle. The popular basis of the republican cause – embracing communists as well as non-communists – might well have encouraged Britain and France to offer assistance, but their non-intervention was prompted by their suspicion that the republicans were too left wing and their fear that by intervention they might be risking general war. In practice, Britain and France, by their official non-involvement, assisted Franco's cause. The timely, generous aid bestowed on the nationalists by the fascist powers was made the more effective by the unity imposed on the nationalist cause by Franco. Heavily conditional communist aid to the republicans, however, exacerbated the disunity in the republican camp about what their ultimate objectives should be.

Conclude by emphasising that there was no clearly defined ideological divide between nationalists and republicans, and that the giving of aid – or the withholding of it – and the terms on which it was bestowed were important determinants of the outcome of the Spanish Civil War.

Related questions

1 'Unlikely to survive.' Discuss the validity of this verdict on the Spanish Republic of 1931–6.

In 1931 the Spanish Republic was hailed as a 'new dawn'. Five years later it collapsed, the victim of increasing, seemingly irreconcilable divisions. The shortcomings of the parliamentary system had ensured weak governments – there were 18 between 1931 and 1936. Additionally, regional aspirations complicated the devising and implementation of policies. Above all, reforms of the Church, the land and the army, initiated by governments of the left between 1931 and 1933, and sought again by the Popular Front government in 1936, raised expectations among the underprivileged without satisfying them, while the mere existence of these expectations and of the parties promoting them was regarded by the right as the prelude to social revolution. The repression of the 'Two Black Years' (December 1933–February 1936) was the right's response in a period of quasi-fascist government. The precipitate reversal of policy by the left in 1936 persuaded the right that there was no alternative to a violent counter-revolution based on an army uprising. Arguably, in a society that had become so thoroughly politicised, no regime could survive indefinitely when characterised by such intensity of political polarisation.

Many aspects of the Spanish Republic need to be examined in detail in order to answer the question set – the weakness of the political superstructure; the development of a determined opposition to the government of the republican–socialist alliance by 1933; the difficulties inherent in effecting reform; the attitude of the army to government by the left; the divisive issue of regional autonomy; the culmination of the process of polarisation in Spanish politics, as shown by the narrow victory of the Popular Front in the general election of November 1935. In 1936 Spain was still an agrarian society in the process of industrialisation. Such a society was delicately poised and susceptible to a determined minority who were disposed to rally conservative interests that were hostile to the emergence of the mass politics of an industrial society. The circumstances were well suited to the military, who were alone capable of seizing power. They were able to exploit the collapse of order as a symbol of general social collapse, in the context of irreconcilable differences over crucially important policies.

2 'The revolt of the Spanish army in Morocco on 18 July 1936 was the flashpoint of the resentment and the discontent existing between right and left in Spain in the 1930s.' Discuss this view.

3 'An international conflict.' How far do you agree with this judgement on the Spanish Civil War?

Question 35

How far was foreign intervention responsible for Franco's victory in the Spanish Civil War (1936–9)?

Tackling the question

Sir Simon Hoare, when British ambassador to Spain in 1940, described Franco as 'a small rather corpulent and bourgeois figure, who seemed insignificant'. Appearances may deceive, clearly. In reality, contained and composed as he always seemed, he was formidable. Paul Preston, his recent biographer, has claimed that he was utterly ruthless, his early experiences with Spanish forces in Morocco persuading him that he should disdain half measures and give no quarter when dealing with Moorish rebels. He inspired fear and it may well have been his awesome inscrutability and coldness, combined with his known capacity for brutality, that persuaded the disparate elements who were hostile to republicanism to combine against it. He may not have been a military genius, but he had the implacable resolve to secure his objectives. Calculatedly, Preston argues, he prolonged the civil war unnecessarily 'in order to annihilate his political enemies on the left and his rivals on the right and to consolidate the mechanisms of his power'. He was, he says, loath 'to move to the definitive victory before further destruction and demoralisation of the Republicans' human resources'. Hugh Thomas counters this by arguing that the republican armies were led by many fine professional officers who were not easily overcome. Moreover, Franco realised that he would encounter serious risks if a European war were to break out – as it seemed that it might do before the Munich agreement in September 1938 – prior to his winning his own conflict.

He was better served by foreign aid than his republican opponents, but the benefit to Franco would have been seriously diminished had he not imposed a unity of purpose upon the differing political elements, who, temporarily at least, could share his view that he could be the saviour of Spain from a godless enemy. In assessing the value of external aid to Franco's cause, his foresight, cunning and political skills were prerequisites for maximising its usefulness, which should not be underestimated.

Answer

Before Franco's death (1975), historians often attributed nationalist success in the Spanish Civil War (1936–9) to German and Italian aid, supplied consistently and almost unconditionally. In contrast, the Republican Government received Soviet aid accompanied not only by stringent financial demands, but by

Guidance notes

Consider concisely foreign intervention on Franco's behalf in the context of other factors that helped to determine the outcome of the Spanish Civil War.

unremitting political interference that probably damaged rather than nourished republican resistance. Indirectly, the nationalists were assisted by the decision of Britain and France not to aid the legitimate government in the crisis. Yet foreign intervention – its availability or its scarcity – did not alone, or even principally, determine the war's outcome. The conflict, fought mainly by Spaniards, was an eruption produced by internal political, social and economic divisions. Such factors played their parts in the outcome, as did the efficacy and limitations of military strategies and tactics employed by both sides. Crucially, and arguably most importantly, the nationalists' political unity, forged by Franco's perspicacity and good fortune, contrasted with the political divisions and regional autonomy of the republican-held territories, which bred unconcerted efforts.

Examine in some detail the nature and timing of the aid that Franco received from Hitler and Mussolini.

The nationalists were the beneficiaries of substantial, timely and consistent German and Italian military aid. Tanks, aircraft and armoured vehicles were supplied to them. While Hitler made available, *inter alia*, squadrons of the élite Kondor Legion and thousands of military advisers, Mussolini – with ambition to make the Mediterranean *mare nostrum* – contributed some 50,000–60,000 troops, aircraft and warships, which, qualitatively, were inferior to German assistance. Immediately, such aid enabled Franco (5 August 1936) to mount his invasion of Spain from north Africa, thus changing the strategic balance in favour of the rebels, whose attempted coup (18 July 1936) had seemingly stalled. By 1938 the provisions of modern aircraft gave the nationalists air superiority as they mounted their final offensive. Moreover, the aid was provided on easy credit terms and usually without specific political conditions.

What were the value and limitations of the Soviet Union's military aid to the republicans? Why did Soviet aid diminish at the time of the Munich Conference in September 1938? What strings were attached to the aid, which handicapped the republican cause?

Although initially hesitant, Stalin supplied the Republican Government with tanks, aircraft and military – and political – advisers. Furthermore, during the war there were 60,000 foreign volunteers, some of whom were recruited and trained in the Soviet Union. As with the aid to the nationalists, it could be timely – as when it gave the republicans temporary air superiority (October 1936). It played a part in saving Madrid from the nationalists. However, the Soviet Union's efforts were limited by the Italians' Mediterranean naval blockade, Stalin's caution and the implications of the Munich agreement (September 1938), which, to Stalin, suggested that the Soviet Union should look almost exclusively to its own defences. Thereafter, the Soviet Union's aid dwindled, its benefits already eroded by political interference in the composition of cabinets, the formulation of strategy, the undermining of incipient social revolution and the ruthless persecution of political enemies. Arguably, the Soviet Union had always been interested less in promoting republican victory than in ensuring a protracted conflict that might eventually stimulate a general conflict against fascism – a prospect seemingly undermined at Munich.

It was to the Republic's disadvantage that Britain and France adopted a policy of non-intervention. The Republican Government's legal right to purchase arms abroad was discounted. Anti-communist sentiment and fear of the conflict spreading influenced the British government in its decision. Blum, France's Popular Front prime minister, might have been expected to sanction aid, but he deferred to Britain not to do so, and was anxious not to provoke conservative and Catholic opinion that was hostile to the Republican Government. Feebly, the 'institutional hypocrisy' of the Non-Intervention Committee failed to frustrate German and Italian aid to the nationalists, thus aggravating the republicans' difficulties.

> Why did Britain and France decline to assist the republicans in defending Spain's legitimate government?

Abroad, the nationalists acquired financial credit, exported wheat for foreign exchange and bought oil supplied from the USA, despite the Neutrality Act (1935). It has been estimated by R. Whealey that the nationalists spent $76 million on foreign exchange purchases of war-related supplies – 12% of their total foreign aid. Moreover, they occupied the main grain-growing areas and avoided the acute food shortages experienced in republican zones, where, especially latterly, starvation threatened.

> Explain how Franco was helped by financial credit acquired abroad.

Ultimately, the outcome depended on military operations, fought mainly by Spaniards, but linked indissolubly to the degree and timing of foreign aid and political considerations. Both sides made costly miscalculations. Had the republicans been less preoccupied with defending Madrid in 1936, Franco might have been checked in the south. Franco was overtly cautious, often insisting on taking strategically unimportant territories. He found no way of subduing Madrid and delayed until 1937 a northward advance that yielded crucial gains in industrial output and manpower. Even though the republicans possessed a disciplined Popular Army after October 1936, autonomous actions by regional governments weakened the impetus of offensives. The fall of Teruel (February 1938) decided the conflict irreversibly in the nationalists' favour. Thereafter, unavailingly, the republicans launched a despairing offensive in the Ebro before conceding defeat. Laboriously and unspectacularly, Franco's forces prevailed.

> How did Franco's strategy and tactics contribute to his final victory?

Stress the importance of the nationalists' political unity in determining the outcome of the conflict.

Perhaps most important of all, the nationalists enjoyed a greater degree of unity than the republicans. The fortuitous deaths of potential rivals – including that of José Antonio Primo de Rivera, the Falange's leader – helped Franco to establish his authority over autonomous political movements like the Carlists and the Falange. Right-wing militias were brought firmly under army control. Franco's initial prestige, as commander of the intervening army from Africa and the specified recipient of German and Italian military aid, enabled him to secure his political and military leadership of the nationalists by September 1936, aided by traditions of conformity and obedience to military authority by right-wing groups. By contrast, republican divisions increased as the war progressed. The unity of purpose established under Caballero (September 1936) soon gave way to insoluble divisions as to whether the revolution was the means for securing victory or whether social change should be postponed until after the war's end. The Soviet Union insisted on the latter view prevailing as a condition of its aid.

Conclude by emphasising the complexity of the factors involved in Franco's ultimate victory in 1939.

The differential impact of foreign aid and non-intervention upon the two sides seriously threatened the prospects of the republicans. But other factors also contributed to the republican defeat. Franco's willingness to fight a war of attrition slowly but surely wore down his opponents. Apart from the initial phase of conflict, ampler material resources favoured the nationalists. Perhaps above all, the effectiveness with which the nationalists utilised foreign aid depended very much upon their unity of purpose – an element that consistently eluded the republicans.

Related questions

1 To what extent is it appropriate to describe the Spanish Civil War (1936–9) as a dress rehearsal for the Second World War?

Although volunteers who assisted the Republican Government in the Spanish Civil War believed that they were involved in a crusade against fascism, the conflict was essentially the product of Spanish political conditions. Overwhelmingly, those who fought were subjects of Spain. Franco enjoyed German and Italian military support – the former's qualitatively superior to the latter's – but the Soviet Union's material help to the republicans did not include servicemen fighting. Britain and France pursued a policy of non-intervention. Therefore, strictly militarily, it was scarcely a dress rehearsal for all participants in the Second World War. Rather it provided a foretaste of techniques that were to be employed on a vaster scale than in Spain. It also foreshadowed the potential for civilian suffering in wartime. Additionally, the civil war helped to consolidate and fashion political alignments and to precipitate developments elsewhere – especially in Central Europe – that brought major conflict nearer. Thus, it permanently alienated Italy from Britain and France, and ensured that Hitler was fatally encumbered with Italy's military incompetence in the coming conflict.

In the short term, the Rome–Berlin axis of 1936 enabled Hitler to pursue policies in Central Europe leading to *Anschluss* (March 1938) and the Czech crisis (September 1938). Anglo-French territorial concessions in the Munich agreement soon persuaded Stalin that the Soviet Union's survival, in the short term at least, demanded an accommodation with Hitler. This was secured in the Nazi–Soviet Pact of 23 August 1939, which helped to precipitate the outbreak of European war in September 1939. Meanwhile, the USA's aloofness from the civil war, reinforcing its established 'isolation' and its preoccupation with domestic problems, was encouragement to Japan to entertain expansionist policies in the Far East and for Hitler to consider that, whatever his actions in Europe, American intervention was extremely unlikely. In these ways, the war in Spain may have influenced the decisions leading to the Second World War.

Beyond these considerations, Germany gained most from the intervention. Its new weapons were tested and *blitzkrieg* techniques were refined during the civil war. Intimations of Italy's military shortcomings warned Mussolini that his armies were ill prepared for major war. Some volunteers who survived translated their acquired skills to service in resistance movements after 1940, especially in France and Yugoslavia. But there was no practice in Spain for the Soviet Union or the USA – and Britain and France too were non-participants.

2   Assess the importance of Franco in securing victory for the nationalist cause in the Spanish Civil War.

3   'Merely the latest and the fiercest battle in a European civil war that had been under way since 1917.' How far is this a valid judgement of the Spanish Civil War?

Question 36

Why, and with what consequences, did France elect a Popular Front government in 1936?

Tackling the question

The interwar period seems to have been one of virtually uninterrupted gloom for France. There were political strains aggravated by there being a plethora of political parties – the left having split, in the aftermath of the war, with the formation of the French Communist Party; the right having become divided among factions, most of which opposed social reform and sought a nationalistic foreign policy. Radicalism, so important and influential before 1914, was a spent force. There had been a brief improvement in the robustness of the flagging economy after a devaluation of the currency in 1928, but in the early 1930s it was again weakened by the effects of the world depression. Provocative actions by the new right, which embraced fascist-style characteristics and had roots in Action Française before 1914, erupted into violence in 1934. By 1935 the conduct of the Croix de Feu, a fascist organisation, was enough to prompt the various elements of the left to try to co-operate with each other. Communists, hitherto bitter rivals of the socialists, became conciliatory, encouraged to be so by their political masters in Moscow, who were alarmed by the dangers posed by Nazi Germany. Progress was soon made towards a Popular Front. Believing that a serious danger was posed to France's political stability by the right, Leon Blum wrote that 'when the Republic is threatened, the word Republican changes its meaning'.

In a context of worsening economic conditions, the Popular Front gained a convincing mandate from the people in the general election of 1936. Weakened by financial problems, however, by 1938 it collapsed. By this time France was ill equipped to face the challenge posed by Hitler to the security of Europe. The damage done to France by the rigours of the First World War, a declining population, acute economic problems and a humiliating deference to British decisions in policy towards Germany by the late 1930s all combined to sap French confidence. This was no more plainly demonstrated than in the defensive mentality symbolised by the building of the Maginot Line.

Answer

What factors led to the formation of the Popular Front government in 1936? What were the consequences of electing that government?

In the 1930s the fragility of democratic institutions was exposed by the gravity of the Depression following the Wall Street Crash (1929). It encouraged authoritarian sentiment in all European countries and Hitler's triumph in Germany (1933). In France, economic crisis aggravated political and social divisions. After

1918 French parliamentarians were discredited because of a paucity of all kinds of reform – social, financial and constitutional. Evidence of corruption in government prompted anti-parliamentary feeling. Politics were becoming polarised between a right, seeking the smack of firm government, and a left, moving towards co-operation with communists. An alarming confrontation threatened. Republicanism and democracy seemed in peril. The Popular Front – based on compromise between communists, radicals and socialists – was an attempt to save French democracy. Electorally successful (May 1936), Blum's government endeavoured to enact belated social reform, rejuvenate industry and rearm against the menace of Germany. Such an expensive combination of policies was unlikely to succeed. Nor was any conviction established in foreign policy. By 1938 political tensions remained acute and, troubled and confused, France was acquiescing impotently in Chamberlain's appeasement of Germany.

The existence of extra-parliamentary movements after the late 1920s, mostly demanding strong government, some anti-Semitic, like Maurras' Action Français, others, like the Croix de Feu, unashamedly nationalistic, together represented more than an irritant in French political life. Their hostility to the left promised a paralysing polarity between political extremes. The evidence of widespread corruption in the Stavisky scandal (1933) precipitated the expression of anti-parliamentary feeling and rioting in Paris (February 1934), provoking ungrounded fears of a coup. Concern about internal collapse, activated by burgeoning fascism and Hitler's unchallenged breaches of the Versailles settlement – which had grave implications for France – encouraged a union in 1935 of left-wing opinion to rally the nation in defence of democracy. Social reform, managed capitalism and divisions over rearmament, masked by a common resolve to promote collective security, were the hallmarks of the new Popular Front (1935).

> Why did the Popular Front emerge as a political force in 1935?

Equipped with a manifesto proclaiming 'Peace, Bread and Liberty', the Popular Front won the election of June 1936 convincingly. Nevertheless, widespread strikes followed immediately and, coupled with France's deteriorating international position – the Rhineland had recently been reoccupied militarily by Germany (March 1936) – the right manifested alarm. In this context the government was unable to restore social peace. Employers, ultimately but reluctantly, made agreements with their employees, through Blum's mediation, which established an eight-hour day, a five-day week, paid holidays and a 12% increase in wages. These concessions were little encouragement to an economy already ailing. Confidence in the economy was so sapped at home

> On what platform did the Popular Front win the election of 1936? Explain why it was unable to preside over a recovery of the French economy.

and abroad that a rapid outflow of capital obliged the government to devalue the franc by almost 60%. A persistent budget deficit dogged the government and industrial investment declined inexorably. Trade was not revived, wage increases were soon outpaced by inflation and unemployment fell little. France's financial problems were further aggravated by plans for expenditure on housing and social welfare as well as on increased armaments, necessitated by Germany's aggressive acts and posturing.

Why was the political right not reconciled to the Popular Front?

The right suspected that the communists, hitherto ostensibly pacifically inclined, by associating themselves with the policy of rearmament, were merely seeking to drag France into assuming some responsibility for the defence of the Soviet Union. Thus, the right, now that the left was linked with a strategy of preparing for possible war, adopted a policy of appeasing Hitler. This was a strange reversal of roles for, since Boulanger's time, the right had supplanted the left as ardent nationalists, supporters of France abroad, proponents of revanche before 1914 and advocates of the rigorous implementation of the Versailles settlement. Yet essentially the Front politicians were supporting rearmament reluctantly. Indeed, some socialists, disenchanted by Blum's leadership, were inclined to accept the right's verdict on communist intentions.

Now consider how the Spanish Civil War increased the difficulties of the Popular Front. Why did Blum sanction the policy of non-intervention also pursued by Britain?

When the Spanish Civil War broke out (July 1936), deep rifts in French policies were evident. The right, sympathetic towards Franco, demanded a policy of non-intervention. The communists, mindful of German and Italian participation in support of the rebellion, sought a crusade against fascism in defence of the Republic. Many socialists merely wanted peace. With the nation sharply divided and conscious that Britain discouraged intervention, Blum chose non-intervention as alone politically acceptable, although he was aware that Franco's success would make France vulnerable to governments of the extreme right on three of its frontiers. The Soviet Union was disappointed at Blum's decision, so it was more difficult thereafter to rely on the Soviet Union to counter Hitler. In practice, the Franco-Soviet Pact (1935) was inoperative, the right being hostile to any association with the Soviet Union and sceptical about the Soviet Union's military capacity, while Blum was loath to strengthen ties with the Soviet Union that would increase communist influence within the Front. Thus, the Front failed to strengthen France internationally after Hitler's remilitarisation of the Rhineland (March 1936), which had been acquiesced in timidly despite the grave threat that Hitler's move posed to France's security.

After Blum's resignation (June 1937), the Popular Front survived until Daladier became Prime Minister immediately after the *Anschluss* (March 1938). Problems of finance had enfeebled it. While the Front had taken steps to remove France's social backwardness, it was unable to mitigate the harsh political divisions in French society. Its legacy was government paralysed by indecision as Hitler engineered the Czech crisis (1938). Abjectly, France followed Britain's lead in appeasing Hitler and accepted passively the ignominy of the Munich agreement (September 1938). That French communists advocated going to war to defend Czechoslovakia, and that other shades of opinion were persuaded that only Bolshevism would gain from another European war, was a contradiction in France's nationalism that was a response to France's experience of the Popular Front.

> What was the legacy of the Popular Front government?

Related questions

1 By what diplomatic means and with what results did France seek to achieve security in Europe during the interwar period?

France, twice invaded by Germany since 1870 and mindful in 1918 of defeated Germany's greater industrial and commercial potential, regarded as its priority the establishment of durable guarantees for its security in the event of a revival of German power. Briefly, a projected Anglo-American guarantee seemed to offer this, but the American Senate's repudiation of the Treaty of Versailles and membership of the League of Nations frustrated it. During the 1920s Anglo-French relations were often cool because Britain, unlike France, had reservations about the prudence – even the justice – of some of the terms of the peace settlement made in 1919. France's anxieties about Germany prompted it to make a series of agreements with the new states of Eastern Europe, although these were largely undermined by an agreement with the Soviet Union in 1935. However, in that agreement there was no firm guarantee of Soviet action against Germany. Once Italy was pursuing policies in the Mediterranean inimical to French interests and Hitler was openly violating the Versailles settlement, France acquiesced meekly in Britain's ultimately unsuccessful attempts to find an accommodation with Hitler.

Thus, France failed to find a system of security that would prevent Germany from renewing aggression against it. In 1939, France – with Britain – guaranteed Poland against German aggression, but when Germany attacked Poland in September 1939, Poland was defeated within weeks. The Nazi–Soviet Pact of August 1939 meant that, when France was itself attacked in May 1940, there was no second front in Eastern Europe as there had been in 1914, which might have done something to diminish the ferocity of the invasion.

2 What were the objectives of French foreign policy in the interwar period, and to what extent, if at all, were they realised?

3 'Little was achieved or changed in France during the interwar period.' Why, and to what extent, was this so?